Praise for *Your Call Is (Not That) Important to Us*

"If you've ever been mildly frustrated, extremely irritated, or driven just plain mad by automated customer service lines, rude telephone service representatives, or agents who can't speak intelligible English, this book is for you. Yellin dives into the often dysfunctional world of customer service, exploring the multibillion-dollar industry from various points of view."

—*Publishers Weekly*

"An in-depth look at the increasingly international customer service industry. Yellin's prodigiously researched book is a useful cautionary tale. Companies that farm out customer service, she makes clear, divorce themselves from their customers."

—*Fortune Small Business* magazine

"Probably the best book on the state of customer service and how to do something about it I've read. . . . Very strong on the actual agent-based customer service world, and its failures and the best practices for doing it right. Very important book."

—Paul Greenberg, author of *CRM at the Speed of Light: Essential Customer Strategies for the 21st Century*, from his blog on ZDNet.com

Also by Emily Yellin

Our Mothers' War

Your Call Is (Not That) Important to Us

Customer Service and What It Reveals
About Our World and Our Lives

EMILY YELLIN

FREE PRESS
New York London Toronto Sydney

Free Press
A Division of Simon & Schuster, Inc.
1230 Avenue of the Americas
New York, NY 10020

First Free Press trade paperback edition August 2010

FREE PRESS and colophon are trademarks of Simon & Schuster, Inc.

For information about special discounts for bulk purchases,
please contact Simon & Schuster Special Sales at
1-866-506-1949 or business@simonandschuster.com.

The Simon & Schuster Speakers Bureau can bring authors
to your live event. For more information or to book an event
contact the Simon & Schuster Speakers Bureau at
1-866-248-3049 or visit our website at www.simonspeakers.com.

Designed by Ellen Sasahara
Manufactured in the United States of America

1 3 5 7 9 8 6 4 2

The Library of Congress has cataloged the hardcover edition as follows:
Yellin, Emily,
Your call is (not that) important to us : customer service and what it reveals
about our world and our lives / by Emily Yellin.
p. cm.
1. Customer services. 2. Customer relations. 3. Corporations—Public relations.
I. Title.
HF5415.5.Y47   2009
658.8'12—dc22   2009002468
ISBN 978-1-4165-4689-4
ISBN 978-1-4165-4690-0 (pbk)
ISBN 978-1-4165-9457-4 (ebook)

Dedicated to
Chuck, Peyto, and Ezra

Contents

Introduction to the Paperback Edition

Welcome to the belly of the beast—the place where the disconnect between companies and customers plays out—customer service.

I wrote this book to see if I could figure out why customer service on the phone had become such an ordeal for us all. Of course I had my own bad experiences. Everyone has them. But I thought if I could go in and examine what was going on, I might be able to help those of us who are customers get along better with those who answer phones for companies. I thought I might demystify the current maze of aggravation for myself, and for my fellow customers.

One of the first things I found was that the people who run customer service call centers are often just as frustrated by how bad things have gotten as we are. They are in a bind. They live with the problems and see the need for change. But often they are working in corporate cultures with long-standing traditions of marginalizing customer service—of not giving their workers the backing they really need to support customers well. So workers have to adjust to a rickety system, where call center success is often measured in the same ways that manufacturing success was always measured. How many widgets can they produce for the least amount of money, in the least amount of time, and with the fewest number of employees?

It doesn't take a business genius to realize that makes no sense. You can't measure a function that is all about human interactions and human relationships in the same way you would measure a function that is all about machines and widget production. But common sense has not prevailed among corporate leaders in their attitudes toward customer service.

Measuring the number of calls an agent takes in an hour, first and foremost, and rewarding agents for taking more calls and spending less time on each call regardless of the problem, produces the kind of customer exasperation we all know to be epidemic in telephone customer service. Time and again, studies have shown that customers leave when service is bad, and that losing customers and getting new ones costs much more than caring for and keeping the ones you have. Even companies with hordes of customers clamoring for their products or services end up losing when their monopoly ends, as it always does, unless they have nurtured a lasting relationship with their customers through good service.

Squeezing the relationship further by making people who call your company wait on hold for excessive amounts of time after buying your wares, is not the right way to treat a fellow human being either. At least your employees are paid something for the time they spend on a call. The customer is not. If time and money are so important to companies, then how do they justify routinely disregarding their customer's time and money?

We have been beaten down by all this. Customers are left to try to find ways to get around the broken system, or to find companies that don't make us work so hard to get the service we thought we had purchased. The bar has gotten so low that common courtesy in customer service has become a luxury. A company that merely answers phones quickly and doesn't make us wait long to connect to a human being is considered top of the line.

People don't like to feel ignored. People don't like to be treated like machines. People don't like to talk to machines when they need human help. People don't like it when their needs are blatantly disregarded.

In the current frenzy to brand every move a company makes, customer service is often overlooked, and ends up being like a piece of toilet paper trailing on the shoe of someone who is wearing a Gucci suit. Everyone sees it except the one who is so well-dressed. Most companies with sizable budgets for marketing and advertising relegate customer service and call centers to the outer reaches of their corporate hierarchy, or even exile it to distant lands to boost their quarterly profits. They brand themselves like crazy to sell to their customers. But then their lowest paid and least experienced employees are often the only ones who interact personally with their customers after a sale. Or they take human workers out of the equation altogether, and funnel us to an incomplete website or to an automated agent with no option for escape, even when we know we need a person. No wonder we are enraged, and are crying out for relief from dealing with the very people who are supposed to help us.

The good news is some people and companies are doing better. The common element I see among those bellwethers is an ethic of skillful service at the heart of their corporation's culture and mission. Customer service is not treated as an afterthought or a necessary evil. The call center is viewed as a strategic information hub and vital cultural pacesetter for the company. Every decision is run through the litmus test of how it will improve the lives of customers, not just how it will increase the bank accounts of executives and shareholders. The newest gadgets, and even outsourcing, are not used as panaceas, they are seen as tools only to be brought in if they contribute to the larger goal of helping customers. Those companies are about more than making money. They are about providing able service. The great thing for everyone is that as long as they stay true to that principle, the profits follow. It might not be in the next quarter, but over the long run, the same policies that lead to untiring service also seem to be the trick to sustaining business success. Likewise, the cost of perpetrating the policies that lead to feeble service is always higher than it may seem in the short run.

More good news is that the technology is out there to help address many of the problems that arise and persist in providing intelligent service, if it is used judiciously. Also, a lot of people are trying to develop more and better technology to improve shortcomings. Technology is also making it harder for companies to hide deficient service behind their corporate firewalls. Customers can come together, hear each other, and speak as one like never before through the Internet. That new power has forced more and more companies to listen and learn.

Still, getting customer service right is a much more sophisticated prospect than most companies seem to understand. It is part art and part science. But it is not draw-by-numbers art or an exact science. It takes painstaking design and engineering. It takes diligence in making sure all the elements of proactive service are continually adjusted and aligned for the good of all. And it takes a commitment to follow-through that is unsinkable, even in a crisis. Merely throwing some lip service and the latest technology at customer service and hoping it sticks is another mistake many companies seem to make.

Not many people dispute that customer service as we know it has to change. Conservative estimates say that Americans make upwards of 43 billion calls to customer service each year. That averages about 143 calls per year for every man, woman, and child in the nation.

Customer service is a prolific contributor to the tone of our public life, but we have not bothered to understand it very well. That is the goal of this book. I am not trying to indict. I am not trying to blame. I just want to find reasons for all our bother, and along the way, perhaps find some hope for a more agreeable future.

So I talked to everyone across the board. I considered as

many angles as I could. I talked to more people who are innovating to make things better than I did to those who are simply complaining about how bad it is now. Most customers are already experts in bad service, because we have all experienced it. Most call center workers are already aware that their profession is not exactly beloved. But the promise of change lies with those who have broken through to the people who pull the strings and inspired them to find ways of increasing profits without alienating the very people who pay the bills—their customers.

It is clear that making customer service a core business tenet has to come from CEOs and board chairs before anything will change in a significant way. One of the premises I started with when I decided to write this book was that I couldn't believe that so many people who ran companies intended to do such a bad job at customer service. It turns out they don't. Still, they are doing a bad job in spite of their intentions. They are doing a bad job because they have been conditioned to make decisions based on outmoded or shortsighted business philosophies. They see customer service as separate and auxiliary to other, more tangible outcomes of business. They consider it a "soft skill," when it is one of the hardest things for a business to get right.

The problem is compounded because top-level executives are often cut off from those who have to live with their decisions—their employees and their customers. Executives get very little, if any, regular, unfiltered feedback from the customers or from customer service agents who interact every day on the inhospitable turf those executives have created and must play by the untenable rules those executives set. Uninformed decisions lead to policies that might improve quarterly profits, but also foster lasting incivility between employees and customers. It can't go on. But only after it is too late do top executives and shareholders come to see the most dire and enduring consequences of all that ignorance and neglect, as customers (and even some of their customer service workers) grow to distrust and even hate their companies. As soon as they can, both the unhappy workers and customers leave—sometimes in droves. Everyone loses.

There is hope. Things have to change. Getting to know the terrain is a good place to start.

Welcome to the belly of the beast—the place where the disconnect between companies and customers plays out—customer service.

Author's Note to the Hardcover Edition

In the course of writing this book I've learned that customer service is all about expectations. So, in an attempt to provide readers with good customer service, I feel the need to clarify what this book is and isn't meant to be.

The majority of sources in this book are original. However, I did turn to other people's reporting about certain incidents that happened before my work began or for which I was not present and original sources were not available. For any detailed descriptions of such incidents, I consulted more than one trusted account. All of those sources are credited in the narrative itself or in notes at the end of the book. Anything else is my own reporting. And although the customer service industry is in constant flux, I did my best to include the most timely information possible.

To get an up-close look at outsourced foreign call centers, I could have traveled to just about anywhere in the world, since they are that widespread. But I chose to focus my on-the-ground reporting in two emerging outsourcing locales—Latin America and Africa—rather than in the more established locales of India and the Philippines, which have been much reported on by others.

This book is not intended as a comprehensive analysis of the industry's problems or as a prescription for its future improvement. Instead, it is an attempt to seek out the humanity and reason behind the customer service experiences that many people find to be inhuman and nonsensical. My efforts were grounded in the idea that it is important for those of us who are customers (and everyone is somebody's customer) to know more about the inner workings of global customer service and its ever-increasing impact on us all as we try to navigate successfully through our daily lives.

1.

Random Acts of Rudeness

As the twenty-first century dawned, most people were feeling fed up. A public opinion poll in 2001 reported that 80 percent of Americans believed the constant coarseness, disrespect, and lack of consideration they encountered in society was such a "serious, pervasive problem" that it affected them "on a personal, gut level" and had grown into "a daily assault on their sensibilities and the quality of their lives." At the same time, it seemed people didn't believe they had much power to change things, so they simply resigned themselves to all the insidious incivility they encountered.

The Pew Charitable Trusts sponsored the poll, called "Aggravating Circumstances: A Status Report on Rudeness in America." Public Agenda, a national policy research group, conducted it. And in their introduction, the authors made sure to justify their examination of how we get along with each other in public every day: "At first, it might seem that conducting a survey on courtesy and rudeness is less serious or important than exploring citizens' views on, say, health care or education or retirement policy. Yet how people treat each other in their daily interactions—whether they take steps to be respectful of one another, whether they are willing to moderate their own desires and comfort to accommodate the needs of others—seems to us to be profoundly important and indeed central to the definition of a 'civilized' society."

The report immediately zeroed in on one area of society that most respondents agreed offers perhaps the ripest examples of rude and infuriating public behavior. "Americans say that the way they are treated by business and customer service employees is frequently exasperating, and sometimes even insulting." One particular customer service channel came under the heaviest fire. "When it goes wrong, perhaps nothing embodies greater exasperation than customer service by phone."

According to the survey, 67 percent of Americans sometimes have to "make a fuss to get a problem resolved." And nearly everyone—94 percent—finds it "very frustrating to call a company and get a recording instead of a human being." Even if callers do finally speak to a live customer service agent, the irritation doesn't always end. In a Florida focus group, one man said, "Half the time they have no idea what they're talking about. And they don't care. They'll tell you anything just to get you off the phone."

To be fair, the report also notes that "it seems the rudeness cuts both ways. Disgruntled customers bring frayed nerves, previous frustrations and their own personal shortcomings when they deal with those responsible for helping them." A Connecticut customer service representative told her focus group, "They think you're at their beck and call. They may want something, and they're not getting it as rapidly as they think they should. I answer the phone, and they just immediately go off on me."

It probably doesn't take a scientifically conducted public opinion poll to find evidence of the contempt most Americans harbor toward bad customer service or to elicit testimony about the effects of that kind of antipathy in their lives. Merely bringing up the subject at any gathering will generate at least one horror story from just about everyone. But in the years since that survey officially highlighted and validated the displeasure bubbling just under the surface of our everyday dealings with customer service, a few of those tensions have boiled over in very public ways. The news media, in tandem with various websites and social media, have played increasingly larger roles in amplifying them. Just ask Comcast, for example.

Trouble for the nation's largest cable television and broadband provider started in earnest with the story of LaChania Govan, a mother of two in her mid-twenties who inadvertently became a public symbol of mistreated customers everywhere. Govan lives in suburban Chicago. She goes to work all week and attends church every Sunday. She has a pleasant and welcoming voice. She also has a strong sense of fairness.

In July 2005, Govan's digital video recorder wouldn't work. She called Comcast's customer service line in Chicago but couldn't get through. During the course of four weeks, she called more than forty times. She was repeatedly disconnected, put on hold, or transferred to inept or inert representatives and technicians. One customer service representative transferred her to the Spanish-speaking line. Govan knows only English. She just wanted someone to resolve her seemingly simple case.

She says she never raised her voice, but she was resolute. "Calling Comcast became my second job," Govan said. "I had to ensure the cordless phone was fully charged and the kids were content. And I sat and called. I cooked and called. I cleaned and called, and just called." Almost every day, Govan prodded the big company's customer service department as best she could. Finally, she found a rep who heard her out and took her case in hand. A technician was sent to replace her cable box at no charge, and she was credited with a free month of service. Govan's perseverance paid off. Her headaches seemed to be over.

Then Govan's August cable bill arrived. Her name did not appear on the bill. Instead it was addressed to "Bitch Dog." Someone at Comcast had changed her account name. Govan said, "I was so mad I couldn't even cuss."

Instead of becoming just another unnoticed casualty in the adversarial relationship between many companies and their customers, Govan went public. The *Chicago Tribune* ran her story. Within days, the mainstream news media, bloggers, and consumer advocates from everywhere were spreading her tale of woe. She appeared as the number-one story on MSNBC's *Countdown* with Keith Olbermann. A Comcast executive left an apology on Govan's home voice mail. The company claimed it identified and fired two employees responsible for changing the name on Govan's bill. She was offered all sorts of free service, which she refused. She wanted nothing more to do with Comcast.

Govan, who also happens to be a customer service representative for a major credit card company, is studying criminal justice with plans to go to law school one day. Eventually, she says, she hopes to become a judge. Her inherent sense of justice is what drove her to persevere. So she was speaking with conviction when she told the *Washington Post* that she believes customer service means "being friendly, helpful and respectful. I know how it feels to be a customer service rep and a consumer on the other end. You do not have to settle for less, and you do not have to be mistreated."

In 2006, Comcast was dealing with another public display of customer service missteps. A subscriber in the Washington, D.C., area found the technician that Comcast sent to fix his cable system had fallen asleep on his couch. The worker was kept on hold for so long by his own company when he called for help that he dozed off. The customer shot video of the napping technician and posted it on the Internet, where it went viral. Comcast issued another apology, and again said the worker in question had been fired.

Then in August 2007, Comcast suffered what was perhaps its worst embarrassment to date when seventy-six-year-old Mona Shaw took her outrage with its customer service a few steps further than any disgruntled customer had done before. As she has told the story, it started when a technician scheduled to come out to her suburban Washington, D.C., home on a Monday didn't show up. Comcast was supposed to install what it calls its triple-play service, which included the company's new telephone service, along with its traditional Internet and cable television connection, all for under $100 per month. Shaw, a retired military nurse and secretary of her local AARP, as well as a square dancer who fosters stray dogs until they can be adopted, waited all day Monday. When Comcast finally arrived two days later, the technician left the job half done and never came back. On Friday, the company cut off what service Mona and her husband, Don, still had.

Without phone service, the Shaws couldn't call to get help, so they drove over to their local Comcast office in Manassas, Virginia. They asked for a manager and were told to wait, outside, in the August heat.

They say they sat on a bench for two hours, until the same woman who had asked them to wait leaned out the door, told them the manager had gone home for the day, and thanked them for coming. Shaw told the *Washington Post*, "They thought just because we're old enough to get Social Security that we lack both brains and backbone."

By Monday, after a weekend with no phone, TV, or Internet, Shaw was so angry that she took matters into her own hands, literally. She got her husband's hammer, and they went back to the local Comcast office. This is how *Washington Post* reporter Neely Tucker described Shaw's account of what happened next:

> Hammer time: Shaw storms into the company's office. BAM! She whacks the keyboard of the customer service rep. BAM! Down goes the monitor. BAM! She totals the telephone. People scatter, scream, cops show up and what does she do? POW! A parting shot to the phone!
>
> "They cuffed me right then," she says.
>
> Her take on Comcast: "What a bunch of sub-moronic imbeciles."
>
> Being a responsible newspaper, we must note that this is a misdemeanor, a crime, a completely inappropriate way of handling a business dispute.
>
> Noted.
>
> Who among us has not longed for a hammer in this age of incompetent "customer service representatives," of nimrods reading from a script at some 800-number location, of crumbs-in-their-beards plumbing installation people who tell you they'll grace you with their presence between 12 and 3, only never to show? And you'll call and call and finally some outsourced representative slings a dart at a calendar and tells you another guy will come back between 10 and 2 next Thursday? And when this guy comes, pants halfway down his behind, he'll tell you he brought the wrong part?

And there is nothing, nothing you can do.

Until there! On the horizon! It's Hammer Woman, avenger of oppressed cable subscribers everywhere! (Cue galloping "Lone Ranger" theme.)

"It had never occurred to me to take a hammer to a phone company before, but I was just so upset," Mona Shaw told the paper. "After I hit the keyboard, I turned to this blonde who had been there the previous Friday, the one who told me to wait for the manager, and I said, 'Now do I have your attention?'" Shaw, who has a heart condition, said during the incident her blood pressure rose and she started hyperventilating. In addition to calling the police, someone called an ambulance. By the end, she was fined $345 and given a three-month suspended sentence for disorderly conduct, as well as a one-year restraining order prohibiting her from going anywhere near the Manassas Comcast office.

For months afterward, Shaw was a television and Internet celebrity of sorts, appearing on *Good Morning America*, *Nightline*, and *Dr. Phil*. A Mona Shaw fan club formed with a website, and she was hailed as a folk hero on numerous blogs, as well as on ComcastMustDie.com.

That website was initiated in fall 2007, two months after Shaw's Comcast encounter, by Bob Garfield, *Advertising Age* columnist, author, and cohost of National Public Radio's *On the Media*, who had his own customer service dust-up with Comcast. Garfield describes the ComcastMustDie mission on his site's home page: "Actually, I have no death wish for Comcast, or any other gigantic, blundering, greedy, arrogant corporate monstrosity. What I do have is the earnest desire for such companies to change their ways. This site offers an opportunity—for you to vent your grievances (civilly, please) and for Comcast to pay close attention."

In conversation, it isn't hard to get Garfield to air some of his own frustration. "I don't know about anybody else, but already, as I'm dialing 1-800-COMCAST, my blood pressure is 180/140, because I know what's going to happen. I try to start on an even keel, but my worst fears are realized within the first few minutes. And then, you can't really sob on the phone—that's unmanly. But I've tried everything else. I've tried begging, I've tried reasoning, I've tried threatening. I've tried it all. Nothing works. You just hope the gods align on your side.

"I've had real tragedy in my life—really painful stuff, the stuff of real life. But I have never been as close to blowing an aneurysm as I was on the phone with Comcast. It is just so frustrating and so infuriating— the combination of rage and the sense of absolute impotence. It's not a happy feeling. It gets back to the golden rule. You would never treat somebody this way yourself. It's against everything we've ever learned, from the time we were ambulatory. The experience we have is antithetical to everything that we ever have been told about what constitutes the way to get along with others."

Garfield believes Comcast and other companies ignore a changing business landscape at their own peril, a landscape in which the Internet is giving new power to customers. "Now we can aggregate to have our voices heard and to put pressure on these people. Customer service and customer relations management is going to be so critical to all corporate futures. Marketing, as we have known it, is all about customer relations in the future. I mean, forget advertising. It is over. We are seeing the last dregs of advertising being the prime marketing tool. It's going to be all about cultivating, exploiting, and collaborating with consumers. And you can't do that if they hate you."

Hundreds of customers posted their complaints on ComcastMust-Die right away. Many then reported online about getting a personal call from a Comcast customer service worker who was monitoring the site and made sure to solve their problems. Garfield was happy with that but thought the company should go further. "It's not just servicing the customer; it is befriending, exploiting, collaborating. And they have to create a technical infrastructure, and also empower employees to deal with customer complaints in a logical, honest, straightforward manner. They are very far from being there."

On the site, Garfield told Comcast, "You must recognize that none of this is a PR move you have to make through gritted teeth. It is a golden opportunity to exploit the unprecedented potential of a connected world." Garfield pointed out that ever since the founding of Comcast in Tupelo, Mississippi, in the 1960s, it has been laying the wiring for what has become the Internet. "Yet you don't even realize you have created the very conditions for all of us to band together against you. At this moment it must seem like Frankenstein's monster, but take our word for it: It's Comcastic," he wrote, using the company's own advertising slogan to mock it.

While all this public turmoil was taking place on the customer side of Comcast, the shareholders were getting restless and squeezing the company from their end as well. Heretofore in the cable television and broadband Internet industry, only one of a handful of companies provided service in any local market. But those local monopolies started to face serious competition from the dominant national players in the telecommunications industry, such as Verizon and AT&T. Those companies began offering broadband Internet access and television just as Comcast was breaking into the telephone business. Comcast lost some customers, but it also poached some from its new competitors. By the end of 2007, apparently due to pessimism about the company's ability to compete, share prices for Comcast had fallen 35 percent despite the fact that revenues were up and the company was still profitable.

In a speech in early January 2008 at a major Las Vegas consumer electronics show, Brian Roberts, Comcast's CEO and the son of the company's retired octogenarian founder, said Comcast's "customer service has got to continue to reach new levels of excellence."

A few days later, a high-level conflict that had been brewing for months came to a head when a major institutional investor in Comcast, Glenn Greenberg of Chieftain Capital Management, wrote a scathing letter to the board calling for the ouster of Roberts. Greenberg, son of baseball great Hank Greenberg, noted the falling stock prices and called the management of the company a "comcastrophe." As examples, he pointed to slow response to competition; large management bonuses; a multimillion-dollar, five-year death benefit for Roberts's father; and what he saw as too much emphasis on acquiring other companies while ignoring investors.

In a blog for *BusinessWeek* magazine a few days after the letter, reporter Jena McGregor also spoke about the customers who were feeling ignored and expressing their discontent on the Web. McGregor wondered: "When will investors focus on customer service as an issue they should address?"

By Valentine's Day 2008, Comcast was making moves to stem some of the most immediate shareholder criticism. They did away with the founder's death benefit, reduced executive bonuses, and announced that they would reinstate a shareholder dividend they had not paid since 1999. Roberts assured investors that rumored plans to acquire Sprint or Yahoo! were untrue. At least temporarily, stock prices rallied, and an investor uprising was quelled.

But a Fortune.com news brief about the Comcast shareholder initiatives garnered some representative public comments that again highlighted the company's customer problems. One *Fortune* reader said, "Returning profits to their shareholders is good, in the short term, but Comcast needs to invest some of that profit in improving their extremely poor customer service." Another *Fortune* reader said, "This week my wife and I have talked to a total of 9 individuals at their customer service center, including 4 supervisors, and they have yet to resolve our current issue. Unfortunately I'm starting to see that horrible customer service is actually the norm these days in EVERY industry here in the states. As a people we have no desire to properly serve others."

Rick Germano, the senior vice president of customer operations for Comcast, was charged with the huge responsibility of taking on these issues. By early 2008, he had begun a listening tour of Comcast cities. In an open letter to customers on Comcast's website, he announced the company's new commitment to customer service. "We are putting a tremendous amount of resources into making it easier for you to do business with us. This is part of a company-wide effort to improve service that will continue for several years." He then listed some of the first changes, including the hiring of 12,000 new customer service agents and technicians in the two previous years, opening six more call centers, weekend appointments for service so it is more convenient for customers, and shorter windows for appointment times so that customers aren't spending entire days waiting for service.

Germano is humble, and surprisingly frank, when discussing his role. "I would look like a corporate suit," he says, "trying to bury a problem if I said we have no problems. We do have problems." He has been at Comcast since 1986, first in the corporate office in Philadelphia and then managing the West Coast region. In that time, he has seen the company grow and evolve as it expanded from cable television into new markets and industries, such as providing high speed Internet and, now, telephone service. "Telecommunications has become quite competitive, and that's new for us. Cable was a monopoly for all intents and purposes up until very recently. If you don't have any competition, you're the only game in town. People really aren't going to leave you. They're beholden to you.

"Now they have a lot of choices. And we went from not being in the phone business, to being the fourth largest telephone company in the United States in less than three years. And I think we took our eye off of the customer service ball. There were other, more important priorities, like rapid growth, product innovation, integration of acquired properties. We grew way too quickly, and now customer service is playing catch-up. We weren't always big. When I first started, we were tiny, and nobody cared what we did. So I think, in some cases, we're a victim of our own success. But the critical piece is: How do we handle it moving forward? Now we're going up against some of the largest corporations on Earth. And it's fascinating to me to watch AT&T and Verizon, two very large, well-respected corporations, get into the television business. They are learning the hard way, just like we're learning the hard way in the telephone business. And customer service is a key differentiator. It has become much more important. So we have to go back and fix customer service, and it has to be sooner rather than later."

Germano says to do that, the company will continue to adjust to its new competitive landscape, where fast change is inevitable and where employing the tools of the marketplace to keep their corporate eyes and ears open is key. "Customers have higher expectations. They want what they want, and they want it now. Companies have to listen, they have to understand—particularly larger companies. Social networking and blogs are very, very powerful. One unhappy customer, in any company, can become a national sensation in less than twenty-four hours. In our case, we've had a couple. And our reputation has been harmed. I think we accept that fact. A company can't hide its problems anymore. But now we're trying to go out and listen to people, listen to our customers, listen to our employees, and say, 'Okay, what do we need to do to get our reputation back?'"

———ᴍ———

When Claes Fornell enlisted for mandatory military service in his native country, Sweden, during the late 1960s, he was given aptitude tests to determine the job for which he would be best suited. "Apparently, I tested well for putting patterns together that nobody else can see." He was sent to work in cryptology, or code breaking. "I started trying to figure out what was crawling under the surface of the Baltic Sea. We had some very murky pictures from the bottom of the sea." They also had sonar readings that indicated something was there. But nothing was self-evident. By making connections between the incomplete measures and other data they had, Fornell and his colleagues were able to come up with a plausible theory, even if they never found a conclusive answer. "We figured out there was a strong likelihood that it was Russian submarines, unmanned submarines."

Well after his Swedish soldier days, Fornell would go on to develop his skill at determining "what something is even though I can't see it" as a professor of business at the University of Michigan in Ann Arbor. And now, instead of trying to pinpoint suspected Soviet subs, he has turned his expertise toward measurement of a less subversive but equally elusive enigma: how well companies are doing at keeping their customers happy. Fornell is the founder of the American Customer Satisfaction Index, the ACSI, which is now considered a national standard in the United States. Through 65,000 customer interviews each year, Fornell and his staff come up with scores, on a scale of 0 to 100, for more than two hundred major U.S. companies and government agencies. They segment the results into forty-three industries and ten economic sectors and calculate scores for them as well. The numbers have reflected customers' satisfaction with the leading goods and services in the American economy since 1994, when the ACSI started.

"The modern economy has changed so much more than its measurement," Fornell says, "particularly in the United States. This country had a great economic model in terms of producing more with less. And that worked well in manufacturing. But if you apply the same economic model and the same types of measurements to the service sector, it's much more difficult. We were trying to run companies that are mostly service oriented as if they were manufacturing companies, and I just don't think that is healthy. So I thought not only should we look at the quantity of economic output, but we should measure the quality. Because you can easily increase quantity, and quality suffers. And vice versa. They need to be better balanced. It's something that has been neglected in economics, primarily because quality is a bit more difficult to measure."

And measuring it from the consumer's point of view is what Fornell says is unusual about the ACSI. "Traditional accounting leaves customer relationships off the balance sheet. It produces a distorted view of how a company makes money. With ACSI, we are able to capture a much better understanding of a company's current condition and its future capacity to produce wealth." Fornell says this is partly because "spending to improve customer service is usually treated as a cost center rather than an investment." Returns on an investment in one quarter might not come back in the next quarter, or even in the next year, after the initial investment. And when they do come back, Fornell says, they aren't necessarily seen as relating to the initial investment and are often credited to other factors. He is convinced, based on about fifteen years' worth of data, that customer satisfaction is a leading indicator of a company's long-term market value and financial health.

The exception, he says, is in businesses where the customer has no real choice. "In the cable TV industry, forget it." Comcast has had one of the lowest ACSI scores (59 in 2009) in the already low-scoring cable and satellite TV industry as a whole (63 in 2009). Fornell blames that in part on the fact that Comcast has had a monopoly in many cities. Customers had few, if any, other options. So the company, and the industry, did not have the incentive "to treat their customers well. And they still have made a lot of money. Now recently, if you look at the return to investors, it hasn't been that great. But as long as we have a system, or a particular part of a system, where there's not punishment for being bad, then you can make a lot of money by actually treating your customers like dirt. The airline industry is another interesting example. But it's a little different. We're not treated very well there either, but airlines are not making money."

The airline industry as a whole had an average ACSI score of only 64 in 2009, down 11.1 percent from 1995, the first year it was measured. By contrast, one of the highest-scoring industries is Internet retail, which scored an average of 82. The leader in that industry is Amazon.com with a score of 86, up 2.4 percent from its score of 84 the first year it was measured in 2000.

Fornell believes that as the way we measure our economy grows more nuanced, customer service will improve. "Maybe I'm too optimistic, but I think it will be much more difficult in the future for companies to hide from the power of the buyer." Increasingly, he says, the rule will be, "If you have consumer anger directed at your company, you better do something about it." He is not much for clichés like "the customer is always right," because, he says, "that is obviously not true. But what I do think is true is another saying: 'Take care of your customer, or somebody else will.'"

—⚬—

Scott Broetzmann has been paying attention to angry customers for much of his career. He majored in psychology and communication science at the University of Wisconsin, and went on to work for the Better Business Bureau, first in his native Milwaukee and later nationally in Washington, D.C. A husband and father in his mid-forties, Broetzmann (pronounced Brets-man) is friendly, smart, and levelheaded—just the kind of guy most people would trust to analyze problems fairly and solve them humanely. After he left the Better Business Bureau, Broetzmann became a consultant on what the industry calls "the customer experience." He collects data on it, analyzes it, and helps companies see the value of investing intelligently in their own customer service.

A few years ago, Broetzmann was reading a *Washington Post* article about store owners who were having a hard time holding on to staff because working in retail was so low paying and high stress. Broetzmann remembers the article depicting customers as "a bunch of jerks." It immediately reminded him of actor Michael Douglas's wry portrayal of an aggrieved customer gone wrong in the 1993 film *Falling Down*.

Douglas's character, Bill Foster, is a man broken by the stresses of commuting, crime, job loss, divorce, and the cynicism of the everyday world. He reaches a breaking point in a fast food restaurant where he asks for breakfast at 11:32 one morning. The guy behind the counter says, "We stopped serving breakfast at 11:30." Foster appeals to him to help anyway. The worker refuses. Out of patience, Foster looks the guy in the eye and says, "Have you ever heard the expression, 'The customer is always right'?" The worker says, "Yeah." Foster then says, "Yeah? Well, here I am, the customer." Driven by what he interprets as continued disregard by the worker, Foster pulls out a machine gun and waves it around the restaurant until he gets his way. He continues his armed tirade against bad service across Los Angeles. After ransacking a convenience store where he felt mistreated, he tells the frightened owner, "I'm just standing up for my rights as a consumer."

Broetzmann also believes that customers often get a raw deal these days. But his motives and tactics for combating that are nothing like those of Michael Douglas's character. Broetzmann prefers to mediate between aggrieved customers and companies gone astray. He takes care always to approach both with understanding and a goal of helping each to see the other's point of view.

That is why he felt a need to counter what he saw as growing hype about irrational customers. He started his quest with an Internet search of the word *rage* and got a smorgasbord of terms: *road rage, air rage, retail rage, computer rage, travel,* and *leisure rage*. But he saw little on the justified indignation of reasonable people, which he had a feeling was more common than indicated in the sensational accounts he found. "Rage was being positioned in the marketplace," Broetzmann says, "maybe unfairly, maybe fairly, as a bunch of crazy people who did wacky things. It just didn't seem right to me."

Then the social scientist in him took over. His company, Customer Care Measurement and Consulting, based in northern Virginia, teamed up with Arizona State University's business school to gather some hard evidence on the phenomenon he was sensing. They created the Customer Rage Study and reported their first results in 2003. The study was based on a telephone survey of a random sample of national households in which respondents who had trouble with a product or service during the past twelve months answered a series of questions about the problem they considered most serious. The study showed that approximately 68 percent said they were either extremely or very upset about their problem. Broetzmann and fellow researchers identified those people as experiencing "customer rage." Another 28 percent were somewhat or a bit upset. Just 3 percent were not at all upset.

But the study went on. It asked those who were found to have "rage" to answer questions about the various ways they might have expressed their displeasure. Ninety percent said they shared their maddening story with other people, and 77 percent complained to the company that caused the problem. Of those who complained, customers reacted in one or more of the following ways to the company's handling of their complaint: 57 percent decided never to do business with the company again, 28 percent yelled or raised their voice at a company employee, 8 percent cursed, and another 8 percent threatened legal action.

The Customer Rage Study came out again in 2004, 2005, and 2007, and not much had changed from 2003. The percentage of people with a complaint who reported experiencing rage rose or held steady each year, never again dipping below 70 percent. But in 2007, 44 percent reported being "extremely upset," as compared with an average of 41 percent in previous years. Each year the study became more detailed. Perhaps in homage to Michael Douglas's movie character, or maybe just to make sure rage wasn't about to get out of hand as it did in that movie, the 2004 study began asking about revenge. Each year since, on average, 15 percent of respondents have wanted revenge on the company they felt had wronged them. Only 1 percent reported getting it. The study didn't specify how, but Mona Shaw's hammer and Bob Garfield's ComcastMustDie website come to mind.

—⁓—

A few years ago, Junius Harris was moving into a newly renovated apartment in New York City. He had been a star elementary school teacher in Los Angeles and New York since the late 1980s. His friends say patience, forgiveness, integrity, and a wry humor seem to be embedded in Harris's DNA. But the customer service at AT&T and Verizon pushed him past his limits during his move.

Harris and his partner, David Lebow, were set to move in on August 15. On July 15, Harris called to switch their current Verizon landline number to the new place. Moving it didn't cost anything; he just had to get it done early so the line would be working when they moved in. But Verizon told him the previous tenants had not cancelled their account with AT&T, so the new apartment's phone lines were still live. Before his phone service could be established, the previous phone service had to be cancelled. The Verizon customer service agent told Harris they could not cancel an AT&T customer's account. He would have to get AT&T to do that. Verizon knew the account holder's name and the phone number but couldn't tell Harris, so he would have to cancel the account without any of the information or authority he needed. Harris called his new landlord for help, only to find he was in Greece for the month. Harris called Verizon one more time just to see if there was any other way. The agent told him they could install new lines into the apartment, but that would cost $300. Harris decided to go ahead with it. The agent immediately made the appointment for Saturday, August 15, move-in day.

Then Harris called AT&T, on his Verizon phone, to see if he could get anywhere with them. He couldn't proceed too far into the voice response system because he didn't have an account number (an AT&T phone number). When the system asked if he was a customer, he said yes, just to get through. He was asked again for his account number. Finally, he shouted "agent" and "operator" at the voice response system. At first it told him it did not understand his response. But he just kept shouting "agent" repeatedly. Eventually it connected him to a live customer service agent, in India. Harris explained the situation. But when she asked him for the number of the line in the apartment, he couldn't tell her. When she asked for the name of the customer, he didn't know. Finally, she told him that all she could do was report it as an abandoned line. She would file the form, but it would take two weeks to turn off the line. So by the beginning of August, the line should be free to set up his Verizon service. He was skeptical and asked her to give him a number he could call to check on it. She assured him the old phone line would be disconnected and gave him a confirmation number instead. He asked again for a phone number to check on it. She wouldn't give in. Harris hung up, warily.

Then he called Verizon back to cancel the appointment to put in new lines. They transferred him to the maintenance line. The technicians advised him not to cancel the appointment unless he was positive the line was free, because then he might be left in the lurch. He agreed, and so they transferred him back to the agent. She told Harris that if the line was free when they came out and they didn't have to install new wires, the service call would cost only $80. Then without really saying it, the Verizon agent mentioned that one way to get around this was to call AT&T and pretend to be somebody who could get the line cancelled. Harris understood her point, but lying was not really in his nature.

Three weeks later, about five days before moving day, Harris and Lebow were at the apartment cleaning it. Harris called AT&T again from his cell phone to see if the line had been cancelled. He somehow maneuvered himself to something called AT&T Local. The agent was in the United States this time. Harris told his story, replete with the confirmation number. The agent told him that the line had not been cancelled. No form had been filed. She said the confirmation number he had meant nothing. It was a fake. They didn't issue those kinds of numbers. She said the only way to cancel the account was to have the person who owns the building or the account holder do it. Then she asked, "Who are you again?" Before the call, Lebow had run down to the mailboxes for the apartment and gotten the two names of the previous tenants off it—a male name and a female name. So Harris didn't lie, but answered that the account holder was one of the two names. The agent told him it was the woman he mentioned. That helped. At least he had the name now. But the AT&T agent said all she could do was try to expedite a new order to cancel the abandoned line. She wouldn't promise it would be done by Saturday, but he was welcome to call back and check then.

On Saturday morning, a few hours before Verizon was due to arrive, Lebow was unpacking, and Harris went in the back room to call AT&T one more time. He now knew which buttons to press and which prompts to use to get where he needed to be. As he waited on hold, he planned what he would say.

Harris was born and grew up in Jamaica, Queens, in New York City. His father was a bus driver and his mother a nurse. He had gone to Columbia University, the first in his family to make it to the Ivy League. Sitting on hold that morning in his new apartment, Harris says something clicked. "I realized they weren't going to give me a straight answer." Then he thought of the woman at Verizon who seemed to be nudging him to do what he was about to do.

When the AT&T operator came on the line, he found himself yelling into the phone in a Greek accent. "Yes, hello. My name is Stavros Papadopoulos," the name of his landlord. "It all came together," says Harris. "It was such a big lie, and it just felt so weird because everybody had been saying that they were taking care of this, and they weren't." He went on impersonating his landlord. The agent told him the line was not cancelled yet. He did a whole riff on how he was a very busy man and had no time to deal with their incompetence. "What kind of business are you running?" he asked, his Greek accent holding strong. "I need this to end now." Suddenly, the agent was very apologetic. "But I blustered on," says Harris.

Lebow had heard the yelling and wondered what was going on. He came to the door but didn't go in. He heard Harris bellowing into the phone in a Greek accent. Thinking he might ruin it for laughing, he stepped away. "Tell me who to call. I want names and numbers. My tenant needs to move in. What kind of people say they will do something and then don't do it?" In the end, the woman said she would take care of it right away and that the line should be free in minutes. She apologized profusely and thanked him for calling AT&T. Harris said, "Thank you. I apologize for yelling. It was nothing against you. How do you say—you seem like a very nice lady." When Verizon came an hour later, it was done. Harris felt a little guilty but says, "It was so frustrating. They make you do things you wouldn't normally do."

In that 2001 rudeness survey by Public Agenda, 69 percent of respondents said they believed the problem of a lack of consideration and courtesy in our society was getting worse. And 52 percent of respondents said the residue from these infuriating incidents stayed with them for a long time afterward. But one point in the study raised a question that is debatable: 73 percent of respondents said they believe Americans used to treat people with more respect and courtesy in the past, while 21 percent believe that is simply nostalgia for a past that never existed.

A look back at how customer service has evolved (or devolved) in this country, especially customer service by telephone, not only confirms the merit of both those opinions about the past in the rudeness study, but also shows how we got to where we are today.

2.   What Would Alexander Graham Bell Say Now?

Mildred Lothrop was roused from her sleep in the wee hours of Monday morning, May 31, 1920, by the sound of a ringing switchboard. As the chief telephone operator for Northwestern Bell in Homer, Nebraska, her home in the heart of that small town was the area phone company's main office. She hopped out of bed and ran to answer the call. Mildred knew that if someone was ringing her in the middle of the night, it must be important. Sure enough, a customer five miles up the Omaha Creek from Homer was calling to alert Mildred that heavy rains had caused the creek to overflow, turning the entire valley above Homer into a sheet of water, and the torrent was heading toward town. Sitting at the switchboard, still in her dressing gown, Mildred sprang into action. She rang and woke the fire chief and the mayor. Then she methodically began calling all her sleeping customers in the path of the flash flood to warn them of the coming waters and urge them to get to higher ground.

She sent the youngest of her five sons out into the rain to ring the fire bell, knowing that would wake the residents she might have missed, causing them to call her at the central office to find out what was happening. As the heavy storm kept coming for more than four hours, Mildred stayed at her job, providing a lifeline for her inundated customers. Even as water rose around her and the mayor and her sons begged her to abandon the switchboard for her own safety, Mildred wouldn't budge. She was the pivotal communications point for the whole area, directing help where it was needed and assuring stranded customers that someone would rescue them soon. Mildred did not leave until the flood waters had risen so high that her switchboard would no longer function. The water was up to her shoulders when they finally pried Mildred away from her work post to safety. About a hundred homes were damaged or destroyed by the flood, but because of Mildred's dedication, no one died. Later she said that though she was frightened, "At times like that, you just don't think about yourself."

In recognition of her heroism, Mildred Lothrop was the first person ever awarded the Vail Gold Medal, accompanied by a $1,000 check. The award, still given to telecommunications industry workers today and accompanied by checks as high as $10,000, is named after the first general manager of AT&T, Theodore Newton Vail. The award was created after Vail's death in 1920 to honor employees who lived up to his legendary devotion to what we would call customer service today. But Vail called it "public relations," before that term took on its current meaning. Vail believed that taking care of the customer—good relations between the customer and the company—was the most important thing a corporation could do for its long-term health and profit. He believed that corporations had a public trust with their customers as much as they did with their investors. Bucking the trend of the time, he advocated that profits should be funneled back into the company for service improvements and not solely doled out to investors. He preached that the long-term health of the company and satisfaction of its customers should not be subordinated to the short-term gain of shareholders.

Vail's disagreements with other business leaders of his era, including the Boston financiers of AT&T, caused him to quit his post as general manager after nearly twenty years. Vail said the early investors in the telephone and telegraph industry were running the show and thinking only of milking all the technology patents they had for the benefit of the stockholders, at the expense of the customer. Vail knew that strategy was a shortsighted collision course that would produce disastrous results for the customers and for long-term profits.

Vail was proven right. In 1907 he was brought back as AT&T's president by financier J. P. Morgan after most of the early technology patents had expired. The company was losing money, and the public's distrust of it was at a zenith. To great success, Vail implemented his pioneering idea of one unified long-distance phone service for all the country, reinforced by his ideas of "public relations."

Vail came by his interest in communication technology naturally. His great-uncle was Samuel Morse, who invented the Morse code, a forerunner to the telephone. Just before coming to the telephone industry, Vail had been in charge of the U.S. Postal Service, where he implemented some of the systems the post office still uses today, including the idea of carriers delivering mail every day. He has been credited more recently for making the post office into the FedEx of its day, creating a new, efficient message delivery system. So the concept of creating a national phone service that connected the entire United States was a natural outgrowth of his previous work and even his ancestry.

In the 1910 AT&T Annual Report, Vail summed up some pitfalls of the customer service business then, which endure today. He talked about business from the point of view of both the customer and the company. Such compassion, or even compassionate lip service, was not common among corporate leaders in those days. "There has always been and will always be the laudable desire," said Vail, "of the great public to be served rightly, and as cheaply as possible, which sometimes selfishly degenerates into a lack of consideration for the rights of those who are serving. On the other hand there has always been the laudable desire of the 'server,' or the producer, to get a profit for his services or production, which sometimes degenerates into a selfish disregard or a lack of consideration for the rights of those who are served."

Vail's ideas about humane treatment of customers by companies also extended to employees. Under his leadership, AT&T became the first corporation to provide pensions for its workers. And when government regulators were breathing down the neck of the company, it was Vail who engineered the regulated monopoly structure that kept the company private, a structure that endured at AT&T until deregulation in the 1980s. In a regulated monopoly, a company agrees to government oversight; in exchange, the government makes it illegal for other companies to compete in the market. "It is contended," he wrote in 1907, "that if there is to be no competition, there should be public control." That idea too came from a sense of being fair to the customer and the belief that one unified long-distance service was better than many, even though the phone company—as AT&T came to be known until deregulation opened up the market to competitors—did not always live up to Vail's most noble ideals.

—⦵—

Just after Christmas in 1890, a letter complaining about local phone service was sent to Gardiner G. Hubbard, the father-in-law of telephone inventor Alexander Graham Bell, from a well-known citizen of Hartford, Connecticut. It was addressed to "The father-in-law of the Telephone" at Hubbard's home in Washington, D.C., and signed, "Mark Twain." It read in part:

> The Hartford telephone is the very worst on the face of the whole earth. No man can dictate a 20-word message intelligibly through it at any hour of the day without devoting a week's worth of time to it, and there is no nightservice whatsoever since electric-lighting was introduced. Though mind you they *charge* for night-service in their cold, calm way, just the same as if they furnished it. And if you try to curse through the telephone, they shut you off. It is this ostentatious holiness that grovels me. Every day I go there to practice and always get shut off. So what it amounts to is, that I don't get any practice that can really be considered practice.

Twain facetiously held Hubbard and Bell responsible for the troubles (including not being able to get practice at using curse words) with his local phone company's version of the mechanism he implied they had foisted upon the world.

Some of the challenges and public sentiments surrounding early telephone service in the late 1800s and early 1900s were eerily similar to troubles abounding in today's world of customer service by telephone. If customer rage had been measured among the first telephone subscribers, who were mostly affluent white men, it might well have registered somewhere near the percentages we see today, or higher.

In November 1882, the *New York Times* said, "There is nothing that will so excite the irritability of a person, apparently, as the telephone, and the man who can use it and keep an even temper at the same time is a paragon of patience and forbearance." A month later in December, an article headlined "Swearing by Telephone" described a Cincinnati case in which a man got angry when an operator connected him to the wrong number and he said, "If you can't get the party I want, you may shut up your damn telephone." At that, company representatives came to the man's house, took his telephone, and barred him from being a customer because of his profanity. The man filed suit and lost, so he appealed to the district court. He lost there too. Part of the ruling read: "The question is whether in a business communication, where a party is somewhat excited, having failed to get a proper communication, and uses the words, 'Damn your telephone,' that is a sufficient ground for cutting off permanently the use of the telephone for which he had paid and depriving him of a vested right." Apparently it was.

By 1902, swearing at operators had become illegal in many places. In Chicago, John Laskowski was charged with disorderly conduct and fined $20 for shouting what the prosecution called "cuss words" after an operator told him that not only was the line he wanted busy, but also that he couldn't get back the money he had deposited into the pay phone he was using. Laskowski admitted to swearing at the phone and the operator. "But," he told the court by way of explanation, "I was hungry and wanted to telephone for my dinner." The court said that was no excuse for swearing. In St. Louis, also in 1902, Dr. Gettys, a physician, was arrested for cursing at an operator. In court he was asked, "Did you swear over the telephone?" He responded, "Yes, Sir, I did." But he clarified, "I cussed the system, not the employees." Dr. Gettys was found guilty of using abusive language and fined $5.

Much like customer service agents today, in the early days of the telephone, it was the frontline workers, the operators—not senior management—who directly bore the brunt of customers' frustration with their system. As the telephone was becoming an instrument for communication in the late nineteenth century, human operators were required to connect customers through switchboards. And the first switchboard operators were teenage boys, a logical choice because they were the ones who had successfully operated all the telegraphs that came before telephones. But they didn't need to talk to customers to get their telegraph jobs done. When they suddenly did have contact with customers, the boys proved to be too unruly. Customers complained that boy operators were rude and cursed at them. In the switching rooms, the boys had to run from one board to another and yell to each other to connect the calls. It sometimes took awhile because the technology was slow. Apparently, during the waits the boys also had wrestling matches, threw spit wads, played practical jokes on customers, and some even drank beer. The various local phone companies had a hard time reeling in their wild operators.

In 1910, thirty-four years after the telephone was invented, Herbert N. Casson wrote a lively account of the early years in which he described the operator problem. "By the clumsy methods of those days, from two to six boys were needed to handle each call. And there was usually more or less of a cat-and-dog squabble between the boys and the public, with every one yelling at the top of his voice." He concluded, "Boys, as operators, proved to be most complete and consistent failures. Their sins of omission and commission would fill a book. What with whittling the switchboard, swearing at subscribers, playing tricks with the wires and roaring on all occasions like young bulls of Bashan, the boys in the first exchanges did their full share in adding to the troubles of the business. Nothing could be done with them."

Knowing that to lure customers away from the telegraph they would have to improve their operators' service, the phone companies eventually fired the teenage boys, a solution that Casson applauded. "In place of the noisy and obstreperous boy came the docile, soft-voiced girl. The quiet voice, pitched high, the deft fingers, the patient courtesy and attentiveness—these qualities were precisely what the gentle telephone required in its attendants." He also said, "Girls were easier to train; they were more careful; and they were much more likely to give 'the soft answer that turneth away wrath.'"

Rather than being a quality inherent to women, the female operators' civility might have had more to do with the fact that a woman with a yen for some independence, or income, did not have many other job options outside the home in the late nineteenth and early twentieth centuries. Another bonus for the company was that the women could be paid less than the boys, who were already low paid. But a century ago, not many people would have worried about any of that. Instead, Casson went on to praise the operators' part in the proper running of the newest technological wonder: "These telephone girls are the human part of a great communication machine. No matter how many millions of dollars are spent on cables and switchboards, the quality of telephone service depends upon the girl at the exchange end of the wire. More is demanded of her than any other servant of the public." He believed that the telephone company was providing a public service, though that was not necessarily the common belief of his business colleagues.

Casson also foreshadowed the respective plights of telephone customer service agents and their customers a century later when he said, "Her clients refuse to stand in line and quietly wait their turn. They do not see her work and they do not know what her work is. They are in a hurry, or they would not be at the telephone; and each second is a minute long. Any delay is a direct personal affront that makes a vivid impression upon their minds."

The women selected to become operators were chosen for their manner and malleability. Perhaps in reaction to the disastrous experience with the boys, phone companies all over the country kept a tight rein on these women, carefully picked to project a certain image. Many more applied than were selected. They were required to be unmarried and usually between the ages of about eighteen and twenty-six. If they married, they were let go. Dress codes meant they had to look prim and proper always, even though, as Casson had noted, no subscribers would see them doing their jobs. Also in line with the tenor of the times, phone company executives rejected any African American or Jewish women who applied, and they would not hire anyone with a foreign-sounding accent. The women who were hired were given elocution lessons as part of their rigorous training. They were taught to draw out certain words for clarity because early telephone lines were noisy. So the word *please* would be pronounced "pleeeyazz." The number nine became "niyun," and the word *line* turned into "liyun."

Corporate executives also commissioned management teams to come in and marshal the women to the company's needs. Much as management does in some call centers today, these early telephone operators had their humanity regulated down to the smallest detail, all in the name of efficiency. The women had to sit facing the switchboard at all times. They were not to talk to each other and were not allowed to look around for fear they might miss a light flashing on the switchboard indicating an incoming call. They were to answer those calls within four and a half seconds. They had strict limits on what they could and could not say to the customers, and they were always required to use "pleeeyazz" and "thank you." They worked ten to twelve hours a day, six days a week. Supervisors watched over them at all times. They had to ask for permission to go to the bathroom or get a drink of water. And without the operators or customers knowing it, some supervisors even listened in on their conversations. No recording back then warned anyone that "your call may be monitored for quality assurance."

The women came to be called "hello girls," because when subscribers took their receivers off the hook to place calls, instead of the dial tone that came later, they would hear the operators say "hello" on the other end. The early phone systems did not use numbers, so the operators had to memorize the names of all the customers. Once phone numbers became standard, the operators were required to pick up the call by asking for the number the subscriber wanted to call, saying only, "Number, please." Often subscribers became impatient waiting for a connection, so managers began monitoring and calculating the wait times. In 1882, the average wait time for a Chicago subscriber to be connected to another local subscriber was five minutes. By 1897, that wait time had been reduced to 45 seconds. By 1900, the average wait time was down to 6.2 seconds.

Despite the civilizing influence the women were supposed to have had on their customers, during those waiting periods the operators heard the brunt of customers' frustration at the amount of time a connection was taking and at the poor quality of the early connections too. A Cincinnati operator quoted in the local paper in 1920 described some of her customers as "discourteous, inconsiderate, chronic complainers." She said the customers often didn't speak clearly or loudly enough and then got angry when the operators didn't immediately catch what they were saying. "Their society manners are forgotten when using the telephone." Another employee told the paper in 1920, "The public has forgotten the operator is a human."

An anonymous poem of the time conveys the prevailing public conception of these early operators and is telling for its similarities to current-day attitudes toward customer service agents:

> *The Girl We Call "Hello"*
> There's a certain kind of people, very useful, yet
> obscure,
> Who receive small approbation from the public, I am
> sure.
> Yet the service which they render none of us could
> well forego,
> Still 'tis rare we kindly speak or think of the girl we call
> "Hello."
> The Public simply take her as a cog in one great
> wheel,
> Placed there for their convenience, to promote the
> commonweal.
> And it's rare indeed a kindness to these girls we show,
> But oftentimes we "cuss" aloud the girl we call "Hello."

We grasp our "phone," a number give, and should
  there be delay,
We frankly are ashamed to own the awful things we
  say.
We seem to think that ours must be the only call, you
  know.
When perhaps some forty others, quite insistent, call
  "Hello."

Around the turn of the century, automatic switching technology
was developed that began to make these local operators' duties obsolete. They no longer had to be involved in connecting one caller with
another at local phone companies. Newer phones started to have rotary
dialing mechanisms so customers could dial each other directly in local
systems. Hello girls began to fade. In 1892, LaPorte, Indiana, became
the first city in the country to have a fully automated local phone system. A news brief in the *New York Times* on November 3, 1892, noted
the milestone with the headline "Does Away with the 'Hello' Girl." It
said that the city was celebrating the new system by declaring the following Thursday "telephone day" and that "a special train load of capi-
talists from Chicago, New York, San Francisco, and Europe" would be
arriving to join the festivities.

Years later, nostalgia began to mark the continued fading away of
local operators, as more systems integrated the automated switching
technology. In 1906, the *New York Times* ran a Sunday magazine feature "The Passing of the Telephone Girl: A Retrospect," which started
by reporting that "there has been some anxiety felt in 'Hello' circles as
to the future of the telephone girl in case the automatic girlless phone
should be adopted." The article estimated there were more than 5 million
telephones in the United States at that time, and that more than 45,000
"girl" operators responded to more than 25 million "hellos" each day:

Her familiar voice is heard wherever the telephone wire
leads. From the isolated prairie homestead to the hurry

and bustle of Wall Street is a long step, but the voice of the ubiquitous telephone girl is heard all along the line. So familiar has her presence been in the growth of the country at large that any development in the art of telephony which would do away with her services would appear to be a radical departure from the accepted methods in vogue.

The 1906 article then went on to mourn the seemingly inevitable nationwide loss of the operator at "central," as the local switching facilities where the hello girls worked were called. And the article foreshadowed public laments a century later about the loss of human contact on today's customer service lines:

> The telephone business does not differ from any other, inasmuch as the process of evolution always tends to eliminate the personal factor as much as possible, substituting mechanical means for manual operations.
> Stop for a moment and think what this means.
> A machine, no matter how ingeniously constructed, cannot think. In the adoption of the automatic telephone we eliminate the girl who has placed her intelligence at our command, and instead assume the entire responsibility of our actions.
> The feeling of assurance given by the friendly voice of central will be missing, and instead there will arise a sense of incompleteness which will be difficult to overcome.

—⟋⟍—

By World War II, the hello girls' time had passed. But for at least the first two-thirds of the twentieth century, operators, who continued to be almost all women, were still needed to connect long-distance calls. Then, in the late 1950s, direct dialing of long-distance calls became possible, and the operators' role was reduced further, mostly to handling collect calls.

The middle of the twentieth century also saw the first incarnations of the term *customer service*, as businesses started to answer customers' questions and take orders by phone. In 1950, an article in the *New York Times* reported that for the previous ten years, the New York Telephone Company had employed eleven courtesy experts they called "customer service consultants." These experts had analyzed phone operations and conducted workshops for about 1,500 subscribers, "including manufacturers, department stores, banks, lawyers, universities, newspapers and theatres," teaching them how to "speak pleasantly, cheerfully and courteously over the telephone." In one telephone order–taking section at a department store, the consultants found that the women taking the orders "sounded bored, made customers hang on and did not apologize for delays." The way the women answered the phone especially shocked the consultants. Instead of a more professional greeting, the workers picked up the phone and said, "It's your nickel, brother, talk fast."

The consultants found the main reasons for the women's sour moods were that the forty female telephone workers had to function in cramped quarters and they did not think they had the information they needed to do their jobs properly. As a result, the consultants suggested that the phone order area be expanded, which it was. The women were given more information to use. And the courtesy experts also instructed them on how to answer the phone politely.

In 1965, the chairman of the Macy's department store board was considered bold for making "customer services" a central theme of his speech to the Macy's annual shareholders' meeting. Jack I. Straus said the highest-level executives in retailing were not being deployed to supervise the handling of after-sale issues such as customer questions and complaints. Instead, these functions were put on the back burner, while top executives spent the bulk of their time overseeing all aspects of making sales. Straus said that the effects of that kind of management were being noticed by customers. He told the board of a recently completed six-month review by thirteen task forces within Macy's looking at all aspects of customer contact, from employee attitudes and store policies to delivery, billing, and advertising. Based on their findings that customers felt neglected, he announced a major program at Macy's to "re-emphasize the importance of impressing on the customers that we are really interested in their problems, that we really care."

Then he waxed poetic about the dehumanizing technological and social changes that were proliferating around them. "We live in a world where we are a number," he said, "to the tax collector and to the Social Security department." Referring to new postal innovations and the new seven-digit phone numbers that replaced the old system of exchanges, where neighborhood names were combined with numbers, he continued, "We are getting all-number telephone dialing and we live in zip code areas." The anonymity of all these numbers, he said, has led to a general sense of alienation. He then spoke of what he considered the antidote: a policy of "caring" he was reinstating at Macy's. He said that such an attitude was not just a program that all retailers needed to consider, but a philosophy with an impact beyond retailing, to caring about the quality of government, education, and public safety. "Someone has got to get religion on this matter," Straus said.

By the early 1960s, the stage was being set for a wave of consumer advocacy in the United States, in sync with the widespread political unrest and social rebellion that spread through the decade. President Kennedy had focused attention on consumer issues with his Consumer Bill of Rights in 1961, which established the Consumer Protection Agency. Among other things it stated that consumers had a right to be heard. Then President Johnson created a new position, the special assistant to the president for consumer affairs, and appointed labor activist Esther Peterson to the job.

Ralph Nader made a splash in the 1960s and 1970s with his consumer advocacy as well, especially in addressing the safety and quality of U.S. automobiles. His 1965 book, *Unsafe at Any Speed*, shook the automobile industry and led to the implementation of what were called lemon laws to protect consumers against getting stuck with badly built cars. His advocacy also led to other stricter regulation of product safety and quality-of-life issues across the board, such as mandatory seat belts in cars and clean water and air legislation.

In 1969, the U.S. Chamber of Commerce called for a program of voluntary business reforms to respond to growing consumer pressure. An advisory panel report by thirty-two business leaders said, "Current consumer activism, which has gone beyond protest to the formulation of legislative reform programs, represents a 'new consumerism' much as the civil rights movement of the fifties sought redress through programs and policies designed to stimulate Government action." The chamber report came up with the voluntary reforms "to minimize ill-conceived legislation and to offset the impact of new Federal regulatory programs which could impose onerous burdens on industry." In other words, business had gotten the message of the times: the masses, or at least a lot of people under thirty, were rebelling against what they saw as corporate greed and disregard for the consumer. They were using legislation to address their concerns, and businesses had better cover themselves. The chamber advised companies to change how they operated, especially in their marketing and advertising practices, "to reflect a greater awareness and sensitivity to the public's evolving ethical values and nonmaterialistic aspirations." The report warned executives, "It is of paramount importance to recognize that the consumer movement is well-established and is likely to gain strength in coming years."

It didn't gain as much strength as its leaders hoped or business feared in the 1970s. But some of the Chamber's suggested voluntary, preemptive reforms struck right at what we now call customer service. The 1969 report advised businesses to come up with "a workable feedback system for customer complaints and inquiries." It also suggested rethinking the role of the Better Business Bureau, making it into "a consumer ombudsman" to strengthen the systems that businesses had set up for dealing with questions, complaints, and problem solving. The report ended, in part, by saying, "Businesses will need to become more attuned to the changing values of a better-educated younger generation which is quite critical of orthodox business practices." The establishment was on alert.

Also in the late 1960s, AT&T introduced a service for businesses called WATS, which stood for "wide area telephone service." Because so many businesses were receiving collect long-distance calls from customers, 800 numbers or WATS lines were meant to make such customer contact less expensive. Instead of costly collect-call rates, businesses could pay a more reasonable flat fee for the long-distance calls from their customers regarding sales, repairs, questions, and complaints. But WATS lines were also AT&T's response to the fact that its long-distance operators were becoming obsolete. While collect calling persisted into the 1990s, phone company operators spent an increasing amount of their time during the 1970s handling directory assistance calls. And in 1973, the phone company began charging for those as well. It wouldn't be until the 1980s and 1990s that 800 numbers took off, becoming a mandatory part of doing business in most industries and the main channel of communication for the industry that sprang up around customer service. The birth of that industry was spurred by the consumer movement of the 1960s and 1970s, but also by a budding social-science focus on the customer in the 1970s and 1980s.

—⁂—

By the early 1970s, change was happening. One editorial writer in 1972 summed it up: "Ralph Nader has become a folk hero. Congressmen are standing in line to attach their names to consumer legislation. And the word on the tip of every board chairman's tongue is consumerism. The dissatisfied customer, once a loner, has become a political and economic power—part of the loosely knit but potent consumer movement."

Much of the focus of the consumer movement was on product quality and safety, not on how well businesses handled customer problems. But in the early 1970s, the news media reported a heightened emphasis on customer service at major corporations, and many mentioned the consumer advocacy—or what was then often called "consumerism"—of the mid-1960s as a direct cause. Companies developed consumer relations or consumer affairs departments to handle questions and complaints. In 1971, Ford Motor Company started a division within the consumer service department devoted specifically to analyzing customer complaints and addressing them in Ford's products and services.

In 1972, the budget for consumer service at Ford had increased by $10 million. In 1972, the Whirlpool Corporation spent $45 million on consumer services.

Companies such as Hallmark, Pan American Airlines, RCA Corporation, and Chase had created the corporate ombudsmen by 1971 that the Better Business Bureau recommended in its 1969 report. The companies touted these executive-level ombudsmen as being higher up in the company than many previous complaint department workers, affording them more power to cut across different departments in order to get things done. The Chrysler Corporation called its ombudsman "Your Man in Detroit." He was Byron J. Nichols, a thirty-year Chrysler veteran who became its first vice president of consumer affairs. "I have enough experience in the corporation," Nichols said in 1971, "to know exactly whom to call. And by handling our customers' problems well, it will have a good psychological effect."

Suspicion lingered about the sincerity of the business world's motives and about its true commitment to these efforts. "I think there's an awful lot of P.R. in it," said one consumer advocate in 1973. "Companies ought to try to cut out conning the public and give us the facts." Philip Schrag, a Columbia University law professor at the time, said, "The most important consumer issues require federal legislation, but business is doing everything it can to fight it."

In the mid-1970s, studies of consumer attitudes started to appear in public more frequently than before. A 1976 newspaper ad by the Better Business Bureau mentioned the Corporate Priorities Study, conducted by a market research firm, which showed what consumers wanted most. "Consumers care about human decency and courtesy," the ad said, summarizing the study. "They want to be treated like people, not statistics. They desire enough information to enable them to make intelligent buying decisions. They want a guarantee expressed in plain English. They want a merchant to make good on defects promptly, without hassle."

An academic survey of consumers in 1977 found they were unhappy with one out of five purchases, but it found that fewer than half who were dissatisfied complained. And of those who did complain, one third were not happy with the way the company handled the complaint. Often people just threw away defective products without complaining and never bought from the company again. One of the professors who ran the survey said, "Complaints are too costly for the consumer and frequently unproductive," and noted that this had caused resentment against business.

In 1976, Gerald Ford's administration released a report on how well customer complaints were being handled by American business, non-profits, and government. The study, Consumer Complaint Handling in America, was commissioned in 1974 by Virginia Knauer, the special assistant on consumer affairs to President Richard Nixon and then to President Ford. The results on how business handled its complaints were bleak. Sixty-nine percent of the people who had a consumer problem complained. Only 22 percent of those people who complained said they were completely satisfied by the response from the company to which they complained. And of the 31 percent who didn't complain, 55 percent said it was because it wasn't worth the effort, and another 21 percent said they decided that no one would be concerned about or interested in their problem.

Until that 1976 report, informally called "the White House study," conventional wisdom held that handling customer complaints was merely a cost of doing business. Despite some corporate efforts to accord customer service new value in the 1960s and 1970s, within some companies it was almost considered a leech. But the White House study and others conclusively showed that customers were unhappy with their treatment by companies and that the bad experience had a significant impact on their loyalty to the company. Those were terms businesses should have understood, because they knew customer loyalty had an impact on their bottom line. So by the late 1970s, some were beginning to recognize that customer service was more fertilizer than leech.

In addition, the mid-1970s to mid-1980s was a time when most of the main technology now used in customer service was just emerging.

Rotary dials gave way to touch-tone phones starting in the 1960s, paving the way for early automatic response systems requiring a caller to press a number to reach a department. Automated recordings began to replace long-distance operators on collect calls. Answering machines arose, the precursors to voice mail. Then personal computers became standard at home and work, replacing typewriters. With them, telephone help lines sprang up to assist customers in dealing with their computers. The lines were open twenty-four hours a day, seven days a week. That started to cement the idea that customer service could be available around the clock.

Updates of the 1976 White House study published in 1981 revealed that 70 percent of the people who complained and were satisfied with a company's response became repeat buyers. Those customers remained more loyal to the company than if they had not complained, and they told their friends about their positive experience. They were more satisfied and loyal than customers who never had a problem. The idea that companies could profit from handling complaints well began to gain currency. That led General Electric to open its GE Answer Center in 1981, one of the earliest customer service call centers. It was created by the marketing department of the company's appliance division. By the late 1990s, the answer center's nearly two thousand employees were handling 3.1 million calls a year. And because of the customer loyalty it fostered, GE credited it with returning profits of about twice what it cost to operate.

Back in 1981, the United States had just about completed its transformation from a predominantly manufacturing-based economy to a predominantly service economy. At that time, Japanese companies, with their emphasis on service and high quality, were outshining American companies on American soil. Management consultants gained prominence. Tom Peters, for instance, wrote a bestselling book, *In Search of Excellence*, that emphasized the importance of attention to customers. These consultants started training programs for companies on how to handle their customers. By the end of the 1980s, the term *customer service* had become a part of our everyday lexicon. With toll-free 800 numbers, the telephone had become the main tool of the burgeoning customer service industry. Desktop computers made it possible for agents to access customer records instantly, while customers were on the line. And call centers had been installed in most major corporations.

—ɯ—

Much of the same kind of rage we feel today already existed in 1987 when *Time* magazine ran a cover story, "Why Is Service So Bad?" Tom Peters was quoted in one article in the issue saying, "In general, service in America stinks." The magazine declared, "Economic upheaval is to blame. First came the great inflation of the 1970s, which forced businesses to slash service to keep prices from skyrocketing. Then came deregulation, which fostered more price wars and further cutbacks. At the same time, managers found that they could cut costs by replacing human workers with computers and self-service schemes. Americans tolerated, even welcomed, self-service during an era of rising prices, but now a backlash is beginning." Later in the article that idea was reinforced. "Sensitive to the mounting criticism, the business world is starting to make amends." A business professor was quoted as predicting that as prices bottom out, which they had by then, "the next major battlefield is going to be service." A "quality-service guru" said his advice was in great demand, and he had been giving lots of speeches to top managers, always preaching the same message: "We teach them the financial impact of good customer service. They're interested only in hard dollars and cents."

That was in 1987, but much of the article rings just as true today—particularly this one anecdote about bad service: "Even when they speak up and get their money back, consumers often come away with a feeling of being abused. Earlier this month, when a Los Angeles homemaker took back a foul-smelling piece of fish to a supermarket on the city's west side, she got a refund only after answering brusque questions and signing papers. At no time did anybody apologize or give the slightest sign that they regretted spoiling her dinner."

In the 1990s voice mail and calling cards came into being, so busy signals and long-distance operators effectively became things of the past. Faxes were a new step forward, cell phones took hold, and much of customer service had migrated from the store itself to the telephone. By the late 1990s, the Internet had blossomed. And soon it became the boon it is today to the business practice of requiring customers to do more and more of the work of customer service. That self-service goal was also aided in the customer service world during the past decade by increasingly sophisticated customer service software to manage customers and redirect them away from agents to other channels, especially the ever-more-advanced automatic voice response systems.

But as the technologies become ever more sophisticated, customers seem even more turned off by it all. That creates a paradox that many corporate executives struggle to understand. Looking at the balance sheets of their customer service departments, they keep thinking they have addressed the problem. After all, best estimates of the total expenditure for customer service in America are in the billions of dollars, but customers keep telling companies that they haven't addressed much of the problem at all. "From a corporate perspective," says Scott Broetzmann, co-creator of the Customer Rage Study, "the investment in customer care has been on a big slope up for the past thirty years. But at the same time, from a customer perspective—and the rage study shows this—everybody to a person would say customer service is lousy today, and getting worse. To oversimplify: Though a lot of money has been spent, the impact from a customer perspective has been negative."

As even newer technology emerges, the ways we connect with each other are continually in flux. The telephone, though imperfect, remains a powerful business tool. As much as the industry may want to change it, the phone continues to be the centerpiece of the relatively new customer service industry. The latest customer rage studies show that 62 percent of all customers prefer to use the telephone to communicate with companies. Toll-free numbers have made it possible for companies to pay for the calls we make to them, but the numbers have also allowed them to keep us on hold as long as they need to because they aren't billed for the length of the phone calls. And companies say they can't afford to pay for enough agents to answer all our calls.

All the while, the ones who make and sell the phones, the telecommunications industry, are lagging in customer service—even though the customer service industry would not exist in any familiar form without telecom products. Many customer satisfaction studies cite today's phone companies, along with cable providers, as the sectors with the lowest customer service satisfaction rates—sometimes as low as 10 percent. Just as a century ago our great-great-grandparents (and Mark Twain) were frustrated—with both the incivility that telephones seemed to foster and with the seemingly indifferent telephone companies that hawked those phones to them—many of us today are too.

But no matter how much we rage, the customer service industry, with all its complexities, is not going away. And the telephone probably isn't either, even if its prominence in the industry might someday be displaced by newer technology. Yet in response to the familiar failings of today's customer service industry, a new consumer movement has begun to take hold. It is akin to the one in the 1960s and 1970s—but is fitted out with more high-tech tools, fewer lawyers, a greater sense of business savvy, and in some cases a readiness to collaborate with companies for the good of us all.

3.

"You're Going to Listen to Me"

In the summer of 2006 Vincent Ferrari called America Online to cancel his personal account. This was before the company began offering its e-mail service for free later that year. Having heard stories of how the company made becoming an ex-customer hard to do, Ferrari, who works in information technology and lives in the Bronx, decided to record his phone conversation so that everything would be documented. After hanging up, he posted the audio recording of his exchange with John, the AOL representative, on his own blog. Ferrari had no idea what a sensation the posting would become.

After many minutes of automated recordings and waiting on hold, Ferrari reached John and explained that he had opened the AOL account a few years earlier but had stopped using it long before this call, so he was ready to close out the account. Barely two minutes into the conversation, it was clear that John's intent was to thwart Ferrari's exodus:

> AOL: Okay, I mean, is there a problem with the software itself?
>
> Ferrari: No. I just don't use it, I don't need it, I don't want it. I just don't need it anymore.
>
> AOL: Okay. So when you use this, I mean, use the computer, I'm saying, is that for business or for, for school?

Ferrari: Dude, what difference does it make? I don't want the AOL account anymore. Can we please cancel it?

AOL: Last year was 545, last month was 545 hours of usage . . .

Ferrari: I don't know how to make this any clearer, so I'm just gonna say it one last time. Cancel the account.

AOL: Well explain to me what's, why—

Ferrari: I'm not explaining anything to you. Cancel the account.

AOL: Well, what's the matter, man? We're just, I'm just trying to help here.

Ferrari: You're not helping me.

AOL: I am trying to help.

Ferrari: Helping—listen, I called to cancel the account. Helping me would be canceling the account. Please help me and cancel the account.

AOL: No, it wouldn't actually—

Ferrari: Cancel my account.

AOL: Turning off your account—

Ferrari: Cancel the account.

AOL: —would be the worst thing that—

Ferrari: Cancel the account.

AOL: Okay, 'cause I'm just trying to figure out—

Ferrari: Cancel the account. I don't know how to make this any clearer for you. Cancel the account. When I say

cancel the account, I don't mean help me figure out how
to keep it, I mean cancel the account.

AOL: Well, I'm sorry, I don't know what anybody's done
to you, Vincent, because all I'm—

Ferrari: Will you please cancel the account.

AOL: All right, someday when you've calmed down
you're gonna realize that all I was trying to do was help
you, and it was actually in your best interest to listen
to me.

Ferrari: Wonderful, okay.

The exchange went on for five agonizing minutes. At one point,
John asked Ferrari, who was thirty at the time and married, if his father
was there. Ferrari explained that the account was in his name and billed
to his credit card, not his father's. At another point, John also scolded
Ferrari, saying: "You're going to listen to me."

Finally, John canceled the account. A few days later, when Ferrari put
the recording of the conversation on his blog, InsignificantThoughts.com,
he also alerted other popular sites about his posting, including the consumer advocacy site Consumerist.com and the social networking site Digg
.com. Within eight hours, Ferrari's site got so much traffic that his server
went down. Soon the story was all over the mainstream news media, and
Ferrari appeared on *The Today Show*, where Matt Lauer interviewed him
and played much of the recorded conversation. AOL issued a public apology to Ferrari, condemned the actions of John, and said it had fired him.
The recording has lived on YouTube ever since.

Reporting in the aftermath of the incident, the *New York Times* said,
"Before the advent of the Web, an encounter with inept customer service was ours to bear alone, with little recourse or means to warn others.
Now, Mr. Ferrari can swiftly post on the Web a digital 'documentary' that
recorded his dismal experience, and news-sniffing hounds do the rest."

Ferrari is still happy to talk about his AOL encounter and continues to marvel at how it demonstrates the power that new technologies offer consumers. "It used to be that the multimillion-dollar corporation could just do whatever, say whatever, and that was the end of it. They would get away with it nine times out of ten. But now, that one time is going to be me."

Ferrari believes customers are starting to wake up to the changing equation, along with the companies. "In general, the customer service industry doesn't put an effort into treating customers the right way. Customer service is an ancillary thing to making money. Now, customers have just had it. And it's only going to get worse for companies. Because more people are learning about what they can do online. And maybe companies are learning that you can't treat every customer like crap, because one day it's going to bite you."

AOL did seem to learn something like that. An internal memo soon after Ferrari's story got out warned employees to treat every call as if it were being recorded by the customer. Ben Popken, the editor of Consumerist, says the posting of Ferrari's AOL recording is "a perfect case study of what we do, how it operates and the ultimate effect it can have. Our job is to empower consumers. We dip our toes in consumer advocacy and consumer rights and try to make a difference and balance the playing field between consumers and companies—give people a voice, and leverage it across our millions of viewers."

Indeed, the trouble didn't end for AOL. A few weeks after Ferrari's media sensation, an employee inside AOL's retention department leaked to Consumerist the more-than-eighty-page manual that John and other retention agents at AOL received in training. In it, the agents are given a detailed process for trying to hold on to the customers, including asking multiple questions and then relentlessly trying to change their minds.

Keith Dawson was the longtime editor of *Call Center* magazine and is now a senior analyst at Frost & Sullivan, a consulting firm. In mid-2006, soon after the Vincent Ferrari incident, he wrote in the magazine that Ferrari was an example of a new, more formidable kind of angry customer. "His tools are far more powerful: social networking websites, blogs, video and audio recordings, on and on. His platforms reach far more people and they take what would once have been an indignant letter-writing campaign and turn them into overnight global outrage."

Dawson then pointed to the *Exxon Valdez* oil spill in the early 1990s as the level that corporate misconduct had to reach in the pre-Internet days to garner a similar outcry. "Essentially, if you wanted to mobilize thousands of angry customers against you and have them screaming obscenities at you in public forums, you had to dump a shipload of oil on a pristine coast. Now all you have to do is irritate the wrong, highly motivated customer with a blog. The degree of company transgression needed to get to a critical mass of customer frenzy is far lower today, thanks to the amplifying technologies."

But Dawson went on to stress that while the Ferrari-AOL story was a handy and graphic example of the phenomenon, the company "shouldn't be made scapegoats" for what is a larger, industry-wide syndrome. He said that in the AOL incident the rep did exactly what he was trained to do. The core problems in such call centers are the "strategies and objectives set forth by the company's management and the actual effects they have on the customer experience." Based on his work editing Consumerist, Ben Popken has honed his own view of corporate culture and the problems it fosters for customers. "Before, I viewed companies as very self-aware and self-directed entities, with everything working in tandem in a very organized operation. But what I'm coming to realize is that it's kind of more like Soviet Russia, with a central governing authority. You have all these different levels and factions. And in every silo, they have their own goals and metrics that they have to meet. And sometimes they are doing them at cross purposes, because everyone has to look out for their best interests. So a lot of customer complaints arise from that disconnect."

Consumerist was created by Gawker Media in New York and is now owned by the publishers of *Consumer Reports*. The site describes itself as "biased towards the consumer. We're not anti-capitalist; we're anti–stupid capitalist. Our premise is that good customer service isn't a goal in and of itself, it actually makes and saves more money in the long run."

Popken, who grew up in New Jersey and now lives in Brooklyn, became the editor of the site in 2006, just a few years after graduating from the University of Colorado. "When I started, the main goal was to let people vent, and poke fun and point out errors by companies— to just kind of have fun at companies' expense and post people's complaints and stuff like that." But as the site began to get more attention, priorities changed. "Before it was sort of to entertain and inform, in that order. And now it's been reversed and it's to inform and entertain."

The viewers inspire much of the site's substance by sending in stories or tips that the editors sift through, and sometimes, Popken says, he and his staff add "some puns and some jokes and do a couple of elbow digs. It's calculated, because we know that's a delivery mechanism that will get people to listen. Oftentimes, though, we're really more like curators, and the readership is really driving the flow of the site."

At every turn, he says, Consumerist strives to keep its focus on "the human element" on all sides of the customer-company equation. "I think to a decent extent there are executives and VPs who want to improve customer service, but they're stymied within their own company by the layers of bureaucracy and middlemen and the reports. And then all the technological innovations that companies have used to lower the costs of their customer service centers look like efficiencies. But they're decreasing the efficiency of how they are actually dealing with people's problems. You send off an e-mail to one of them, and you get this robot reply and you just know that the person skimmed your e-mail and selected a pre-filled out form from a drop box and sent it back to you. And it doesn't actually relate to what you said. That's not an efficiency, it's a deficiency."

Vincent Ferrari says that before the Internet, customers mostly believed that those kinds of bad experiences were happening to them in isolation. "I don't think people realized, up until the advent of sites like Consumerist, that, 'Hey, this isn't just you. You're not just unlucky. This happens a lot.'"

While exposing corporate missteps and posting people's most enter-taining or exasperating stories are part of what keeps the site popular, Popken says he finds it most satisfying when Consumerist breaks down the process and gives its audience the tools they can use to get better customer service for themselves instead of "just perpetuating a cycle of victimhood and powerlessness that is one of the roots of people's frus-tration." Along those lines, the site includes the "Consumerist Guide to Fighting Back," which offers tips and inspiration beyond the daily posts. Popken says they try to get across the idea that "customers need to think and behave like businesses more often, and be more profes-sional. That's how they should talk to the company, because the com-pany is not a human. You might be talking to a human, but they're not going to do anything for you unless it makes sense in business terms. So people need to couch their complaints and their issues in business terms."

Readers seem to be absorbing the message. Popken says, "I had someone the other day who said, 'I just wanted to say thanks for your site, because before I had no idea I had so many ways to get a company to listen to me.' I think people are becoming more informed and savvier, and definitely they're becoming more informed and savvier at a faster rate than companies can react to undermine those efforts."

One of the first consumer rebellions on the Internet that really changed the way a company interacts with its customers was started by Jeff Jarvis, journalist, media critic, blogger, and head of the new media department at the City University of New York's Graduate School of Journalism. Most recently, he has written a book about Google called *What Would Google Do?* In 2005, Jarvis had problems with a Dell computer, and his contacts with the company were fruitless. So he wrote about it on his blog, buzzmachine.com, under the headline "Dell Sucks." His original blog post garnered thousands of comments and links, all with essen-tially the same "me too" message. Then Jarvis wrote an open letter to company founder Michael Dell, which he posted on his site. He began by linking the underlined words to articles that backed up his points. "Your customer satisfaction is <u>plummeting</u>, your marketshare is <u>shrinking</u>, and your stock price is <u>deflating</u>. Let me give you some indication of why." Jarvis went on to urge the company to listen and join in with bloggers and the other Internet conversations about Dell that "your customers are having without you."

A few months later, much to Jarvis's surprise, the company began reaching out to bloggers and even started its own, Direct2Dell. In 2007, the company also launched its own social networking site, IdeaStorm.com, on which it asked customers to tell the company what it can do to improve its products and service, and then to vote on others' ideas. In the first year, customers gave Dell's IdeaStorm 8,600 suggestions, which gathered 600,000 votes and 64,000 comments. From that, the company implemented more than a dozen of the ideas. In April 2008, Michael Dell told reporters that the new connectedness of communications has forced companies to listen to their customers differently. "Listening used to mean commissioning a customer survey. Now it means engaging directly with customers and critics and using those relationships to create a smarter business. Tapping into the ideas of our customers is like having an open source research and development lab. It's incredibly exciting, both for Dell and for our customers."

A few large companies had already realized what Michael Dell was espousing. Mostly driven by their marketing departments, companies that began to blog early on, before Dell, included General Motors and Microsoft. A few more companies learned from watching Dell. Rick Germano, the executive at Comcast who conducted the listening tours, said when they were venturing into the social arena on the Web, they studied the way Dell had used the Internet to connect with their customers after their tangles with bloggers.

Other channels on the Internet have also gained ground as popular environments for customers to talk among themselves about their problems with customer service. Groups formed on social networking sites like Facebook where customers could complain about specific companies. And the microblog site Twitter became a potent tool for complaining customers as well. Users could transmit messages of up to 140 characters to a network of other users. The conciseness often made them especially damaging for a company's reputation. Soon, many companies appointed people to monitor all mentions of them on the Internet each day and to respond in kind. Comcast set up an e-mail address for the head of its Internet monitoring to use with customers. Comcast was learning, along with Dell, that Jeff Jarvis was right when he warned companies they would have to learn to engage in the conversations taking place on the Web about them.

The first of those conversations began appearing in the earliest days of the Internet, with the rise of relatively simple websites devoted solely to airing customer complaints. One of the first such sites was started by a disgruntled United Airlines customer named Jeremy Comstock, who started a website called Untied.com in 1996 after a bad flight between Toronto and Tokyo. And long before ComcastMustDie.com started in 2007, other sites aimed at individual companies included:

PayPalSucks.com
AllstateInsuranceSucks.com
MicrosoftSucks.org
Amexsux.com
WalMart-Blows.com (the site explains, "Wal-Mart doesn't just
    suck . . . It blows!")
IHateStarbucks.com
IHateDell.net
IHateDell.org
VerizonPathetic.com

In a 2005 article entitled "Top Corporate Hate Web Sites," John Westphal, who started Amexsux, told *Forbes* magazine that he started his site because of a minor complaint in 2001. Two years later, he had 20,000 postings. He believed he was "doing a real public service by alerting the public to the dangers of dealing with Amex." But Westphal said he received threatening letters from the company's lawyers, and they filed an unsuccessful arbitration claim against him in 2004, trying to take away the domain name. American Express "does everything but clean up its business," said Westphal. In the late 1990s and early 2000s, a handful of websites arose dedicated solely to giving hundreds of thousands of customers each year a forum on which to vent their frustrations toward companies of their choosing. These more general complaint sites included Complaints.com, My3cents.com, PissedConsumer.com, PlanetFeedback.com, ConsumerAffairs.com, DamnCompanies.com, and Drive-you-nuts.com.

The practical influence of these sites was an open question. The Customer Rage Survey found that only about 5 percent of people who had a problem with a company use the Internet to voice their complaints. Others said the number who voice complaints on the Web is not as important as the impact that opinions of people who do use the Internet to complain can have on their fellow consumers. Jon Berry and Ed Keller, both veteran marketers and market researchers, work for the Roper Organization. In their 2003 book, *The Influentials*, they identify a type of person, dubbed an "influential," who holds sway over the opinions of about ten other people in any community on what to buy, how to vote, and where to eat. According to their premise, the average influential is a mid-forties, college-educated, white-collar, technologically literate home owner, with children. Their studies found that almost twice as many influentials reported having a problem with a product or service in the previous three months as compared to the general population. And virtually all of the influentials took action on their problem. Many did more than one thing, ranging from complaining in person to calling the company, to telling friends not to buy from the company. And influentials made up more than one-third of the people who posted their complaints on the Internet. The book summed up the message for companies: "The bottom line: Those influentials who come forward when they have a complaint represent a vastly larger problem of potential customer dissatisfaction."

Many other marketers took that idea to heart and added it to the larger concept of word-of-mouth advertising and marketing. Pete Blackshaw was one of the founders of PlanetFeedback. In 2004, he also cofounded the Word of Mouth Marketing Association, the premise of which is expressed well in the title of his 2008 book: *Satisfied Customers Tell Three Friends, Angry Customers Tell 3,000: Running a Business in Today's Consumer-Driven World*. Blackshaw worked in marketing for Procter & Gamble and is now an expert on branding for Nielsen.

Other marketing consultants have written and preached along the same lines, including Jackie Huba and Ben McConnell in their 2002 book, *Creating Customer Evangelists: How Loyal Customers Become a Volunteer Sales Force*. Huba and McConnell also have a very active blog, Church of the Customer. The concept of customer evangelism has so captured the imaginations of some in the corporate world that a few companies have even given staff members an official title as head of customer evangelism.

Blackshaw also writes extensively in marketing industry blogs about customers' growing voice on the Internet in what he calls "customer-generated media" (the word *media* as he uses it essentially means "advertising," as it does in marketing lingo). He points out that marketing, advertising, and customer service are no longer separate and distinct functions in a company. To the customer, he argues, all three areas are an integrated whole, even if companies don't perceive it that way yet.

In conversation, Blackshaw expresses a lot of enthusiasm about the change he says he is beginning to see in the way companies value customer service. "There's a whole renaissance taking place right now among people who run call centers. There's an awakening to the advocacy-building benefits of phone interactions. And the Internet is raising the stakes for good customer service, because bad customer service is what tends to flood Google search results. Anything that's really grounded in emotion tends to get a lot of link love, a lot of online conversation from others. So what really wakes up the executives in charge of the call centers is when you tell them they don't really understand those broader consequences of getting the phone interaction wrong."

Blackshaw has been telling some executives that recently. He is a consultant to Comcast and helped steer the company through its latest round of bad customer service publicity. "If you poll consumers, they trust other consumers more than advertisers. So, negative consumer commentary on the Internet can have a huge impact. And if you're a brand like Comcast where you've just got a lot of negative advocacy, you look at that and say, 'My gosh, I don't want people advertising against me, putting up billboards against me, in effect. That has real cost. I have to address it. I have to understand the root cause.'"

Blackshaw says he tells companies that "if you really want to tackle this issue of favorable or unfavorable consumer commentary in the marketplace, you're going to have to fix the call center, deal with customer service—make it more of a marketing engine. But those are long-term strategies. So you may have to take a step back. You may need to give the call center agent a little bit more latitude to solve the problem. Or you might need to spend $2, not $1, on training."

Up to now, "everyone in call centers got rewarded for getting more consumers through the pipe, faster. The irony of it is, on the flip side of the equation, marketers are all waxing poetic about engagement. They're like, 'Gosh, we can't even get the consumers to engage with us. How do we pull them in? How do we interact with them? How do we get their attention as long as possible?' All the marketers are throwing all this money toward viral campaigns. They're asking for feedback," while the call centers and customer service in general are busy pushing customers away. "Those are two opposites," says Blackshaw, "that need to be joined."

Of course, there is a potential pitfall to marketers' hyperattentiveness to customer-generated media. Some marketers have posed as consumers in Internet customer conversations, thus co-opting customers' voices and compromising their authenticity and reliability. And some companies have paid consumers to write favorable comments about them on blogs or customer complaint sites without disclosing that relationship. The Word of Mouth Marketing Association, for its part, came up with a code of ethics to guard against those kinds of dangers in 2005. In addition, the Federal Trade Commission, prompted by Commercial Alert, an advertising and marketing watchdog group in Portland, Oregon, said in 2006 that companies must disclose ties to those they pay or otherwise compensate to promote their products in public or to their peers.

Thor Muller, a founder of Get Satisfaction, believes corporate survival in the new, more transparent customer service landscape fostered by the Internet depends on an absence of guile: "If companies try to exploit the goodwill of their customers, that's very self destructive." The Silicon Valley–based company's GetSatisfaction.com website has merged the idea of genuine Internet word of mouth with the advocacy of complaint sites and blogs, and added sophisticated technology, design, and social networking to create an open forum in which companies and customers can engage in a constructive conversation. The site was started by Muller, his wife, Amy, and a friend and fellow Internet entrepreneur, Lane Becker, in fall 2007. The site is free to customers and to company representatives. It is funded by venture capital investors. With more than 2,500 companies being talked about on the site by their customers within its first six months, Get Satisfaction drew the attention of companies such as Apple, Twitter, Zappos.com, and even Comcast. As Get Satisfaction grew to more than 2 million unique visitors by early 2010, it began to garner revenue from selling software it developed to help companies increase their ability to interact peacefully and productively online with their customers. The goal is to promote understanding, not foster contempt.

"Part of the trick we're attempting to pull off here," says Muller, "is to get a fair, more balanced environment, a more respectful space that would free people from both sides to come together for communication that actually breeds trust. You have some communities online, and lots of blogs, where snark is the rule of the day. The crueler you can be to people around you, the more street cred you have. It's like the schoolyard bully syndrome. We're creating this new community-driven approach—a Switzerland for companies and customers."

Muller says they believe the business world is "at the tail end of the industrial age where companies thought from inside, out to the edge of their organization. The whole point was to preserve power and control, inside the organizations. Companies hedged and avoided being straightforward because of fear that if they actually told the truth the customers would jump on them. And consumers got used to this closed—maybe not dishonest, but certainly not candid—behavior from companies. So they assumed the worst. They assumed they were being screwed. We ended up with this kind of polarized relationship. It's a vicious cycle."

He says with Get Satisfaction they are "trying to turn it into a virtuous cycle, with more openness and more human interactions that are based on mutual respect, so that new trust can emerge. We believe we can change organizations from the outside in. We have created a platform and built it in a way that is a win-win for both customers and companies. We see a lot of people who hit a wall through the formal customer service channel. They come to Get Satisfaction. They are able to talk amongst each other about the company and its products, and they can then invite the company to respond." In turn, some companies have adopted Get Satisfaction as a new kind of customer service channel where they can invite their customers to engage in a civil dialogue with them. "Much like a social network," says Muller, "where people get invitations—maybe they ignore them at first. Then after a while, after somebody you respect invites you, or enough people invite you, you say you guess you need to sign up and respond. And that's exactly the thing we're doing with this. And in some ways it may be increasing the pressure on companies."

The tone of the site is one of shared responsibility. "Consumers who want a more candid, honest relationship with companies need to be willing to assume the best of companies who are communicating with them in that context. And the companies need to act human, and not talk in corporate doublespeak, and actually use real names. And be up front with people when things go wrong."

Get Satisfaction sponsored a summit called Customer Service Is the New Marketing, in San Francisco in early 2008. Muller says the idea was to elevate the customer's status in corporations: "Customer service is the primary place where companies interact with individual consumers. Every customer is a potential transmitter of a company's brand. And yet customers are treated as cost centers. So this is a huge mismatch in the value of a customer. But the center of gravity has moved from inside companies, out into the hands of increasingly empowered consumers. In the industrial era, to communicate with customers required access to broadcast media," which companies had and customers didn't. "Now anybody with a computer can communicate to hundreds of thousands of people."

Muller says, "We're really about empowering customers to have a positive impact on those whom they do business with and the products that they use. A lot of what we're doing is changing minds and hearts. That's a cliché, but we honestly believe it. Our goal is to make a safe space for companies to respond and to engage with users who may have an issue. And we look at technology as a means, not the end."

—⚏—

The concert in the lobby of Kiasma, the Museum of Modern Art in Helsinki, Finland, was packed almost beyond capacity. A ninety-six-person chorus serenaded more than three hundred receptive listeners with seemingly earnest songs that reeled off a litany about such common Finnish annoyances as crowded saunas, cold winters, and always losing to Sweden in ice hockey. It was the first public concert of the Helsinki Complaints Choir, an idea hatched by two Finnish artists. The concept came from a Finnish expression, *Valituskuoro*, which translates literally into a "choir of complaining," or less poetically, a lot of people complaining at the same time. The artist couple, Tellervo Kalleinen and Oliver Kochta-Kalleinen, thought it would be an interesting experiment to form an actual choir of complainers.

The idea took hold, and now they have traveled to more than twenty cities worldwide, from Europe to Australia to Israel, Canada, Russia, and beyond, helping other cities set up their own complaint choirs. Videos of the various efforts are available on YouTube. The Complaints Choir in Birmingham, England, grouses in harmony about expensive beer and bad public transportation. The Singapore Complaints Choir laments the effects of humidity on hairstyles, noisy stray cats, and men who do not like independent women. And the Chicago Complaints

Choir melodically whines about rude fans at baseball games, apples that cost more than Twinkies, and the price of gasoline. "We say you should sing complaints out," the Finnish couple told the Associated Press in Chicago. "Acknowledge things aren't as they should be. It's therapeutic." They also declared they had come to the United States to set up choirs as beachheads against "the tyranny of the positive attitude in America."

A worldwide survey conducted every year by the Roper Organization might give clues as to why the founders of the Complaints Choir adopted this stance of nurturing and celebrating complaining. It could have something to do with their Scandinavian upbringing. The survey ferrets out the attitudes, values, and behaviors of more than thirty thousand consumers, from cities and rural areas in thirty developed and developing countries worldwide. A tiny part of the survey addresses the issue of complaining and customer service by trying to discern which country has the highest rate of customer complaints per citizen. The clear winner since 2005 has been Sweden (the only Scandinavian country included in the survey). The English-speaking world is not far behind, with the United Kingdom, Australia, Canada, and the United States rounding out the top five countries, in that order. The lowest rates of complaint consistently were found in Taiwan.

"I'm not surprised that the Swedes complain the most," says Claes Fornell, founder of the American Customer Satisfaction Index, business professor at the University of Michigan, and former military decoder in Sweden, his native country. "The Swedes are like mini-Germans. If the train is not there within thirty seconds of when it was supposed to arrive, something is wrong, and they have difficulty coping." He believes that has to do with the expectations Swedes have of orderliness. "If society is organized too much, you're relying on the organization. When it fails you don't feel so good. And I think it's probably worse now, since the French have bought the Stockholm subway system, because the trains never run on time anymore."

That phenomenon of industriousness leading to complaints when the world doesn't conform to expectations seems to prevail in other

Scandinavian countries as well. A line from the song composed by the complaints choir in Bøda, Norway, again suggests such a worldview: "I'm so bloody sick of there only being 24 hours available. It's nowhere near enough."

But those high expectations can also lead beyond complaining to constructive results. While Ralph Nader was decrying how dangerous American-built cars were during the 1970s, the Swedish Volvo became a hit on the world stage, setting a new standard for safety in automotive design. And as Walmart became the world's largest retailer in the 1980s and 1990s, spreading the idea of low cost above all else, the Swedish furniture chain IKEA also rose worldwide, showing that value didn't have to mean a sacrifice of style. And of course there are Ingmar Bergman's films, which showcased the Swedes' particular knack for making even their free-floating angst into something seductive, artful, and somehow orderly.

A strong sense of justice also seems to motivate the Nordic penchant for complaining, and probably spawned another omnipresent feature of Swedish life: the ombudsman. That word comes from the Old Swedish word for *representative*, and also appears in other ancient versions of all the Scandinavian languages. The term was reintroduced in Sweden in the early 1800s when the parliament of Sweden appointed its first ombudsman to give people a place, separate from the king, where their complaints about the country could be heard. Today, says Fornell, "there is an ombudsman for everything in Sweden."

It's true. The parliamentary ombudsman for Sweden is still around. But the government has also created a consumer ombudsman, an equal opportunities ombudsman, an ombudsman against ethnic discrimination, a children's ombudsman, a disability ombudsman, an ombudsman against discrimination because of sexual orientation, and an ombudsman for equality in sports. Recently there was embarrassment all around when it was reported that the woman Sweden had appointed as its ombudsman for equal pay was earning 17 percent less than her male predecessor. You can bet everyone complained about that, including her predecessor.

Claus Møller is a management consultant from Denmark. In what could be seen as a nod to his Scandinavian roots, he was a coauthor of the 1996 book *A Complaint Is a Gift*. In it, he was among the first to make the argument that companies needed to stop treating customer complaints as an annoyance and see them instead as one of their best feedback and marketing tools. By welcoming complaints, he said, and taking what they can learn from them, their products and service will improve.

Claes Fornell's measurements of customer satisfaction reveal how well companies are doing at preventing the problems that lead to complaints and how well they are addressing and fixing the complaints that do arise. But it is without a hint of self-interest that he says he thinks the rest of the world should probably take a page from his native culture when it comes to speaking up about what is wrong. "I'm Swedish, and I say the Swedes probably do it right. Now, you can complain too much. That's not terribly pleasant. But you should complain. Why suffer in silence? That makes no sense."

—◠◡◠—

It's a good thing the Finnish artists, the Norwegian singers, the Danish business consultant, and the Swedish professor didn't try to take their messages of reverence for whining to Kansas City, Missouri. They might have run into resistance from the Reverend Will Bowen, pastor of the Christ Church Unity there. Not that he would complain about them, of course.

In July 2006 Bowen challenged his congregation to stop complaining for twenty-one days. To reinforce the message, he gave them each a purple silicone bracelet and instructed them to switch the bracelet to the other wrist and start over if they found themselves complaining. The idea was a hit, and Bowen wrote a book, *A Complaint-Free World*, to help individuals and groups institute their own twenty-one-day complaint fast. He has been featured on *The Today Show* and *Oprah* and maintains a popular website. The church has sent out more than 5 million bracelets, free of charge, to people requesting them from all over the world, including Sweden.

In 2007, a Danish film crew followed Bowen around for a few days as part of a documentary they were making about complaining. And in 2009, Bowen hosted a six-day, complaint-free cruise through the Caribbean. In 2010, he hosted an Alaskan cruise. Bowen told the Associated Press, "When you're not articulating complaints then they have nowhere to go, and your brain literally stops producing them, and you become a happier person."

Bowen is no Pollyanna though. He says he did more than his share of grousing when he was younger. "I grew up in a family where if we did sit down to dinner without the television, it was to complain about what happened in our day. And so that was programmed into my mind." And when it came to contacting customer service, "Oh, I was a bully. I was customer service's worst nightmare. Because I was going to prove how big, strong, and tough I was, and I had a litany of what I was going to do before I even called. I would just get on them and make the customer service person responsible for the problem. I would call the company names and I would—now this was before I was a minister— but I would swear and everything else. I mean, that was just sort of my modus operandi."

Bowen says it was only when he began to look at the underlying dynamics of those sorts of encounters that he changed his ways. He now sees a complaint simply as an unmet need. "I'm not saying that we all don't have unmet needs, and that we want those needs met. What I'm saying is that just to gripe about them and say, 'This is the way it is,' keeps you in the way it is."

Bowen believes that kind of dead-end complaining is particularly prevalent in customer service encounters. "People may have a past expectation that their need is not going to be met unless they are rude, or strong, or verbose in their request. Unfortunately, I think we've all had experiences where we don't get what we want or need, and then we raise our voice and we get it. Then, if I have another bad experience, all of a sudden I'm creating a story in my mind of: 'They're probably not going to work this out. They're going to put me on hold. They're not going to take care of me.' And so I'm coming in with a preconception of having been injured by them, or hurt, and I am exacting that back toward them.

"But I believe that people complain for the same reason that babies cry; they don't have the proper tools to communicate what their needs are. My mission is not to get people to stop complaining, it's to get people to start communicating in a healthy fashion. So stopping complaining is step one. Because complaining is just staying in your dissatisfaction."

That is not to say that Bowen thinks there is nothing to complain about in the world. "Are things going to happen that frustrate you? I would invite you to find a day in your life when something has not happened to frustrate you. Life is frustration. Knowing that going in should give you a certain peace of mind and serenity in handling the challenges that come. We need to lighten up somewhat. We need to get our needs met. We needn't excuse people for poor performance. But we need to just not take it personally. A lot of complaining has to do with, 'How dare you do this to me?' And we need to get beyond that."

Despite all this reasoning and his good intentions, Bowen says that he still can get riled when he calls customer service with a problem. But he doesn't look at the call as merely a chance to vent anymore. He now sees it as an opportunity to practice his complaint-free mode by owning up to his part in the transaction and by working to make it easier for the agent to do the same. "I don't believe it is a complaint if you are speaking directly to a person who can effect a change that you are seeking. Focusing on the solution and talking about the solution is not complaining. Focusing only on the problem is complaining. When I call somebody and I'm upset, when I have a challenge with a product or something, I'll call and say: 'Listen, I know you had nothing to do with this. And you're going to hear some frustration in my voice. It's not directed at you, so please don't take it on. I just need you to help me.'"

And his advice for the customer service agent on the other end of the line? "Wouldn't it be better if a customer service person would say something along the lines of, 'How can we work together to get you what you need?' early in the conversation. Because that would make the people calling in partners in the solution, rather than people who are just sounding an alarm, hoping to motivate the troops to give them what they need."

—〰—

News media coverage of bad customer service often includes an obligatory list, such as "top ten ways to get better customer service," "how companies can give better customer service," and "pet peeves about calling customer service." Those well-documented types of customer problems—being kept on hold too long, agents not having the right information to help, or speaking to someone with deficient language skills—are then often accompanied by specific horror stories. Scott Broetzmann, the Customer Rage Study creator, looks at what underlies those customer complaints to try to understand the root causes of the customer anger he measures. He has broken it down for companies to show them what they do (sometimes inadvertently) to foment the situation. He tells them that most customer anger is not because of troubles with the product or the price. What most companies get wrong, he says, is the way they deal with questions about or problems with their products or services. "Complaint handling," Broetzmann complains with utmost authority, "is lousy, just awful, god-awful."

Broetzmann works in tandem on the Customer Rage Study each year with Mary Jo Bitner, a marketing professor at Arizona State University's business school. Bitner agrees with Broetzmann's assessment, saying most customer service horror stories fall into the category of a failure in what is called "service recovery"—an academic term for everything the company does, or doesn't do, to support the product if there is a problem or question after the sale. Failures in service recovery start with a simple foul-up. But then the recovery process becomes worse than the original issue. That is the area, says Bitner, where a lot of companies do their worst job.

She describes the familiar pattern of most customer stories. "They'll say, 'I had this problem and then they didn't answer my question. And then they put me on hold. Then they hung up on me, or they never came when they said they would. Then they charged me and never took it off my bill.' It just snowballs." Customers expect to have a problem fixed promptly, she says, and to receive an apology, be compensated at a reasonable level, and not waste time. "We've found through years of research that there is a huge payback to companies if they do service recovery right. But there are a lot of companies that don't. And if you ask customers, that is a lot of what they are talking about when they talk about bad customer service."

For companies looking to reduce costs, their customer service departments have become likely targets. Often they are seen merely as a necessary expense of doing business rather than as potential profit centers. Corporations want tangible measures of cost. But service is intangible and not easily quantifiable. When trying to cut customer service spending, the most tangible measure is the cost per call, or contact, as they say in the business. Judged that way, the alternatives to traditional call handling become quite enticing to those holding the purse strings. Exact figures vary by company and industry, but the approximate relative cost of offering a live, American-based, customer service agent averages somewhere around $7.50 per phone call. Outsourcing calls to live agents in another country brings the average cost down to about $2.35 per call. Having customers take care of the problem themselves, through an automated response phone system, averages around 32 cents per call, or contact.

Scott Broetzmann says those economics are at the center of the whole mess. "Companies today are in the business of trying to reduce their cost per contact," he says. "That is the root, from the consumer perspective, of all customer care evils." Broetzmann says that companies often say that outsourcing and self-service are employed "to improve the customer experience—to make it easier, faster, simpler, and more under the control of the consumer. But they're really not. Those are done, to be honest, to reduce the cost per contact."

But the rise of consumer power on the Internet brings new pressures on companies to be more mindful of their customer service. "I think we're in for a change," says Claes Fornell. "It's not a matter of just listening to customers; you have to follow up and do something. The general principle here is that it is much cheaper to get a complaint—to deal with a complaint—than it is to lose a customer."

Fornell says the change is good for customers. "But it's not all good, because it puts tremendous pressure on the other side, on workers, employees." He says in some of the proprietary consulting work he does for companies, he also measures employee satisfaction. And he has seen a correlation between customer and employee satisfaction. "It's very difficult to make sure that your customers are well treated if you're not being treated well by your employer."

That was the claim of some unionized Verizon customer service employees in Tampa, Florida, who picketed against the company in early 2008 for creating conditions that the workers said did not allow them to provide good customer service. Union official Doug Sellars told a Sarasota newspaper that Verizon had "failed to address customer service complaints" as it rolled out new television and Internet services in the region to go with its traditional telephone lines. Customer service workers complained of being held to sales quotas even when their customers were calling with serious service problems. Sellars said, "We're nervous about the way the company is directing the work force, which is ending up in bad customer service. We just want them to let us do our jobs. The employees are timed on everything. If they spend too much time on any customer they can be disciplined for that."

A Verizon employee told the *Tampa Tribune* at the protest, "I understand that every company says, 'Let's make money.' But that's the job of a marketing department, not service. I'm supposed to be there to help the customer." In summer 2007, workers in the same union, the International Brotherhood of Electrical Workers, had protested at Verizon in Tampa for similar reasons, citing "unrealistic performance goals." One union shop steward who works in customer service said, "The employees here have to work overtime every day. They're working 10 hours a day and leave here crying, feeling like they've been held hostage."

Almost a year later, in March 2008, just before the workers picketed in April carrying signs reading "Honk for Better Service!" twenty-three customers had called Florida's attorney general with complaints about Verizon, up from six calls in January. One of those filings came from Jerry Weisenbacher and was quoted in the *Sarasota Herald-Tribune*. "I have continually been stalled, lied to, deceived and to date nobody at Verizon seems to have a clue what is going on. It seems to me that Verizon is deliberately playing games with the general public assuming people will get so frustrated that they will simply drop the issue."

A Verizon spokesman said in response: "I want customers to know that we're not taking service with us for granted, nor are we setting out to create a bad customer experience. I don't want to minimize the issues customers are having. We understand that, in a competitive area, customer service is a huge issue. We're learning as we go."

The union was not facing contract negotiations during any of the uproar. They said they were genuinely concerned about what they saw as the company creating conditions that made it almost impossible for their members to provide good service to Verizon customers. The government also took up the issue.

A few days before the first union protest in early April, national Verizon executives met with state and city officials to account for the company's poor customer service. In Tallahassee, the state capital, company executives and lawyers met with the attorney general, the Florida Public Service Commission, and the Department of Agriculture and Consumer Affairs. The union also held a second protest picket in mid-April, saying the company had not addressed its issues. In addition, the Tampa City Council summoned Verizon executives to a public forum in early May where customers could speak to them directly about their customer service problems. The forum was held at 9:00 a.m. on a Thursday.

Only two customers showed up. The *Tampa Tribune* ran a story about the lightly attended meeting. The many reader comments on its website indicated that an online forum might have garnered more customer participation because a frequent complaint mentioned was that the meeting was held while most customers were at their own jobs. One particularly terse posting summed up most of the sentiments: "What?

I told the City I would be there. The Verizon people should have been made to wait for me to testify somewhere between 9 and 5."

Government intervention in response to formal complaints filed by customers was not a novel occurrence. But employees striking in support of the customers' interest was. Coupled with the Internet uproar, the company was forced to handle it all more proactively than it might have done in the past.

Verizon devised one immediate remedy that stood out for its experimental nature. Tampa customers were notified that they could go to a page on Verizon's website for special help. They were greeted by a photo of a seemingly efficient and friendly young woman wearing a telephone headset. Beside her was written: "Verizon Florida has just turned its excellent service up a notch . . . and you are among the first to enjoy this unique customer advantage that is unmatched in the entertainment and communications industry! To provide you with an unparalleled service experience, we now offer you a Personal Account Manager (PAM) to provide that personal touch you deserve as a Verizon customer . . . at no cost to you!" Under the photo of the customer service agent was written, "Who is my PAM? Click to find out." On the next screen, Tampa customers could enter their address and were then given the name of their own personal agent and a local number at which to reach this person.

PAM was the company's attempt to put a more human face on the workers and the company for Tampa-area customers. The union did not immediately object, although it was unclear how many of its members would be part of the new program for customers. Some initial Internet customer comments on the PAM idea were positive.

St. Petersburg Times columnist Sue Carlton wrote about PAM in a column titled, "Even Your Complaint Is Now Bundled," in late April 2008:

> Just the other day, PAM sent me a friendly letter of intro-
> duction, then left a phone message. PAM is apparently
> there to help, a sort of Jenny-on-the-Spot, if you will.

PAM promises "ONE STOP RESOLUTION: No wait times, no multiple calls to different locations, no impersonal 800 #." On the Web site . . . PAM appears to be a pleasant-looking blonde of nice smile and sturdy headset, ready to tackle your troubles. (Never mind that my PAM actually turns out to be, according to a later message on my answering machine, a guy named Ricky.)

—◊—

In some ways, Paul English could almost be the next Ralph Nader. Both have similar working-class, New England backgrounds. Both crusade against corporate arrogance and greed. And both have struck a chord with millions of consumers. But there are differences in their approaches and in the eras in which their consumer advocacy began. English is head of technology at a for-profit company he cofounded called Kayak.com, a travel search engine. He is a full-fledged capitalist—a technology entrepreneur.

In late 2005, English gained notoriety for a volunteer-run website he started that evolved from his blog. He posted a list of how to get around the automated voice systems on the customer service lines of many major U.S. companies and speak to a live person. The *Boston Globe* ran an article about his blog's "cheat sheet" listing what numbers to press or words to say to reach a live person at about two hundred companies. That led to a torrent of national and international coverage in the news media. By early 2006, the list spurred him to create a website, GetHuman.com, which had more than 1 million visits in its first month. English, who is in his mid-forties, became the spokesperson for what he now calls the GetHuman movement. Where others took on specific companies or customer service as a whole, English focused solely on the automated voice response systems employed across the customer service industry.

And everybody he targeted listened. For instance, Citibank began running ads proclaiming callers could always reach a person just by pressing "0." And English was the keynote speaker at the voice response system industry's main convention in August 2006. By that fall, Microsoft joined with English and a leading creator of speech technology, Nuance Communications, to create a set of standards for voice response systems that provided customers more freedom to channel their customer service calls to live representatives without so much ado. And by the end of 2006, English had created the GetHuman 500, in which he and a team of GetHuman volunteers graded the Fortune 500 companies on how well they lived up to the GetHuman standards. Most companies received Ds and Fs.

English insists he is not antibusiness and not antitechnology. He says he just sees right and wrong ways to do business and to use technology. "There are great things about the telegraph, and the telephone, and now the Internet," he says, applauding the fact that each new incarnation of communication technology provides the possibility "of much larger scale contact. The mom-and-pop store could only talk to one hundred people a day." Now one company can talk to millions each day. But he is wary of those who blindly embrace the kinds of technology that eliminate person-to-person interaction. He says, "GetHuman is kind of a reality check, and a cry for the way we should be interacting with each other, the way we should be thinking about our customers. Human contact needs to be the primary thing. There is a use for machines, but machines should be designed to work the way humans want to work, not the other way around."

English says the start of what he calls his "transition from anger to action" came when his mother died in April 2001. The last thing she asked him was to take care of his father. Almost immediately, English realized keeping that promise would mean slowly chipping away at his aging dad's autonomy. First, he had to take away his car keys. Then his dad told him he was having a hard time understanding how the machines answering the phones at his bank and telephone provider worked and couldn't always hear or follow their instructions. Even when his dad could decipher some of what was happening and tried to comply, the systems had a hard time understanding him. "I would help him," says English, "but it always bothered me."

He says his dad was a "great, funny guy," an Irish-American story-teller with six kids who started as a pipe fitter's assistant at the Boston gas company and worked there for forty-nine years. Complex technology, without an option to bypass it, was prohibiting his dad from making his own customer service calls, and English was incensed at the implications. He saw these barriers as a way that companies, consciously or not, were disenfranchising a whole generation. "When people remove your choices," he says, "and they steer you down this technology path, and say, 'If you want to do x, y, and z, you must use this technology,' they remove your dignity."

At the same time this frustration at his father's woes was brewing, English's own encounters with customer service roadblocks at his bank and his telephone provider mobilized him. One day after leaving the bank he had been using in Boston for five years, English realized he had left behind some forms he needed. So he called his banker, Keith, at his direct number. But the bank's phone system redirected English to a call center halfway across the country. "As hard as I tried," says English, "I couldn't get to Keith. I said, 'I know his name. I was just in his office. I need to speak with him.' And they wouldn't let me speak to him. He had been working for five years on my business accounts, and it was impossible to get through to him. It made me furious." English hung up. He says he was "steaming. It screwed up my whole day."

Soon after that, he had some problems with the setup of a new cell phone. When he called his phone provider to get help, the first thing the automated answering system asked was for his cell phone number. Next, he says, it transferred him from department to department. And every time he landed at a new department, the system would ask him for his phone number. "I'm calling my eff-ing phone company," he says, remembering his exasperation, "I'm calling you from my phone, which I'm paying $100 a month for. How can you possibly not know my phone number?" He says he never spoke to anyone who could help him and he kept getting cut off because his cell phone would drop the calls.

That's when he says, "I just had it. I'm thinking, *How did it get this bad?*" He realized that twenty years ago, no one would have believed you could call a company you were paying $100 a month, $1,200 a year, and not be able to talk to someone. "Like the frog slowly boiled in the water, it just happened to us," says English. "We didn't detect it. And what I'm saying here is I just detected it. And this is bullshit. And we have to change it."

Right around that time, in May 2002, the *Wall Street Journal* published an article with the headline "In Search of the Operator—Firms spent billions this year to make it hard to find one; How to reach a real person." It reported that American companies were spending $7.4 billion that year to "beef up their automated customer service," making it more complicated than ever before to reach a live person. The article listed codes to press to get around automated systems at twenty-five U.S. companies. The next day, Ralph Nader wrote an article posted on his website, Nader.org, in which he compared American customers to consumers in the old Soviet Union, who "stood in long lines hoping the shelves would not be empty before they reached the counter." Nader wrote, "In our country, tens of millions of Americans are told to press a bewildering variety of 1, 2, 3, 4, 5, etc. for several tiers sometimes," only to "be put on hold, waiting, waiting, waiting." Nader said "this automated answering binge" on the part of companies resulted in "tens of billions of lost hours that are taken from consumers." He ended the article by urging readers to "figure out a way to fight back and make them pay for disrespecting your time." Paul English was one of those readers.

English's lack of suit-and-tie formality and his boyish quality belie his status as the head of a thriving technology company with thirty-two employees. Kayak's offices are in a corporate office park outside Boston, remarkable only because of its close proximity to Thoreau's Walden Pond. English smiles easily and speaks warmly of his wife and kids. When he starts talking about his GetHuman mission, his eyes get intense, and an air of impatience comes through, heightened by his Boston accent. It almost sounds as if he is frustrated at his mouth for being such an imperfect conduit from the zeal in his heart and all the thoughts flooding through his brain. First he invokes the indie rock band Rage Against the Machine, then Gandhi, then Martin Luther King.

In the 1970s, when English was in fifth grade, school busing to achieve racial integration came to Boston. The city went through the most notoriously violent transition to school desegregation in the country. English stayed in the public schools throughout, getting transferred from one tough school to another, and finally ending up at Boston Latin, the oldest and one of the most prestigious public schools in the country. He says Boston Latin was better managed than the others. The discord there never got out of hand, and he had an excellent education. He went on to a full scholarship at the University of Massachusetts, where he earned undergraduate and graduate degrees in computer science. But the violence he experienced during the early years of busing, as well as the firsthand exposure busing gave him to the social discord of the times, shaped his spirit and in some ways informs his GetHuman crusade. "I had guns pulled on me a couple of times," he says. "I was knifed in the throat. When you grow up in turmoil and you see people get hurt, hopefully you have some empathy for that. I think empathy is a key to success in life and in business. If you can connect with other human beings and relate to them, you can be successful."

Steeped in these antecedents, English is not afraid to compare GetHuman to the fights for civil rights and women's rights of the past century. "I think this consumer movement is about people standing up and saying we don't like this. We want change, and we're going to make a change. If you look at every social justice movement in history, they all started out with people who realized that they had become victims, and they had become disempowered. And a few brave people stood up and said, 'We are going to change this.'"

English acknowledges he might sound a bit dramatic when he talks about customer service injustice. Still, he never apologizes for the importance he places on his GetHuman endeavor. He says the buck stops with "shortsighted and arrogant CEOs." At many companies, he says, CEOs tell the head of customer service that their pay is based on cutting customer service spending. "If you pay someone a bonus for lowering costs," says English, "it doesn't take a very bright person to fig-ure out what that executive is going to do. They are going to lay people off and put machines in place."

In 2006, English spoke about GetHuman as part of a new, larger force in society—one in which the misuse of technology by companies against consumers is turned around on itself because, he said, technol-ogy is also being used for good, and it is increasingly providing con-sumers with new, effective ways to fight back. "It's about giving the consumers freedom, and choice, and power. And the Internet," he says, "is the oxygen."

GetHuman's cheat sheet is still being used and updated. But the site's growth had waned as English tended to his main business of running Kayak. In March 2008, *BusinessWeek*'s Jena McGregor wrote a story about English: "Rebel with a Stalled Cause—How GetHuman.com, a Customer Empowerment Crusade, Lost Steam." In it she described how while the site was still "a treasure trove for consumers, with 500 shortcuts out of phone-tree labyrinths," the standard he created with Microsoft and Nuance never took hold. She said English admitted that "his busy schedule as chief technol-ogy officer of fast-growing travel search engine Kayak.com played a part in the slowdown, but he never intended the site to take up much of his time in the first place: 'I wanted the citizens of the Web to run this.'" McGregor said English had "learned that no matter how effective online consumer crowds may be, full-blown change still takes the passion and energy of committed individuals."

And those committed individuals, it seems, probably have to be working for change from within the very companies that have those customer crowds complaining outside their gates.

4. To Send Us Your Firstborn, Please Press or Say "One"

Dial 1-800-USA-RAIL, and a welcoming voice comes on the line immediately saying: "Hi. I'm Julie, Amtrak's automated agent." Sounding efficient and eager to please, the recorded voice then goes on to instruct callers on what to say to proceed: "Okay. Let's get started. What city are you departing from?" If the caller says Boston, Amtrak Julie might hear it right, but just to double-check, she'll reply, "I think you asked for Austin, Texas. Is that correct?" If told it's not, she'll say: "My mistake." Once she finally understands that the caller wants to leave from Boston, she'll say, "Got it," and move on to the next step.

Amtrak dispatched Julie onto its phone lines in 2002, and since then she has answered every call that comes into the train line's 800 number. In 2007, Julie answered 18.3 million calls, an average of about 50,000 calls a day. She forwarded 13.2 million calls to live agents at the customer's request. But she completely handled 5.1 million calls herself that year. In fact, Amtrak Julie completes more calls in a day than one human Amtrak customer service agent handles in a year. Each of the approximately one thousand live agents at Amtrak's call centers completes an average of about 13,000 calls per year, while Julie averages about 13,972 calls a day. Julie can field calls about train arrivals, departures, and fares and can even complete reservations. Amtrak doesn't say exactly how much the Julie system has saved the company since its rollout, but the initial $4.1 million it spent to get the system up and running paid for itself within a year and a half.

At the Amtrak station in downtown Boston one fall evening, a young professional woman on her way home to her husband in Connecticut had spoken to Amtrak Julie a few hours earlier to complete her reservation. She told fellow passengers that the automated system's pleasant efficiency made her feel that Julie was really "on it." However, Julie's renown goes beyond Amtrak's stations. In fact, it isn't hyperbole to say that Amtrak Julie has found a place for herself in the American psyche. She is blogged about. She is featured in YouTube videos—most of which are variations on the idea of dialing Julie and recording her responses when callers says things to trip the system up, confuse it, or come on to her. She was an answer on the TV quiz game show *Who Wants to Be a Millionaire.* And National Public Radio produced a Valentine's Day parody featuring Julie on a date with Tom, the computerized voice of United Airlines. Eventually the relationship did not work out because Julie and Tom could not agree whether to travel together by plane or train.

Then there were the *Saturday Night Live* skits. Antonio Banderas hosted the show in 2006, and played a guy who met Amtrak Julie, portrayed by cast member Rachel Dratch, at a party. Eventually he asked her to go back to his place with him that night, to which she replied, "Your approximate wait time is zero minutes." And when actor Jon Heder, best known as the star of the film *Napoleon Dynamite,* hosted the show in 2005, he was a shy guy named Gary who had been fixed up on a blind date with Julie. After they greeted each other in a café and sat down, Gary asked Julie what she did. In a cheerful but monotone voice, she told him she worked in customer service. The waiter then came by to see if the couple wanted anything to drink. Here's how the conversation went from there:

Gary: Um . . . what do you think, Julie? A latte or a cappuccino, or something?

Julie: Did you say, latte? Or, cappuccino?

Gary: Uh . . . well, I said both. Do you want a latte or cappuccino?

Julie: My mistake. Cappuccino, would be great.

Gary ordered the drinks. Then Julie interjected . . .

Julie: Gary, before we go any further, let me get some information.

Gary: Sure.

Julie: Please say your age.

Gary: Oh, yeah! I get that a lot. I know I look young, but I'm actually twenty-nine.

Julie: I think you said nineteen. Did I get that right?

Gary: No, twenty-nine.

Julie: I think you said nine. Did I get that right?

Gary: No. Wow. Twenty-nine.

Julie: Okay. Got it. Sorry.

The people at Amtrak got it too, and they liked it. Matt Hardison, Amtrak's chief of sales distribution and customer service, is, in effect, Julie's boss. He was involved in the rollout of the system and has overseen it ever since. "We intentionally wanted to do something that was a little more lively and engaged than the typical voice response system, to make it a little less mechanical." The company is more than pleased with the results, although he says they are well aware of Julie's flaws, which he mostly attributes to the limitations in the state-of-the-art technology behind Julie. "The *Saturday Night Live* skits are really interesting," he says, because they echo what Amtrak's own market research discovered about people's likes and dislikes in the Julie system. For instance, callers' top dislike is when the system misunderstands them. "If we pay attention to those skits, then we can see where people are getting frustrated. It's subtle, but it's very consistent with what we're finding and what we're trying to do to improve Julie."

The real woman behind Amtrak Julie was also impressed with how right *Saturday Night Live* got it. Julie Stinneford lends not only her voice to the system but also her first name. A voice actress in her mid-forties, she lives in Boston with her husband and two sons. Stinneford says Dratch's impersonation captured her verbal style. "She even dragged out the initial M's in words the way I do as Julie, when I say things like 'my mistake.'"

In person, Stinneford tends toward informal. Her knowing smile and straight, shoulder-length, strawberry-blond hair give her a trustworthy, mom-next-door quality. She is warm, accessible, self-assured, and, yes, perky—but not in an annoying way. In short, the flesh-and-blood Julie lives up to the impression created by her automated telephone persona's voice.

Stinneford expresses amazement that the role has made her into what she calls "a pseudo-celebrity." When people find out what she does for a living, they often ask her to "say something like Amtrak Julie would say it"—especially if they are frequent passengers on the East Coast, where the train service is used heavily. She has learned to give in and dutifully respond with a tried-and-true sample of Amtrak Julie–ese. On cue, she pauses and says with a straight face: "I'm sorry. Did you say, Schenectady?" That one almost always gets a laugh. "I've been surprised," Stinneford says, "about how attached people have gotten to Amtrak Julie. I find it funny. Because they're not really talking to me. They are talking to a computer."

The feat of building those computers—able to carry on conversations advanced enough for companies to use them to speak to their customers—is the result of a long line of technological innovations. First, scientists had to figure out how to make the computers talk. Automated directory assistance in the 1980s was an early commercial example of that. But primitive technology meant less-than-human-sounding voices that often gave not-so-accurate responses. By the late 1980s and early 1990s, recorded human voices had generally replaced computer-generated ones. That was around the time customer service call centers had burgeoned too, and the volume of calls they were receiving increased, as did the complexity of some of those calls. Companies began to assign different tasks to separate call centers. Billing, technical help, and orders, for example, were each handled by agents in separate areas within a customer service operation. Routing callers to the right department became paramount. That role was taken over at most companies by the first interactive voice response systems—or IVRs, as they are called.

Early IVR computers could talk, but they still couldn't listen effectively, so callers had to use their touch-tone phone keypads to respond after such familiar spoken directions as, "For billing, press 3." These systems engendered exasperation among customers who had to struggle through byzantine, time-consuming menus, called phone trees, to get their customer service business done—or to find they could not get it done without a live agent. The technology and design of those touch-tone-based systems improved somewhat as the years went by though their legacy of vexation among customers lingered.

By the beginning of this century, through refinements of an artificial intelligence technology called speech recognition, computers began to be able to do more listening—and even to understand many of the variations in human tone and accents. An increasingly natural-seeming phone conversation between humans and computers became possible. Companies started to offer customers the option to speak their responses instead of punching buttons on the phone keypad. As those speech recognition systems continue to evolve, they are likely to remain part of the customer service landscape. In 2005, businesses spent $1.2 billion on speech recognition telephone systems. Each year since, the speech recognition industry has been growing at a rate of more than 22 percent. And in 2009, companies were projected to spend $2.7 billion on speech recognition telephone technology, according to industry analyst Datamonitor. But the technology isn't perfect yet. And in the face of these newest systems' limitations on what they can hear and how much they can understand, customers are sometimes left feeling just as frustrated as they were with the touch-tone systems.

Steve Springer wrestles with these sorts of issues every day in his job as senior director of user interface design at Nuance Communications, a Boston-based leader in the speech technology field. Nuance corporate literature says the company has created more than three thousand speech technology systems for organizations all over the world, and that more than 7 billion phone conversations are automated through their products each year. Springer comes from a background in computer science. He is smart, likable, resourceful, levelheaded, a good communicator, and committed to his work—just the qualities he and his team strive to infuse into the computerized telephone agents they create. Springer was part of the team that conceived and produced Amtrak Julie, widely regarded by people in the speech technology business as one of the first and best standard-bearers for how speech recognition computers should interact with customers. Amtrak Julie has become a guiding light of sorts for the thousands of automated voices that companies use as first responders to customers' inquiries all over the world.

Most people outside the industry don't make a distinction between speech recognition and touch-tone-based phone systems or between well-designed systems and poorly designed ones. Springer knows that. He also realizes that much of the general public simply believes all automated phone systems are public enemy number one when it comes to customer service—rivaled only, perhaps, by outsourced agents in foreign call centers. The fact that Paul English's GetHuman website struck a chord among so many customers and garnered so much attention when it began was the strongest indication yet of that sentiment.

So instead of blocking out the drumbeat against their profession, Springer was among those who worked with English to address GetHuman's concerns. In fall 2006, when Nuance Communications and Microsoft joined with Paul English, they announced the set of industry standards that included designing all systems so that the option to speak to a live agent is readily available to callers at every point in the process. Springer believed GetHuman was "saying something very important. And for the most part, I think any designer in my group is probably 80 percent in agreement with what the GetHuman people want."

But the standards never took off. The point of divergence, says Springer, was practicality. He maintains that companies simply can't shoulder the increasing costs and complexity of having a human being answer every call coming into a company—especially at multinational companies with millions of customers and hundreds of thousands of calls coming in each week. Making live agents answer mundane and repetitive inquiries, such as bank and credit card balance information, is not the best use of their time or talents either and is not efficient for customers. Speech technology, he says, frees agents up to handle more complex calls, reduces hold times for customers, and makes some company information accessible to customers twenty-four hours a day. But Springer is also keenly aware of the need for many companies to pay more attention to how automated service adds to the alienation and exasperation their customers experience when trying to contact them.

"People are offended when they feel a company doesn't want to speak to them," says Springer. "Unfortunately, what I see is a polarization. You have all the GetHuman fans saying, 'Those damn companies, we've got to stop them. We have to hurl grenades at them until they change.'" On the other side, some of Springer's clients were incensed that Nuance and Microsoft were working with English. "They called us up and asked, 'What are you doing?' They didn't use these words, but essentially they were saying: 'You're negotiating with the terrorists. These guys are publishing a cheat sheet that's meant to undermine all of our cost-saving work for the past five years.'" Springer and many of his colleagues felt caught in the middle, believing that both perspectives have merit. Ultimately he sees Nuance's role as that of a broker of conversations between companies and their customers. They try to "help people figure out how they need to talk to each other."

Despite all his best intentions, outside the office Springer rarely escapes the almost universal antipathy toward his work. In social settings, he has had to find a way to tell people what he does without completely alienating them. "At various times I've said I'm sort of a conversational linguist—but no one knows what that is. Then I've said that I teach computers to understand English—and they think, *Yeah, you're a freak.* He also tried saying, "You know when you call the airlines and those automated systems tell you a flight's status?" But before he could even mention that he designs those systems, people would cut him off and say dismissively: "Oh, yeah, I hate those things!" Finally, Springer came up with a description that seems to work. "Now what I say is: 'You know those really awful automated systems that companies play when you call them? Well, I consult with companies to try to help them make those better.' And I get a little bit of sympathy there."

Finding the exact words to convey information clearly and understanding the effects of those words on people's perception and behavior has become second nature to Springer. It is the art in his work and is evident when he describes how much thought goes into writing the script for voice actors like Julie Stinneford. "When we're designing these systems," says Springer, "we're worried about a high level of precision." For instance, a big pet peeve among top speech technology designers like Springer is the phrase, "Please listen carefully, as some of our menu options have changed." It was created to respond to the fact that many callers were pressing the wrong buttons to get around the wordy systems and then were being routed to the wrong places. So instead of making the systems more customer friendly, someone came up with that sentence, which Springer believes essentially blames the customer for the designer's laziness. He thinks it should be banished from all speech systems, calling it "extremely controlling." And he asks, "Why take up eight seconds to say something so condescending?"

Instead, a more elegant and respectful way to convey the same information might be to ask: "Which would you like: reservations, schedules, or fares?" Springer painstakingly points out that the word *which* should be used at the beginning of that sentence, not the word *what,* because saying, "What would you like?" signals to callers that they are going to have to supply an answer in their own words. But using *which* signals that there is a list of options coming up, and the caller can just sit back, listen, and then choose the right option. Designers have to be that deliberate in thinking about every element of their systems. "There are lots of subtle things to consider," Springer says.

To Robby Kilgore, a designer who works with Springer as a creative director at Nuance, creating a high-quality speech recognition system is a multidisciplinary mix of science, technology, and art. In addition, he says, "The people who are really good at it can walk a mile in the user's shoes." And those people, says Kilgore, are not usually the same people who are great at programming, because the programmers "have had their heads buried in computers for all of their lives, and turn out to be terrible conversationalists." So a typical team would include people with backgrounds in linguistics, psychology, and social science, as well as voice coaches, actors, directors, audio engineers, and computer scientists.

Indeed, it was a multidisciplinary path that led Kilgore to the work of creating speech recognition systems. Formerly a keyboard player, he recorded and performed with such artists as the Rolling Stones, James Taylor, Carly Simon, Paul McCartney, Tom Waits, Laurie Anderson, and Steve Winwood. Eventually he ended up at Microsoft doing sound design for Windows 95. That led to work as a creative director in the social user interface group at Microsoft. Using sound, animation, and breakthroughs in artificial intelligence, they designed on-screen help agents for early versions of Microsoft Office, including the paperclip on-screen help icon, which some loved and others hated.

Now Kilgore works in Nuance's New York City office, downtown near Wall Street—not a neighborhood where many people share his rock musician past. And he has managed to blend in a bit, appearing unassuming and soft-spoken—almost corporate at first. But his artistic passion emerges as he explains how he uses his finely honed audio and performance instincts to help companies convey their brands through the computer voices that answer their phones. He often borrows terms from the world of magic in describing the work. For instance, when pointing out that speech is what separates humans from all other species, he starts by saying, "So here's the thing—humans talk. That's their trick." And he calls speech recognition "an unbelievably complicated trick," because it involves teaching computers to talk and listen to callers as humans would do. Its ultimate goal, he says, is creating "the illusion of conversation."

Kilgore is careful to add, "It's not so much that I want you to think it's a real person. I'm not trying to fool you into that. But I am trying to avoid the deal breakers." For instance, Kilgore says that people who create the systems often "forget to map the social thing onto their software. They forget that a conversation is social. And they make the computer do something really asocial. Like if you call up a company and hear, 'Please listen carefully, for your options have changed . . .' yadda, yadda, yadda. Imagine a real person doing that. They're just talking at you and not listening to you or understanding you. If someone did that at a cocktail party—if they talked your face off for forty-five seconds without letting you respond, and then asked you a bunch of questions, and then didn't really hear the answers—most people would get away as quickly as possible."

Kilgore tries to model the systems on accepted norms of real human interaction. "If a system keeps repeating, 'I didn't understand that,' and it loses track of how many times you've had that error message—if it doesn't make you think that it knows that it's on step three of a five-step process—then it just sounds dumb." On the other hand, he says, "There is something reassuring" if the computer signals that it knows it is responding a second time and says: "I'm sorry. I *still* didn't understand that."

The merits of making human-to-computer relationships adhere to the etiquette of human-to-human interactions are not just a hunch. When Kilgore was at Microsoft, one of the consultants for their group was a Stanford University professor of communications and social science named Clifford Nass, who conducted numerous experiments in which he found that people tend to relate to computers and other media in the same way they do to humans. He reported his often humorous results in a 1996 book that has become a bible of sorts to many computer interface designers, *The Media Equation: How People Treat Computers, Television and New Media Like Real People and Places.* He found people like computers that flatter them better than those that don't. He discovered that people respond differently to computers they perceive as either female or male. And he observed people being polite to computers that display some human qualities in the same ways they would be to humans. Nass, who is also a professional magician, concluded that people are more at ease with a computer that appears to have some human-like traits.

Nass's influence has informed the work of many designers of computer-human customer service interactions as they try to find the right balance between making a computer's limitations clear to callers and making the experience easy and intuitive for users. Steve Springer says, "We're of the mind-set that a computer never pretends to be a person. And shouldn't." Making a computerized telephone customer service agent speak and interact like a human is more of a metaphor, says Springer. He compares it to the way a computer desktop doesn't look exactly like a desk, but it suggests one, and serves a similar purpose.

Amtrak Julie may be just a metaphor, but she comes closer to evoking a real human than many among her breed, called IVR personas. Most of them don't have names. And some are not underpinned with Julie's sophisticated speech recognition technology, which allows her to mimic human conversation more accurately than many others. Still, the interactive voice response persona trend has developed since Julie broke the ground in 2002. An actress from the Broadway play *Rent* plays Simone, the automated agent who answers phones for Virgin Mobile USA. She begins the call by saying: "Hey. What's up? This is Simone. Virgin Mobile customers, you rule!" Her tone is more relaxed than Julie's, and her style more targeted to Virgin's hip, young demographic. She even flatters callers, as Clifford Nass's experiments suggested computers should do.

At one time, Yahoo!'s IVR was named Jenni McDermott. She came complete with a profile to help the actress portraying her get into character. It said she was a twenty-four-year-old Leo with an art history degree from the University of California at Berkeley, who worked as a coffee barista in a San Francisco–area café. She was in a band and liked to scuba dive and walk along the beach with her jazz musician boyfriend, Rob, and her dog, Brindle. Another IVR persona named Mia has been used to answer the phones in some Domino's Pizza franchises.

These days, IVR personas span the world as well. There are French ones (Florence and Bernard), Turkish ones (Kerem and Zeynep), and Mandarin Chinese ones (Lisheng and Linlin).

In light of this global spread of nonhuman help on customer service phone lines—and the backlash the systems receive—Julie Stinneford feels the need to advocate for the value of her computer-based alter ego and the peers it has spawned. In fact, she even points out reasons she thinks automated agents might be superior to humans in certain situations. "As a computer," she says, "I'll never give you an attitude. I will apologize 'til the cows come home. 'I'm sorry. It's my fault. I misunderstood.' I'll give you sixteen different opportunities to try again. And it's never the customer's fault." She says some of her most frustrating experiences as a customer have been when she gets through to live agents and they "either don't know what they are talking about or I can't understand them."

She goes on in her own words: "A lot of the people who are doing telephone customer service, in my opinion, are not customer oriented. They're in a call center, and they have to get through x number of calls in x number of minutes. And in their minds, they're not paid to be nice. They're paid to get the job done. It's only when I have reached a management-level person that I have actually gotten someone who has been friendly to me."

She doesn't get an opportunity to speak publicly and off-script much about her work. So perhaps it is some pent-up frustration of her own that spurs her to keep comparing what she sees as the virtues of her virtual self to the shortcomings of getting human agents on the phone. "I'm paid to be nice. Doggone it. You can yell at me, and I'll say, 'I'm sorry, I just can't get it right.' Again, it is never the customer's fault. Even if they are speaking gobbledygook into the phone. It's always my fault." She says she has to keep that attitude in mind when she goes through the many variations on apologies she has to record for a system. "I can't be too schmaltzy about it. I have to have the right tone, where I'm not sounding condescending and being snotty. It has to be that I'm genuinely mystified as to why it is I haven't gotten it right. But clearly

I know I haven't gotten it right. It's the kind of customer service that people expect."

Callers' expectations are among the first things many designers consider when putting together an interactive voice response system. "Often people are at the end of their rope when they call," says Steve Springer. "They've tried the other ways of resolving their problems, and now they feel like the system isn't set up to help them with their situation and they need to talk to somebody." So they press zero or say "agent" until they bypass the automated system.

Figuring out how the computers should field those calls is a challenge that system designers take seriously. Robby Kilgore says, "We have multinational companies that have many, many, many millions of constituents and lots of departments. It's all fine for you to press zero. But I've got zeros in billing in Boise, I've got zeros in tech support in Bangladesh, and I've got zeros in new orders in Tampa." Without more context from a caller, getting them to the right agent can be awkward. So Kilgore tries to find "some way—without being incredibly long-winded—to say, 'Well, there are forty-seven different places I can send you.'" In that instance, Kilgore says he would suggest something like, "I can help you do x, but I need to know y." That is the kind of "very social trade-off" he believes most callers can accept.

It's not for lack of trying by Springer, Kilgore, and their colleagues, but still their best efforts haven't sufficiently broken through much of the general public's resistance toward IVRs. In 2004, Forrester Research found that IVRs met customers' needs only 18 percent of the time. Kilgore becomes philosophical when faced with that kind of rejection. "I think the interesting thing is: What do they hate? What's happening when they're hating it?" And beyond the obvious frustrations that the most antisocial IVRs engender, Kilgore thinks some of the aversion is a reaction to a larger sense of helplessness people feel at the course the world around them is taking. "They hate that they've got to go through a sort of an automated triage to speak with somebody at a company because companies are that big now, and their services are that complex. It's the death of the mom-and-pop shop. And there isn't a local place to call. So there are just things they hate about the state of the world. And there's very little we can do about that."

For the callers who don't "zero out," as it is called, a speech recognition IVR system that meets their needs has to do a few basic things: get and give information, understand callers' responses, and direct them to the right live agent if necessary. It may seem simple, but computers that answer the phones need much more initial basic training than their human counterparts do. For instance, in order for the computer to understand the callers, its designers have to think of every possible way a caller could respond to a simple yes-no question. So it might be "yes," or "yeah," or "uh-huh," or "sure." Then they teach the computer to recognize those responses, as well as the variations caused by individual accents and intonations.

Springer remembers a famous example of how complicated that can be from when he worked on a system for Bell South. His team had created and tested the voice response system using a female voice they were confident would work well. But when they put the system into use down South, it turned out the Boston designers had made one glaring omission: the computer hadn't been programmed to understand the responses "yes ma'am" and "no ma'am." Springer said they had to scramble to add those southernisms to the computer's repertoire.

That collection of possible responses a computer is trained to understand is called a grammar in the speech recognition business. Some of the most basic systems have a grammar of only 250 to 300 words. More complex systems can understand up to 2,500 responses. Advanced systems, such as those that handle looking up names and numbers in a directory, have virtually open-ended grammars. But now the trend is toward an even more sophisticated system, natural language speech recognition, which can understand when callers speak in a conversational way. Callers can say, "I need to talk to the billing department." Or "billing please." Or "gimme billing." Then the system can pick out key words or sets of words and discern the meaning, and route any of those callers to the billing department. Natural language systems also allow for what are called "disfluencies"—when a speaker hesitates or doesn't speak in a linear way, saying things like, "uhhh, yeah . . . I guess I—can you get me to the place to talk about my bill?" Presumably a natural language system could understand those disfluencies and still route that caller to billing.

In addition to understanding callers' responses, speech recognition systems also have to be programmed to ask questions and give information. In the speech business, the things the system says are called the prompts. That is where the human voice of the computer comes in. For Julie Stinneford, the hardest prompts to record are the short ones. "You'd be surprised," she says, "at how many different ways there are to say *and* or *or*." With the longer sentences and paragraphs, she says she has the persona to carry her through. "But it's the little prompts that they have to slip in between, to make it flow right, that get you crazy." For Amtrak, she also recorded 1,047 city and state names for the stations, with some towns having two or three different locations, such as New York–Grand Central and New York–Penn Station.

And then there are numbers. Stinneford has to record every possible way to say a number so that designers can edit them together to make natural-sounding phone numbers and addresses or bank balances. The process is called catenation. One prompt might be, "The hours are from, nine a-m, to, four p-m." Stinneford says that designers "want to put it together so it doesn't sound like Rosie the Robot. So when I say each number, I really think about what is coming right before it and right after it. In some of the applications I have done, they have actually said, 'You're enunciating too much. Can you slur that one together?'"

Stinneford says she records every number and every letter in at least three different ways: leading, medial, and final. "Leading," she says, "would be as though you're starting something and you expect something to follow it. So if I'm going to give you an 800 number, I would say One . . . 800. But the one is a separate entity." She then uses the example of an address, like 167, to show how she would say the medial number. "If you say, 'one, six,' the six is kind of climbing a little bit. But you know it's not done." Then the tone of the seven goes down again to show there is nothing coming after it. "As you are recording each and every number, you're trying to think, *Okay, this is coming at the end, so it has to sound final.*

Telephone numbers are different from addresses. Stinneford treats each seven-digit phone number as three sets of numbers. The first three numbers are leading (6-8-5), the middle two are medial (0-7), and the last two are final (8-3). "I've had systems where I have recorded every three-number combination and every two-number combination," Stinneford says. "Luckily I didn't have to think of them myself; they just appear in front of me on a screen. You'd be surprised at the detail that goes into these systems. And I'm sure I don't know half of it."

Another important challenge for designers like Steve Springer is to make sure the voices and prompts of the systems have the right human qualities to create trust. "But if you go too far with that," he says, "then you mislead people." He speaks of a concept called the "uncanny valley" that many technology designers know. It comes from the work of Japanese researcher Masahiro Mori, who looked into people's emotional responses to computers in the 1970s. Springer explains that Mori "charted how as machines become more anthropomorphic, and you ask people what their comfort level with them is, it goes up and up." But then there is a point, according to this theory, where if the machine gets too close to being like a real person but it is still not quite there, the comfort level plummets. The line on the graph seemed to be steadily rising to a peak and then suddenly dropping off into what looks like a valley. Mori called it the uncanny valley. "It freaks people out," says Springer. "It's like zombies. They look like people, but they're not, and it creeps people out."

Julie Stinneford is well aware of her role in helping to humanize the machines. "People have to be confident that I will do what they need me to do, that the computer will." When she is recording the prompts, she says she thinks about how to use her voice to "empower customers to feel like they want to keep going, without feeling like they've ceded control to a machine." She tries to convey a trustworthiness in her voice. "People want to have self-control and self-direction—to be able to have a say over their surroundings and what happens to them. If they feel they are losing that, if they are on the telephone and feel that somebody does not care and is taking away their power, it's infuriating. Because you are literally at the mercy of these systems. You know what you need, and it may not be giving it to you. I know for me, I can't stand to feel powerless. I think most people are like that. They want to feel, not powerful necessarily, but at least empowered—that they can do whatever it is they have to do, that they are able to be effective without somebody tripping them."

Stinneford's unique view into the phenomenon of speech recognition systems causes her to feel some affinity with live customer service agents working in call centers and even some affinity with the companies she represents. But mostly she feels an affinity with the customers. At no time was that vantage point—somewhere between customer, company, and machine—more tangled than when she called Citibank to inquire about her credit card one day. In a *Twilight Zone*–like moment, she dialed the toll-free number and a cheery female voice answered saying, "Thank you for calling Citibank." As it asked her for her account number, she realized the voice was her own. "That was very strange," she says, "especially because I had forgotten I had done it. So I called, not knowing it was going to be me. It asked me for my telephone number, and I felt like saying, 'Come on. You know my telephone number.' It was very, very odd speaking to me as the voice of Citibank about something I had to do as a customer of Citibank."

—⟋⟋⟍—

IVR telephone systems are part of the broader segment of the customer service industry called "self-service," which includes any kind of customer help besides live human assistance. Companies provide self-service through three main channels: on the phone, on the Web, or at a location (such as a bank's ATMs, a gas pump, a grocery checkout, or a ticketing kiosk in an airport). Self-service saves companies money, gives customers information instantly, and liberates agents from answering repetitive questions. But self-service also can fuel the perception that a company is uncaring or arrogant—not wanting its customers to talk to live human representatives.

In their own defense, some in customer service point to earlier self-service models and the icy reception they received at first, such as the first ATMs in the early 1980s. Many people hated ATMs at first; they found them hard to use and complained they would do away with human tellers. Many banks also gave their ATMs human names to make them appear friendlier. But now there are many more ATMs (and much less need for giving them human names). Surprisingly, there are also many more tellers than ever before as the job has become more complex and customer oriented. And banks have opened more branches, including those in retail outlets such as supermarkets. Customer service industry people also point back to an even earlier time, when customer dialing replaced operators on telephones. Phone customers complained that self-dialing was a sign that society was losing the human touch. Now, the reasoning goes, it is just a matter of time before people accept and appreciate IVRs and other relatively new self-service innovations in the same way they have come to embrace and value the benefits of ATMs and self-dialed phones.

Companies also claim that customers are demanding self-service more and more. It is hard to imagine a company today not having a website or a bank not giving customers the option to check account balances through an automated phone line or on the Internet. Amtrak's Matt Hardison says that 75 percent of the train travelers in New York City who buy their tickets at the station use the self-service kiosks even when live agents are standing ready to help at ticket counters a few feet away. And the self-service trend is not going away. By 2010, the market research firm Gartner predicts, 58 percent of customer service interactions will be self-service, up from 35 percent in 2005.

While the use of IVRs has played a big role in reducing the number of calls handled by live agents, the growth of the Internet has reduced the number of customers who ring companies up in the first place. Hardison says that at one point, Amtrak received anywhere from 28 to 30 million calls per year. By also providing customers with the opportunity to use the Web or station-based kiosks, Amtrak has been able to reduce the number of calls it receives to the current level of about

18 million. "We are trying to give our customers lots of options," says Hardison. "I think people are evolving to where they would rather save time and do what's fast than have the human interaction."

For that, the Internet opens up a whole new world of customer service. Websites across most industries give fast, simple information on services, products, and companies through a list of frequently asked questions, or FAQs. Another convention of most company websites is a search engine where customers can enter keywords to find the information they need. Customers' complaints about websites usually relate to the usability of a site. Frustrations run along the same lines as IVR headaches, and most of the causes are similarly rooted in faulty design. Customers are turned off by websites that make them repeat information at different steps along the way, force them to do too much of the work, present outdated information, contain search engines that bring back too many or too few results, or require customers to answer a barrage of questions before they can get the information or service they need.

Still, the Internet has expanded the playing field of company-customer interactions, and some businesses exist solely on the Web now. Among the most successful of those, customer service is often a rallying cry. Consider three Web-based companies: the Internet retailer Amazon.com, the Internet bank ING Direct, and Craigslist, the Internet classified ad site. Jeff Bezos, Amazon's founder, said at the site's beginning in 1995 that his goal was to make it "Earth's most customer-centric company." More than a decade later he told the *Harvard Business Review*, "Having that kind of bigger mission is very inspiring. Years from now, when people look back on Amazon, I want them to say that we uplifted customer-centricity across the entire business world." In order to keep in touch with that goal, Bezos works in the company's call center once every two years and requires every employee to do the same.

Arkadi Kuhlmann, the founder of ING Direct, the largest online bank in the United States, moved his office from the executive suite to a corner of the company's call center in the fall of 2007 to stay in closer touch with the customers. And on the Craigslist website, Craig Newmark proclaims his official title as: "Founder, Chairman, Customer Service Representative." He told *Business 2.0* magazine, "American corporate culture seems to devalue customer service in a big way. I say, go the other way. Do it right. Trust your customers. Give them power to do things right. Service costs will drop, and customers will become more devoted to your products and services. This ain't rocket science."

A frequent customer of any of those companies can go years without ever having to call or e-mail them. That is by design. And it is an ultimate goal of most self-service in all industries. It is also an objective that can come across to customers as disdain for their needs. But these Internet businesses avow that for them, striving for less human interaction with customers is born of more noble intentions. They try to anticipate their customers' needs and meet them, thereby making it unnecessary for their customers to spend time contacting them. That not only makes happier customers, they say, but it cuts costs, which along with no physical storefronts to maintain helps Amazon offer low prices, ING keep savings account interest rates high, and Craigslist provide no-fee access to its listings.

"Our customers don't contact us unless something's wrong," says Bezos. So Amazon continually strives to reduce the number of contacts their customers make with the company for each unit sold. Those numbers have gone down every year since Amazon's start. "If your focus is on customers, you keep improving," says Bezos. "A lot of our energy and drive as a company, as a culture, comes from trying to build these customer-focused strategies." When challenges arise and decisions have to be made about which way to take the company, Bezos says, "We try to convert it into a straightforward problem by saying, 'Well, what's better for the consumer?'"

That echoes the philosophies of both ING's Arkadi Kuhlmann and Craig Newmark and is partly a by-product of the accelerated pace of the Internet business environment. Amazon, ING, and Craigslist have all thrived. And their founders say they have done so by making the needs of their customers their business priority at all levels of the company.

Bezos points out that "there's so much rapid change on the Internet, in technology, that our customer-obsessed approach is very effective."

But not everything they have done has gone over well. In the beginning, Amazon's phone number seemed impossible to find on its website. That was all part of its effort to keep costs low and pass the savings on to consumers. But the apparent nonexistence of Amazon's toll-free number created a mini–customer backlash in blogs and on consumer websites. One site that found and gave out the number was created by a customer who could not figure out how to reach the company by phone after she had been overcharged $300 for an order. Amazon responded directly to her, apologized, refunded the overcharge, and has since listed the number on its site. But it is still not immediately available. Clicking on the link to the phone number leads customers to a few other contact options first, including a last-ditch offer to get them to give their number instead and let the company call them back. If that is not acceptable, another click will reveal the company's toll-free number. Amazon gets an F on the GetHuman website grading system, which rates companies on how easy they make it to reach a live customer service agent.

Companies that are not solely based on the Internet are also finding ways to connect with their customers on their websites through peer forums, as they are often called, which encourage their customers to help each other. These are an adjunct to help desks and FAQs, especially at technology websites like Dell, Apple, and Microsoft. Users answer other users' questions. Some customers complain that peer forums are a cynical way for companies to outsource the job of helping their customers to the customers themselves, and thus avoid paying anyone to do the job professionally.

But as with much else in self-service, the customer peer forum concept merges a few different business goals, one of which is finding a better way to help customers. Dell's IdeaStorm.com and the San Francisco–based GetSatisfaction.com are both attempts to marry such customer service goals to marketing goals. A GetSatisfaction blog entry describes the ideal behind these types of unions: "To create great service, companies are letting go of control, letting go of fear of embarrassment, letting go of perfection. Relaxing these things gives customers the opportunity to help companies in amazing ways, as their passions feed back into the products and services they use. It allows companies to be real instead of defensive when things go wrong. It transforms customer service from a cost to be controlled into the most meaningful, viral, cost-effective marketing imaginable."

—⟋⟍⟋—

As more and more companies funnel customer service to IVRs and websites, a few companies are finding a way to provide a self-service option that fuses the two. They are adding another dimension to self-service, literally.

At the top right corner of the U.S. website for the giant Swedish furniture retailer IKEA is a little illustrated icon of a youngish, red-haired woman. Beside her appears the message: "Need help? Ask Anna!" Click on it, and up comes a separate, narrow, vertical panel with a larger representation of the same woman, smiling, blinking her blue eyes, and giving her head an inquisitive tilt. She is wearing a yellow polo shirt with the IKEA logo in blue and has on a telephone headset. She looks like a friendly, efficient customer service agent. Underneath the animation of her is, "Welcome to IKEA. I'm Anna, IKEA USA's Automated Online Assistant. You can ask me about IKEA and our products and our services. How can I help you today?"

Typing in "I am interested in chairs" prompts a web page to come up that displays all the chairs IKEA sells. Then, reminiscent of Amtrak's Julie, a dialogue box under the IKEA Anna character says, "You said: I am interested in chairs." In another box under that is written Anna's reply: "Please have a look at the chairs." Much of IKEA's furniture has to be assembled by the customer, but typing in the question for Anna, "Do I have to put them together myself?" draws an odd response. "Well, if you say so," she replies, and then the animated Anna appears to laugh at her own possibly Swedish brand of humor. Rephrasing the question by asking, "Do they come already assembled?" causes Anna to reply:

"I'm very sorry, but I can't really talk about things like that at this time." Typing in "This is frustrating" triggers Anna to say: "I can't discuss those sort of feelings or emotions. Please talk to me about IKEA." And finally, typing in a bit harsher, more personal critique of Anna, like, "You're kind of dumb," will draw this response: "I am not designed to understand or feel insults, although my knowledge will surely improve after this conversation. What would you like to know about IKEA?"

Anna is one of the forerunners of a new breed of human-like customer service agents starting to appear on computer screens. Still in their infancy, they have not even been given a definitive universal name yet. They are called anything from cyberagents, virtual guides, and interactive automated agents to avatars, chatbots, or digital people. They can come in many incarnations and varying levels of sophistication. The most high tech combine the latest speech recognition technology and personas of IVR with the 3-D animation technology of a DreamWorks-produced movie. No such online agent with all those qualities has been put into action quite yet. IKEA USA's Anna moves a bit and shows facial expressions, but she doesn't speak except through dialogue boxes with written text. On IKEA websites tailored to other countries around the world, other Annas have some more advanced features. The online Anna at IKEA's UK site looks different from her American counterpart. She has blond hair and does speak, though in a synthetic, computerized voice. But she can't yet listen to customers speaking. Site visitors type questions into a dialogue box, and British Anna answers them in spoken language.

Other talking online customer service agents include DirectTV's Diane, Bell Canada's Emily, Royal Bank of Canada's May, and Sergeant STAR (Strong, Trained, And Ready), an interactive recruiter on the U.S. Army website. They all speak but don't answer open-ended questions like Anna is supposed to be able to do. Just as with IVR personas, the parodies of online agents have begun too. *Radar* magazine conducted a mock online interview to try to set up IKEA Anna and Sergeant STAR on a blind date. It took on a question-and-answer format, based on the actual responses of the two online agents to the same questions posed to both. One of the first questions *Radar* magazine asked each one was about their thoughts on the war in Iraq:

Sergeant STAR: In times of war, deployment is likely.

IKEA Anna: This is a subject I prefer not to discuss. I'd much rather talk about IKEA.

Radar: Anna, at a time like this, can you really in good conscience retreat into your yuppie bubble of chairs and tables?

IKEA Anna: Please have a look at the tables.

Radar: You've really got a one-track mind.

IKEA Anna: Don't worry about it so much!

Radar: Sgt. STAR, does the Army have any jobs for self-involved, table-obsessed ladies of Scandinavian descent?

Sergeant STAR: There are more than 70,000 women soldiers currently serving with pride and distinction.

Radar: Hear that, Anna? Even you could sign up.

IKEA Anna: I'm only here to answer questions about IKEA so I don't have any outside interests.

More advanced future versions of IKEA Anna, Sergeant STAR, and their ilk will likely pop up on company websites as soon as personal computers and telephones begin to merge, making the technology that allows users to speak into their computers more widespread. And cell phone companies are considering using these human-like guides on the screens of their phones to help users through complicated procedures, sparing live customer service agents that job. Right now, fewer feature-filled versions of these chatbots are used by Comcast and many other companies in the form of instant message–like computer dialogue boxes on their websites, where customers can enter questions and get canned responses, but not necessarily from an animated character with a human name. IBM and Dell have put 3-D avatars of customer service agents on the Web game Second Life at a virtual information desk in their stores on the site. The millions of Second Life residents worldwide can take their questions about IBM or Dell products to that help center in the virtual world. Gartner market research has predicted that 15 percent of Fortune 1000 companies by 2010 will use some sort of chatbot for online customer service.

These and many other breakthroughs in self-service technologies have sprung from artificial intelligence research in technology labs at universities like MIT and Stanford and at commercial research centers within companies like IBM and AT&T.

Rosalind Picard is an associate professor of computer science at MIT. An article about her in the university publication *Spectrum* told the story of another MIT professor who "was on his knees, crying, one day because he and all his best workers from the MIT Lab for Computer Science couldn't crack a computer problem. Picard said, 'If the computer can do this to PhDs in computer science from MIT, what's it doing to the rest of the world?' adding that we have designed computers for technical people and haven't thought about the customer as a human being."

Picard continued, "When you deal with people from different countries, you show respect for them by translating the conversation into their language. You adapt to them; you don't require them to adapt to you. But computers are very disrespectful. They expect us to adapt to them, and if not, we are made to feel dumb. It is not people who are stupid, it's the computer that is stupid, and it is the software that refuses to adapt."

MIT scientists have spearheaded much of the progress that led to computers that appear to speak and to listen. And MIT scientists are among those currently trying to teach computers to think and reason. But Picard and others are trying to go even further. They are working on teaching computers how to feel.

—⟶⟶—

It could be the start of a really bad joke: What do potential international terrorists and callers to most customer service lines have in common? But the answer is no joke. It is the technology called speech analytics. The same technology that the Central Intelligence Agency and the National Security Administration use to listen in on calls domestically and abroad searching for signs of terrorist activity is now being used by call centers all over the world to listen in on conversations with customers. The message at the beginning of most customer service calls, warning that the call may be recorded for quality assurance purposes, doesn't really tell the whole story. With speech analytics, that original intent has been enlarged, and even usurped, as recordings of customer service calls are increasingly being seen as gold mines of all kinds of information for all areas of companies.

Originally, recorded calls were used by call centers only to evaluate customer service agents and make sure that customers were being treated well. But that was a human-monitored system and was never very efficient. Only a small percentage of calls were examined by managers and used for training agents and listening to customer concerns. That sampling was the best a human worker could do, especially at companies that receive hundreds of thousands of calls in a twenty-four-hour period. So the majority of calls were left unheard. But just as computers can perform mathematical equations much faster and more accurately than humans, speech analytics computers can also mine the information contained in huge numbers of phone calls with speed and variations that would prove unmanageable for humans alone. Now companies are adding to the human monitors and catching on to how valuable it can be to use computers to track the themes and trends of customers' concerns in those phone calls. Not only can those findings help to improve customer service, but they also can fuel innovations in marketing, sales, strategic planning, and product development. Speech analytics is now seen as an important tool for unlocking the latent potential in call centers to become invaluable business-intelligence-gathering hubs within companies.

Speech analytics applications employ the same technology used to create speech recognition IVR programs. But instead of recognizing a customer's exact meaning and then triggering the computer to respond, these systems search conversations for patterns and then group them into themes. Companies don't know all the reasons for their customers' calls. Speech analytics, also called audio mining, can help them find out more about the content of those calls. It can search through recorded phone calls and identify trends in conversations by finding and recognizing key words and phrases. So a search could flag every call in which a customer uttered the phrase, "cancel my account," or in which a competitor's name was used. Then those calls could be mined further to find out if those customers actually defected and to try to analyze why, or why not. Speech analytics systems can be programmed to find all kinds of variations on what is said in calls and group that information in endless ways too. More sophisticated programs can even spot trends in calls not identified by programmers—for instance, if the word *hate* is being used by a high percentage of callers when the programmer only told it to look for *angry*. Speech analytics technology is relatively new. It started to migrate from use in government intelligence to business use in about 2004. And in 2007, industry watchers said it was one of the fastest-growing call center technologies.

Some of the analytics tools currently available also go a bit further than word spotting. What are called emotion-detection programs can identify a caller's range of feelings during a customer service phone call. By tracking the pacing, volume, and tone of a caller's conversation, the technology can flag instances in which a caller was particularly upset or particularly happy. "I can't believe this is happening" can be either a positive or a negative statement, depending on the way it is said and the context in which it is used. Simple word or phrase spotting might not be able to interpret that. Presumably emotion-detection technology could, and many are thrilled with that possibility. Others are skeptical. On hearing about the idea of emotion-detection technology, one reporter for *Internet Telephony* magazine, Tom Keating, wondered in his blog whether this technology would allow the computer to understand context well enough to know, for example, the difference between a caller saying: "Angelina Jolie is da bomb," and "I am going to bomb Angelina Jolie's house."

The use of speech analytics and emotion-detection technology by call centers has also raised privacy and security concerns. For instance, companies have to safeguard against outside hackers, or those within the company who might use the technology to mine for customer account numbers and Social Security numbers contained in recorded calls. Also, consumer groups have raised concerns about customer privacy if transcripts of conversations are shared with other parts of a company beyond the call center. The idea that a company can keep a record of the emotions of customers makes some nervous that any time they get angry, their customer record will reflect that and influence the treatment they get from agents in future interactions.

But companies counter that such systems can also demonstrate to executives how one customer's anger is not an isolated incident. Before this technology, they argue, each phone call was a separate entity. Because there was no practical, reliable way to aggregate the complaints of customers and see how widespread one complaint may be, companies often didn't know they had a larger problem. Speech analytics and emotion detection can provide a way to produce tangible widespread evidence of trends that anger customers, thus empowering those who have to fight within a company for changes to address the problems.

Emotion-detection systems, in particular, grew out of voice verification technology, which is also coming into wider use in call centers. Asking for passwords, your mother's maiden name, the name of your first childhood dog, or your favorite flavor of ice cream are some of the more common ways that companies make sure you are who you say you are. But your voice is even more distinctive to you. And unlike a PIN number, it doesn't slip your mind. Unlike photo ID cards, you always have it with you. And unlike fingerprinting, it isn't messy.

When Bell Canada customers want to access their billing information, they need only speak the phrase "At Bell, my voice is my password." And if the voice on the phone matches the voice in Bell's records, that

customer is in, with no more questions asked. This Bell voice identification service uses voice biometrics technology to verify a caller's identity.
New customers are asked to say, "At Bell, my voice is my password,"
four or five times when they sign up for the service. That gives the company a voiceprint to keep in its records. Every time the customer calls
and says the phrase, the computer compares the voice on the phone
against the voiceprint for verification. The company had to work at the
phrase it chose to ask its customers to say. After they tested the phrase
"Bell is my telecommunications company," focus groups told them it
sounded like mind control, so the company went with the more neutral
phrase.

Creators of voice biometrics systems say they are more user friendly
and more precise than many other security verification systems. But
because the best are only about 80 to 90 percent accurate, they must
be backed up by other identification measures. Still, the savings of
using a computer to verify a customer's identity are hard for companies
to ignore.

A study by the British contact center analyst firm ContactBabel said
that American call centers received 43 billion calls in 2007 and that
contact center agents asked questions to verify identities in 41 percent
of those calls. And although it takes only about twenty to thirty seconds for a call center agent to ask the questions, the study calculated
that in 2007, American contact center agents spent 11,000 years' worth
of time, and the contact center industry spent $11.7 billion, checking
callers' identities.

As with all other self-service technologies used in customer service,
companies have to hope that advances in teaching computers to talk,
listen, and maybe even think and feel will continue. And companies
have to trust that sooner or later, their human customers will not only
adapt to the many high-tech systems deployed to help them, but will
even grow fond of the company-programmed machines that are increasingly infiltrating their lives. Robby Kilgore at Nuance Communications
is optimistic that such a peace can be achieved between customers and
automated corporate phone lines and websites across the world. His

pathway to that might sound self-serving, but it also expresses his practical mission in trying to perfect the help systems. "Given that we're kind of stuck with them, I think we need thoughtful human beings to design them."

Besides, he points out, even if all automated customer service were eliminated, technology still wouldn't be banished from the remaining human-to-human transactions. "The human being you get on the other end of the line," he says, "is still interacting with a computer system on your behalf."

5. The Other End of the Line

In a classroom on the second floor of the JetBlue Airways customer service headquarters in Salt Lake City, thirty-five agents sit at rows of tables listening as Kristal Anderson, a teacher from the company's training branch, JetBlue University, presides over a PowerPoint presentation. All of the agents have been answering reservation lines at JetBlue for at least a year, and some for more than seven years. Today's discussion is about dealing with angry customers—or "irates," as they are often referred to in call centers.

A slide of possible responses to irate customers comes up on the large screen beside Anderson. She asks one of the agents to "read this for us, nice and loud." The young woman recites the list:

"You're stupid."

"I'm not going to help you."

"I don't care what you are saying."

"Please shut up."

"You are lying."

There are smiles and giggles. Anderson steps in. "Wouldn't you agree that these things are probably not very helpful if we said them to our customers?" Everyone nods.

These customer service agents usually answer phones from their homes, but about once a month they trek into the call center for team meetings like this one, part of what the company calls continuous training. A potluck lunch buffet of sandwiches, pasta salads, and a variety of desserts—mostly chocolate—is spread out along tables in the back of the room. There are only two male agents in the room, and two infants who accompanied their mothers to this meeting.

Referring to the slide with the nasty responses, Anderson reassures the agents: "I want you to know, we are very comfortable and confident that you guys don't say these things. You don't use these words. Because common sense says that is not very nice." She goes on: "However, look at this sentence—'You were told to be at the airport at least ninety minutes before departure.' Have we ever said that?" A few people smile in recognition. "Never. Not us. Right?" There is a bit more laughter. Anderson continues: "When someone says, 'You were told to be there ninety minutes before departure,' you can almost hear them saying, 'dumb, dumb,' or 'duh.' Right?"

Even if an agent doesn't intend it, Anderson points out, what customers hear in that sentence is, "Someone at JetBlue is calling me stupid." And that, she says, cues customers to fight back. "They start to hear less that you're a human being. They don't even see you as a human being on the other end of the phone. You're a mean person, speaking for JetBlue, who has just called them stupid."

Anderson goes to the next slide, which presents a popular and long-standing psychological theory that 55 percent of what people communicate is conveyed through body language and 45 percent by tone of voice, inflections, and the content of what is said. She points out that according to the theory, even the most effective phone communication misses more than half of how we communicate in person. "They don't get to see if we're smiling at them, or winking. They can only simply concentrate on our words and how we say them." During the rest of the session, Anderson encourages agents to think hard about the 45 percent they can use on the phone. She brings up more examples of how, without intending to, they could convey the rude messages from the beginning of her presentation.

She asks an agent how she might feel if a customer service agent said to her, "I can't do that." The agent replies: "Like I've run into a brick wall." Another agent adds: "I've had my customers say, 'You mean you won't do that? Let me talk to your supervisor.'" Anderson agrees. "It comes across like we're unwilling; we're not going to do it. Right? What about, 'You have to'? How does that make you feel?" Another agent responds: "I feel like I'm a little kid." Anderson nods. "Nobody likes to be told what to do. And as grown-ups, we dislike it even more. We want to make sure we are respected as human beings and as contributing people in our communities. So don't tell me I *have* to do anything."

As a matter of course, airlines do tell passengers to check in at the airport ninety minutes before their flights. They do remind them to bring ID to get through security. "Those are true statements. They are a necessity for travel. But when you tell customers, 'You have to,' it comes across as negative." Anderson then asks how to restate a sentence such as, "You were told to be at the airport at least ninety minutes before departure," so that it sounds "a little bit nicer, more like we're trying to help."

One agent recounts what worked for her in the past. "I've said, 'I'm sorry. I know that it's really hard to listen to someone droning on, recapping your flight and telling you the rules. Maybe you didn't hear that. But it's possible that maybe the reservations agent didn't do that for you. And I am sorry.'" Customers responded by saying they didn't want to get anyone in trouble.

Anderson is pleased with that example. "Empathizing goes a long way. Remember that when they're upset at us, we are not a human being anymore. They couldn't care less about us, and they think we couldn't care less about them. We're just a voice. And then we become two people who are just trying to find out who's right and who's wrong. But when you see someone as a fellow human being, it puts things in perspective."

She goes to another agent response that irritates customers, especially after weather delays in the airline industry: "This is not JetBlue's fault." The agents agree that statement could convey the message "It's not my problem" or "We really don't care." Anderson uses the example of a family on their way to Disney World. "They've been planning this for months. The dad has had to switch the dates three times because he couldn't get enough time off. The mom has had to find everybody to take care of the dog and all that. They've got everything ready. The kids are stoked. They went to the Disney Store and got things on discount so they could wear the cute stuff and save money." Then they get to the airport and find out the flight is cancelled because of weather.

"So for a minute that person is not thinking about safety. They're thinking about their little kids looking at them and saying, 'Gosh, Mom, I can't believe we can't go to Disney World.' When someone is that emotional, they're mad. Think about it. It doesn't matter whose fault it is." Again, she encourages empathy first.

Next Anderson does some empathizing of her own—with the agents. "One of our challenges is we can become callous when we hear the same thing over and over again. Somebody's sad story becomes just another story. We've got to be careful, you guys. Because we might have heard that sob story or that person's problem a lot in the last twenty or thirty calls. But this is that person's one time—their only time to call with it. So it's hard, and challenging. The longer we're here, the more we need to keep that in the front of our minds. We don't want to come across like we don't care."

She moves on to another unhelpful response. "What about this one: 'Ma'am, I've listened to you; now it's your turn to listen to me.' Or 'Sir, if you'll just let me talk.'" Everyone sees how both sentences sound as if they are telling the customer to shut up. Then one agent talks about the need to let angry customers blow off steam, which prompts Anderson to compare an angry customer to a wind-up toy that will go and go. Even if it is picked up and it stops, when it is put down again, it will go on and on until it runs itself out. Anderson reminds the agents: "It does not matter how right we are, what perfect answers we know, or how much we want to help them. The bottom line is that somebody has something to say. And if they just go on and on, we've found that it is more beneficial to let them finish. Then you can say, 'Thank you so much. Let me make sure that I've understood what you said.' First of all, you've let them run out of juice, so to speak. Then you're turning the conversation from the person telling you everything to asking them to listen to what you have to say. And most people will listen. Because they want to make sure you understood them."

One agent brings up the issue of using "sir" and "ma'am," saying she thinks those terms sound rude and distancing, conveying the message, "I don't know you. I don't care about you." The agent says she prefers to call customers by their last name. Anderson agrees and says using a person's name is "an important validation. It says, I'm listening to the conversation. I am engaged with what you are saying, Mr. Jones. I've paid enough attention to know who you are."

They go over another sentence agents might use when customers ask for a change that carries a fee they aren't prepared to pay. If an agent responds by saying, "You clicked on the fare rules when you booked on the Internet," everyone agrees that is tantamount to calling the customer a liar. They note that in such a situation, the use of the word *you* can come across badly. Anderson says, "It's like someone's finger-pointing at the person. '*You* clicked on the fare rules when *you* booked online, *you* idiot.' That's not the message we want to come across, right?"

All people, she says, want to save face. "We don't want to be embarrassed as adults. Even if we messed up." Maintaining dignity is one right that people don't readily relinquish. Anderson suggests the agents try to "take the personal out of it and focus on the process. 'Our process requires that a box accepting fare rules be checked before the system can generate a confirmation number.' That way, it's no longer about who did what. It becomes about our process."

Finally, she asks the agents how many of them have been irate customers in their personal dealings with customer service agents at other companies. Everybody raises a hand—even Anderson. "I've called up and gone off the hook. I have just totally let them have it, and been a really mean person on the phone before. Now, I'm a reasonable, rational individual. I have a gigantic heart. I don't want to hurt somebody. But at the time I was just mad about the process, about the service. I'm not mad at that person, but boy did they get an earful."

Anderson ends her presentation by pointing out that "customer service is not always about doing exactly what the customer wants. Customer service is just doing your very best and helping people within your abilities. It's all about delivering the right message to customers and helping them understand why."

—◊—

On the wall in Tom and Marlene Goudie's home office, a few inches above the photo of their grandchildren that sits on top of Marlene's computer, hangs a framed needlepoint quotation from the ancient Greek slave Aesop, which reads: "No kindness, no matter how small, is ever wasted."

It is tempting to assume that Marlene stitched that precept—which survived for centuries in Aesop's famous fables before it ended up on the wall of her spare bedroom in Salt Lake City—into the fabric herself, and that she and her husband must read it for inspiration before they sit down each day to work side by side as customer service agents for JetBlue. Marlene knows her mostly urban, East Coast callers would probably believe she and her Utah-based colleagues are just that earnest and sappy. But her conversations with customers make it clear she is a kind person by nature, with or without Aesop's encouragement. As for the needlepoint? She won it as a door prize at a Mormon women's conference a few years ago. She didn't know what to do with it, so she put it in their office as an afterthought, hoping perhaps it might help remind them of their commitment to do unto others as you would have them do unto you—even though she knows not all of their customers live by that tenet themselves.

An impatient caller wants to change the date of his flight from San Diego to JFK Airport in New York. He is outraged when he hears about a change fee. Marlene calms him down without mentioning that he clicked on the fare rules when he booked his flight. She already practices much of what Kristal Anderson's PowerPoint presentation reinforced at her team's meeting the day before. She helps the man figure out if changing is worth the extra cost. It isn't. Next is a dejected woman in New York who is going home to visit family in Puerto Rico and wants to leave on the last flight of the night because she has to work that day. She wants to arrange it so she can spend as much of her vacation time on the island as possible, but the late flight is more expensive than earlier flights and beyond her limited budget. Marlene spends a few minutes searching and finds her a cheaper late flight two days later and asks if she can switch her days off. The woman thinks she can. She hangs up happy. Then there is the slightly nervous mother in Florida who is sending her eleven-year-old son to visit his father, obviously her ex-husband, in New York City for the first time. Marlene patiently helps her through the lengthy process of booking an unaccompanied minor ticket, explaining all the rules clearly and stressing how seriously Jet-Blue takes her son's safety and comfort.

All that in just the first twenty minutes or so of her shift. "One thing I do appreciate about this job," Marlene says, "is I get to use my heart." She describes herself as a people person. When she finds out someone is changing a flight because her husband is in the hospital, for instance, she'll ask: "Is he going to be okay?" Marlene also knows the travel industry. Her first job during college, more than thirty years ago, was as a reservations agent with Holiday Inn. Then she worked as a travel agent in Arizona while Tom was in graduate school at the Thunderbird School of Global Management, and later in Salt Lake City. Her husband's work in the international trucking business brought them there in the early 1980s, where they raised their two young sons. Now their older son lives in Ohio with his wife and child. Their younger son is serving in the army in Iraq. His wife and three kids live in Colorado.

The Goudies like the fact that their work at JetBlue gets them out of their own world for a while and gives them a glimpse of the everyday dramas in the lives of such a cross section of Americans. Marlene says she routinely books trips for grandparents to meet new grandchildren, parents traveling to a son or daughter's wedding, businesspeople on their way to high-level meetings, and she is especially attuned to the military families she helps. She's heard a lot—like the newly divorced man arranging unaccompanied minor travel for his daughter to fly from his house in New York to her mother in Florida. Marlene got all the information she needed about the father, including his driver's license number, his child's full name, and his full name. She told him when and where to drop the child off at the airport. Then she asked who would be picking up the child. The man said simply, "That woman." Marlene asked if he meant the child's mother. He said he did but wouldn't give any more details. Finally, Marlene told him gently, "You are going to have to utter your ex-wife's name. That is the only way we can arrange your daughter's arrival." Eventually the man complied.

In her initial training, Marlene remembers hearing the nicknames other agents had made up for some of the more common offbeat types of customers she would encounter. "You've got Pervert Pete and Domineering Dave." When those calls come in, she thinks, *Okay, it's one of these guys,* and then does the best she can.

In the past few years, Marlene has noticed people becoming increasingly hostile. "They are more angry. They don't seem to know how to reduce their stress and want to take it out on everyone." Tom says about two or three times a week, he is asked impatiently if he is based in the United States or at some foreign call center. Marlene has been asked a few times if she was a real person or a recording. But Marlene says, "The ones I have the hardest time with are the people who are extremely demanding. You can tell, within the first three or four words out of their mouth, they're used to getting their way. They don't want anybody to tell them anything other than what they had in mind when they made the call."

Tom says he is also convinced that people treat men and women differently over the phone. He hears Marlene having to deal with more hostility than he does. He has also been on the line when customers talk to his supervisor, who is a woman. "I've had calls where I've started and the guy was okay. But he wants a supervisor. So I get the supervisor on the line, and then he just goes ballistic. They'll just be abusive to her. But they'll talk to me and not be. I think some people feel more comfortable not being polite to women."

Because there has been so much publicity about how JetBlue customer service agents are based in Salt Lake City and many are Mormon wives, Marlene says she has had to field a lot of personal questions.

They start by asking if she is Mormon. "I say I am and just try to get them back to the business at hand." But sometimes the questioners persist, and even go so far as to ask, "Do you have horns on your head?" or, "Do you dance around campfires?" Marlene tries to take it in stride. "I just laugh and say, 'No, I look pretty normal.'" Sometimes they ask about her husband and if he has more than one wife. "I say he's sitting right here next to me, and I'm his only wife. Occasionally, when a Pervert Pete calls, I just say, 'Would you like to talk to my husband? I don't think he would really like the things you're saying to me.'"

But it is during really difficult travel periods that both Marlene and Tom sometimes turn to their faith to help them endure. "I don't think I have prayed about only one, single phone call," says Tom. "But I have prayed that I could get through a day before." Like on Valentine's Day 2007, when a winter storm crippled New York airports and many Jet-Blue passengers were stranded for long hours on the tarmac. Flights were being cancelled so frequently that JetBlue's system couldn't keep up. Then New York delays had a domino effect on the rest of the nation. Passengers were calling from inside the trapped planes, and then all those in the airports whose flights were cancelled were calling, as well as people with upcoming flights. The event got a lot of attention in the news media because of JetBlue's previously sterling customer service reputation.

Tom arrived at his desk that morning at about 7:30, as usual. Marlene was still asleep. "As soon as I got on the phone, there were already four hundred calls backed up." On an average day, the computer system that shows agents and supervisors how long customers are having to stay on hold would register about seventy calls, with an average wait time for customers of two minutes. That day the numbers were higher than anyone at JetBlue had ever seen before.

By the time Marlene got to her phone a few hours later, the crisis was in full swing. Her shift starts later than Tom's, and he let her get her sleep that morning, knowing it might be the last peace either of them would have for a while. Along with most of their colleagues, Tom and Marlene worked almost nonstop for the next fifteen hours, and then for long hours again the following days. They would stop for meals and sometimes to lie down for a few minutes and then go back to the phones. Marlene says she was shocked at the way some customers acted during that time. "I had never heard things out of people's mouths like they were saying. They were vicious—cursing, swearing, calling us idiots." The airline had all hands on deck, even bringing in gate agents from the airport to help field the calls. "The airport people were amazed at the things that people would say to them on the phone," Marlene remembers. "They actually told us, 'There is no way customers would ever look me in the face and say the things that they are saying to us on the phone.'"

Marlene and Tom struggled to maintain their composure. Marlene says all the customers had complaints. That is not what got to her. It was "when they really personalize it and say, 'You guys are all stupid.' Or 'You guys suck.' You can try and say, 'I realize you're frustrated and I know you're upset with me, but I am trying to help you.'" That doesn't always work though.

The Goudies' commitment to service is just what David Neeleman, the founder of JetBlue, who has since stepped down as CEO, had in mind when he decided to base the customer service operations in his hometown of Salt Lake City, even though the corporate headquarters is in New York City. Marlene feels a connection to Neeleman too, since they share the Mormon faith, and she believes he cares about his workers. During the Valentine's Day problems, she says, "He was sending messages to us, saying, 'I apologize for what's happened. Take care of yourselves. But if you can help out, please do.' That meant a lot to us knowing that he actually cared what we were going through."

Marlene has shown that same kind of caring spirit from day one. She says she knew she was in the right place when she answered her very first call for JetBlue. It took her an hour and a half to complete it. But her supervisors didn't complain. Instead, they understood they had hired the right person.

The call came from an elderly African American woman in Florida who had never been on an airplane. Her husband's eightieth birthday was coming up that summer. He had never been on a plane either. She and her kids wanted to surprise him by flying him to New York. She would be traveling with him. She explained to Marlene that her husband had worked all his life. Because he grew up in the South during segregation, if he traveled, he had mostly ridden in the backs of buses. That's why she didn't care what day they traveled or which airport they landed at in New York. The only thing that mattered to her for this special flight was that she wanted him to ride at the front of the plane. JetBlue doesn't have first class, another founding ethic of equality at the airline. But Marlene understood the situation. She spent as long as it took to find the right flights, with two seats in the very front row for this woman and her husband's first, and possibly only, airline flight ever. Marlene says she got them the seats, and after the flight, the woman wrote to the company and thanked them for treating her and her husband so well. "All she wanted was for her husband to have the dignity that had been denied him for so much of his life. I wanted to make sure they got it too. After all, we're taught we are all brothers and sisters of the same God."

Frankie Littleford has been with JetBlue from the very beginning. She is now the vice president of reservations, meaning she is in charge of the whole customer service operation. She is also the recorded voice of the IVR system at JetBlue. When people call in, hers is the first voice they hear. Littleford started in the mid-1980s as a reservations agent at an Eastern Airlines call center in Salt Lake City. She then worked at Morris Air and Southwest Airlines with David Neeleman, JetBlue's founder. Remembering her earliest days, she says a lot has changed. "Customers didn't have the Internet where they could go make their own booking. Now the majority are so Internet savvy. They really don't want to pick up the phone. They just want self-service—to go online and figure it out themselves. More times than not, once a customer calls, they have already tried to solve it on their own. A phone call is reserved for those more intricate, unique, complex situations."

That means training agents to handle calls properly is also more complex than it used to be. The typical training period for JetBlue agents is seven weeks. During that time, they learn all sorts of things, from company policies and computer systems to security measures, and how to handle the callers they will encounter. An important concept in teaching agents to be effective on the phone is what is called "mirroring" the customer—pacing their responses based on how the customer is interacting with them. "If it is the business traveler who's speaking very quickly and not a whole lot of chitchat," says Littleford, "that is how you need to be mirroring to meet their needs. If it's the elderly woman who has more time and is kind of lonely and wants to chitchat, then you don't need to be as hurried on that phone call." Littleford says JetBlue is adamant about not giving their agents scripts to read. They teach the information agents need to impart and then depend on them to convey it in their own words, to personalize it.

Sometimes a customer service agent has to send a particularly difficult call to a supervisor; in the industry, that is referred to as call escalation. At JetBlue, escalated calls are handled by the crew support department. Approximately 168 crew support members work with the approximately 1,200 JetBlue customer service agents. They are experienced agents and have a bit more authority to make decisions about complicated calls than do the reservations agents like Marlene. They also work in the office more often than they do at home.

Walking through the spacious cubicles of the crew support department in the middle of JetBlue's call center in Salt Lake City, it is hard not to notice Rolf DeVries. The sixty-something father of six and grandfather of seventeen is a one-man pep squad, therapy clinic, and motivational workshop. His shaved head and booming voice hint at his previous stint in the military. But his warm manner and jolly demeanor are what cause reservations agents to tell him so often how much they love him. "Thank you for being so perky," says a newer agent who calls in for help with a change request she had never handled before. Another agent tells DeVries, "Thank you for restoring my emotions. They should give you a raise," after he helps her with an angry customer who had lost his confirmation number.

In the early 2000s, DeVries, who is Mormon, moved to Salt Lake City and started at JetBlue as an agent. About six months later, he was bumped up to crew support. Along with freeing agents from having to handle the more complex calls, crew support also answers questions on procedure from agents. DeVries says he considers it part of his job to offer the frontline workers a boost. "The agent will go back and use the same tone of voice that I used with her, to the customer. So instead of just saying, 'We can't give compensation' and being done with it, I would say, 'Oh, I'm sorry, we can't give compensation, as much as we'd like to. But this is a weather-related delay. If it was up to me, I'd push the button and give you a thousand bucks, but we can't. It's weather related.' Then the reservations agent will use the same tone with the customer. If we have a bad attitude, we can infect, in one or two days, all of JetBlue."

He says he sees customer service as "keeping the clouds of negativity from rolling in. They're always around, and you can get taken over by them unless you keep that sort of attitude. These reservations crew members, some of them are on the phone for eight to ten hours, so they want a little schmaltz." That is exactly what DeVries gives them. He has toys that make sound effects in his drawer and sometimes will pull one out and use it to make agents laugh. "Customer service is an art. We're performance artists. We're trying to create a feeling. When you get on that line with a customer, you want to leave them with a warm, fuzzy feeling. They're going to trust you to fly them at thirty thousand feet. They figure, if you can't get customer service right, how can they be sure that you are tightening the bolts on the plane right? They want to get a confident, happy, friendly voice, so they can feel better about the whole experience of flying."

It isn't as easy as DeVries makes it look. Just like a performer about to get up in front of a stadium concert crowd, he goes through rituals before, during, and after each shift. He reads books by motivational speaker Tony Robbins. He arrives an hour early each day and starts to mentally prepare himself. "It's an exercise. It's a discipline. It's something you've got to do with your mind every single day. If you're working a ten-hour shift, you're going to have ten hours of people yelling at you. You've got to be very focused."

When he gets to the phones and puts on his headset, he says a mantra to himself before he goes on the line. "Every time I have to program myself so that I don't get defensive, or meet aggression with aggression. I say to myself, *This person is upset, but I'll bet I can think of a way to make the customer at least happier.* Or, *I hope I can empathize with this person so that they'll know that they're not the only ones concerned about this matter.* When I start off the call, I use phrases like: 'This is Rolf. I'm a JetBlue supervisor. I understand you have a problem I can help you with.' Immediately that switches them to, *Oh, they're not going to be defensive. They're going to try and help me with my problem.*"

Then he encourages the customers to talk. "I say, 'At this point just tell me what happened. I'm going to shut up now. I'm going to make noises just so you know that I'm here and that I'm interested and I'm going to ask questions when I have to. Otherwise, tell me what happened. I'm going to be taking notes, which will go to the people who are most appropriate to understand your problem and make sure this doesn't happen again.'"

DeVries says he likes to take the most challenging callers. "We're trying to turn irate customers around. As impossible as that may seem, it is possible to do. And not by throwing money at them—vouchers. Not by saying, 'We'll give you $150 if you'll just go away and be happy.' It's an attitude of sympathetic listening." The fact that his managers don't judge him solely on the length of his calls is particularly helpful. "I've found that a huge amount can be defused by just taking the time to listen. If you've got an irate call and the person is in tears, the first thing is to take the time and listen—listening for when they're wound down and then resolving the problem. You've got to sound empathetic. You've really got to try to empathize with the customer. I would say the hugest percentage of what that customer wants out of that call is just for somebody to listen. So you start—don't try to do this right away. After they unload, you start asking them specific questions that will get them to the logical side of the brain: 'What time was your flight supposed to leave? What was the number of your flight?' So they're moving from the emotional side to the rational side."

At the cubicle across from DeVries in crew support is Brenda Schultz, who usually works from home but is spending a few days a month at the call center. Schultz is in her mid-forties and came to Jet-Blue after her kids were grown. She has worked in crew support since 2003. She is on the line with an agent who is trying to get a ticket changed for a woman on vacation whose mother has just had a stroke. The woman is trying to go back home to her mother. The agent says to Schultz, "I know how fast a family emergency can come up. If she is cutting her trip short, that kind of bites." Schultz is sympathetic too.

The agent asks Schultz what kind of verification she has to get from the customer. First, Schultz checks the customer's history on the computer to see if this particular customer's mother has ever had a stroke before when she changed a flight. That would signal a ploy. Schultz says such skepticism goes with the job. "There are plenty of people who get away with all kinds of stuff. You really have to try the best you can to find the correct wording to ask questions and find out who's real and who's not. I think being a parent helps. There are always arguments or things that you've got to mediate. Customers will call with things, and you'll think, *This is just like when my kids try to get one past me.* There are a million different situations you're dealing with."

This passenger's story checks out. She has never tried to change her travel dates before. Schultz and the agent begin to work on the switch. Schultz says the challenge is to keep treating the customers as human beings on the other end of the line—"but also not to internalize it. You have to keep some detachment, or you can get sucked into stories."

As she and the agent go through the ticket change procedure, there are moments when the computer is processing the information. Schultz uses those seconds to chat with the agent. This agent is working from her basement at home and has music on in the background, which she turns off when talking to customers. "I get bored sometimes all by myself," she confides in Schultz. "So I put a radio down here." Schultz tells her she knows how it is. Then the agent goes back to the woman on hold and assures her they are sorting out her problem and will be able to change her ticket. She comes back on the line with Schultz, and as they work and wait, they talk casually about other aspects of the job and their lives. The ticket change takes about four minutes, and Schultz is able to give the agent some good cheer during that time. "As nice as it is, working from home can be hard too. You feel like you're alone. So we just have to be that link to real people for them—give moral support to help them survive. You kind of have to be that listening ear."

Just as every customer has a story of bad treatment at the hands of some customer service agent, whenever two or more agents get together, they can easily trade odd-customer stories. Schultz remembers the woman who called very upset that when she popped open her soft drink on a flight, it didn't make the fizzy popping sound she thought it should. She demanded a free round trip. Schultz also tells about a man who wanted a free round trip because his overhead light didn't work on his last flight. Then DeVries remembers the story of a woman who called and said that the door blew off during her flight and people were being sucked out of the plane. She said she grabbed another passenger so he wouldn't be sucked out too. She wanted her money back, even though she couldn't recount any other details of the flight or explain why no one had heard of the incident at the airline.

DeVries and Schultz conduct a half-day class for newly hired agents at JetBlue University in which they impart a lot of tricks of their trade. But Schultz believes the bottom line is that it takes a certain kind of person to do customer service well. "You can't be a callous, I-don't-care-about-you person, because your colors are going to show through and it's not going to work. You have to want to help somebody. It's got to be in your heart to have empathy." There is only so much that they can instill in new agents. DeVries remembers a JetBlue executive who brought that home to him in his initial training. He told the class: "I can teach you how to fly the airplane. I can teach you how to count beans. Given enough time, I can teach every single one of you every operation. But the one thing I can't teach is, I can't teach you to be nice."

Still, Schultz says she has learned some techniques from watching DeVries, a New Jersey native, deal with East Coast customers who, she says, are a bit more "argumentative" than people from the rest of the country. "Rolf has taught us all that it's the battle, not so much who wins or not. They like the fight." Schultz says that helps her not take some of those calls personally.

"A lot of customer service is a cultural thing," DeVries says. But he also believes that some of the hostility goes beyond regional styles of communicating. "It's also about our society. Today it's all right to completely insult people. It's hip to degrade. And you get that both coming and going in customer service. So you've got to decide beforehand how much abusive language you're going to take. Some people just don't like abusive language at all, and they'll disconnect the call immediately when the customer starts swearing. We try not to do that because often the customer, quite rightly, is upset. The question is how you're going to handle it. Some people say, 'Look, let's cut the swearing or I've got to hang up.'"

DeVries handles it a little differently. "Me? I say, 'Harry, look, I'm taking notes. I'm putting down everything you've said. And they're not going to take it seriously if you keep using those words.'" With most customers, DeVries has found that this less direct approach is effective.

Accurate numbers on just how many people work as customer service representatives in the United States are difficult to find. In 2008, most of the best data from consultants and academics who analyze the customer service industry put the number at somewhere around 3 million, which is about 2 percent of the total U.S. labor force. But the definition of who is included in the occupation and who is not varies from study to study, which makes it hard to pin down consistent statistics and projections. A more conservative yet very detailed estimate is produced every few years by the U.S. Department of Labor's Bureau of Labor Statistics (BLS).

In 2006, the BLS reported there were about 2.2 million customer service reps in the United States. It also put customer service representatives third on the list of occupations expected to have the largest growth by 2016, behind nurses and retail salespeople. It projected that the number of reps will rise 25 percent, to 2.74 million, by 2016. The median annual salary of a customer service rep in 2007 was $29,040, according to the BLS, and the median hourly salary was $13.96. States with the highest concentration of customer service workers were Arizona, South Dakota, Texas, Georgia, and Florida. The town with the highest concentration of customer service workers was Sioux Falls, South Dakota, followed by Lubbock, Texas; Jacksonville, Florida; Salt Lake City; and San Antonio, Texas.

The finance and insurance industries have the highest concentration of customer service agents, employing 23 percent of all reps. In 2006 most customer service jobs involved work on the telephone, with much of the work going on in some sort of call center. Most required at least a high school diploma, and many now require an associate or bachelor's degree. Most reps worked a forty-hour week, although many worked at odd hours to keep customer service help available twenty-four hours a day and seven days a week. Seventeen percent of all reps across all industries worked part-time.

The 2006 report also discussed the working conditions in call centers, saying some "may be crowded and noisy, and work may be repetitive and stressful, with little time between calls. Workers usually must attempt to minimize the length of each call, while still providing excellent service. To ensure that these procedures are followed, conversations may be monitored by supervisors, which can be stressful. Also, long periods spent sitting, typing, or looking at a computer screen may cause eye and muscle strain, backaches, headaches, and repetitive motion injuries. Customer service representatives may have to deal with difficult or irate customers, which can be challenging. However, the ability to resolve customers' problems has the potential to be very rewarding."

Some academic studies have focused on those kinds of pressures of the job. Psychologists at Frankfurt University in Germany found that working in a call center could be dangerous to an agent's health. The culprit, according to a 2006 study, is having to exude what they called "fake happiness." In addition to interviewing more than four thousand customer service workers at airports, hospitals, and call centers, the psychologists set up a simulated call center and had eighty student volunteers act as staff. Half of that group was told they could talk back to rude customers, but the other half was told they had to remain positive and cordial at all times. For the group that was allowed to defend themselves, abuse from customers had little lasting effect on their heart rates and overall health. The other group had higher heart rates long after the upsetting phone calls.

The study concluded that most people can handle short bursts of pretending to be happy, but a job that requires people to fake their happiness for extended periods is another matter. "Every time a person is forced to repress his true feelings," said Professor Dieter Zapf, who headed up the study, "there are negative consequences for his health. We all control our emotions. But it becomes a problem when it's over a long period." In addition, the study showed that the amount of latitude a worker is given to make decisions and have some control over a job is another contributing factor to stress levels. "Even though a social worker may experience a great deal of emotional stress in a day, she can choose when to walk away and take a quiet five minutes. Someone working in a call center just has to keep answering the phone, and often finds it hard to take a break, so their stress levels just keep climbing. That tends to lead to burnout and depression."

A British academic study published in 2003, "Psychosocial Risk Factors in Call Centres," reported that "the risk of mental health problems is higher for call handlers and job-related well-being is lower compared to employees in other occupations." The report went on to say that some call center workers had it worse than others, including those who worked in the telecommunications and information technology sectors and those who worked in call centers with fifty or more employees. Some of the elements that made the jobs most stressful for the workers were "high workload," lack of clarity about their roles, and not making "full use of their skills." The study concluded that to improve the well-being of workers, companies should increase autonomy for workers and give them "more variety in their tasks."

Another academic study of call centers, this one in Sydney, Australia, during the early 1990s, surveyed workers and concluded that many companies took a "sacrificial" approach to the well-being of customer service agents. Since the agents weren't expected to stay in the jobs for long, the reasoning went, working them until they burned out was fine as long as it was profitable to do so.

Professor Zapf, the head of the "fake happiness" study in Germany, concluded that people doing call center work are underappreciated. "It's about time we did away with the concept that the customer is always right," he said, "and showed more respect for those in customer service jobs."

Of course, not all customer service work is drudgery, and not all workers are unhappy. But the plight of those who are is not only well documented in government reports and in international peer-reviewed academic studies, it is also well represented anecdotally on the Internet. On Facebook, for example, groups made up of disgruntled customer service workers go by such names as "Customer Service is slowly driving me insane," "Working in Customer Service Made Me Bitter and Hateful," and "If you don't like my customer service . . . I hate you." There is also a British Internet bulletin board created by and for retail and call center workers in the United Kingdom, Canada, and the United States called CustomersSuck.com. The introduction to that site says it is meant to be "a bastion of sanity for those on the frontlines of customer service. This site is a place to vent, share, sympathise, comfort, exchange information of use, share a laugh, and generally relax." Various other call center employees have taken to periodic blogging about their jobs.

The introduction to one customer service representative's blog starts out: "Think it's easy answering the phone for a living? Think again! You might be a nice person, but something happens when people call a toll-free telephone number. I guess they think we have no feelings, since we're only a voice on the other end of the phone."

Another customer service rep writes a blog that sometimes addresses work issues. In an entry called "What Customer Service Reps Have to Deal With," he says:

> Well today, it's time to vent! Today I'm going to bitch about all of the crap we as call center, customer service representatives have to deal with from our customers! Though, I want everyone who reads this to understand that I'm not some kind of disgruntled employee that hates my job. (Quite the opposite.) Nevertheless, these are common frustrations I deal with every single day. . . .
>
> *"I'm Not Taking This Out on You"*
> One of my pet peeves! Irate people yell at me all the time, then promptly say that god-awful phrase because they want to make sure you don't hang up on them. What amazes me though, is that these people continue to take out all of their lives' frustrations on me, even if I had nothing to do with it and I'm trying to help them! Reps often get used as the "punching bags" for customers, which is totally not fair. What typically happens is they get all mad at us, then ask for a supervisor where they are all nice and sweet. Here's a tip: if you can be nice, don't be a jerk towards us. You'll get a lot more accomplished if you stay calm, and very little accomplished if you yell at us.
>
> *"I Hate Your Automated System" & Other Things Outside Our Control*
> We reps have zero control over things like this. If we had it our way, there would be no automated system. We also don't have any control over company policies, only that we're supposed to follow them as closely as possible. (Supervisors can't wave a magic wand for you and change

things instantly, either.) We are not the choice makers in the company.

Being Treated as Machines
You know, it's funny . . . people often complain how much they hate dealing with the "machine" that is the automated system before they talk to a rep. Yet, as soon as they get to us, they treat us as if we're some kind of machine that just spews out whatever response they want from us. I have a good feeling that if it was a face-to-face conversation, it would be different. The thing is though, it shouldn't be like that. We're human. A few "pleases" and "thank yous" would be awfully nice to show your appreciation in speaking with a live person.

A few bloggers wax poetic about what they encounter as agents. One of the most read bloggers, until he quit his call center job after a few years, called himself "Anonymous Cog" and his blog "CallCenter Purgatory.com." His own description of the blog read: "Exploring the mind-numbing insanity and childish corporate culture of an unknown call center employee." In an entry entitled "A Sea of Service," he spoke of the pressures he felt:

When I put the headphone on my head it all started. The calls began like a wave of the ocean. Sometimes I can swim with it, sometimes I actually bodysurf, but more often than not I feel like I am drowning in people's needs for service.

"I need my account updated."
"I've been holding forever!"
"I'm having problems accessing your website . . ."
"This is unacceptable!"
"Someone needs to . . ."
"There is a problem with . . ."

"Every time I call . . ."

"Why won't you . . ."

ENOUGH!!!!!

In an entry called "Wandering Through a Wonderland of Rage," Anonymous Cog said, "If this place has taught me anything, it's that all people have the ability to be evil and unkind, and we all have to fight to be human every day."

The pressures on frontline call center agents certainly abound. In part because of that, one of the biggest problems in the industry is employee turnover. Again, exact numbers are hard to come by, but attrition among customer service agents each year ranges anywhere from 25 to 75 percent in call centers. Personnel costs, including recruiting and training of new employees, are the biggest expenses of most call centers, so attrition is a serious concern. Recent efforts have been made to address the causes of turnover in the industry and to do a better job of retaining employees. Some call centers even have developed elaborate measures to predict when an employee might be about to jump ship and see if they can be kept. In addition, companies are having to become more scientific about whom they hire in the first place, with some conducting psychological profiles of potential agents and picking those with the qualities that will most likely endure and even thrive in a call center.

The sweatshop model of call centers is still the template in a few companies, but most in the industry have become more sophisticated in managing workers and customers. For example, many call centers forecast the volume of incoming calls based on the number of calls they received at the same time of day, week, and month the previous year, so that staffing can be adjusted to best handle higher call volumes.

The call center manager, however, still has to juggle the interests of customers, the company, and its employees. The key is to try to make those interests align. One example of that balancing act is call monitoring, which takes place in most call centers. Recording phone calls can be used to reward good call handling on the part of agents, though it is also, of course, potentially invasive for agents and customers alike. But knowing exactly what went wrong on a call can also validate a customer's claims of bad service and help the company make necessary reparations so it doesn't lose the customer.

As with agents, anecdotal evidence of the challenges that the people running call centers encounter can be found on the Internet. In a blog called "Call Center Steel Cage Death Match," a supervisor discusses some of the issues he faces:

> Of all the components comprising the call center and customer service nothing is of greater importance than the human interaction. It all boils down to two people talking to each other.
>
> So, the crux of the job, from the rep's perspective (and this, I believe, is the most important thing for a call center manager to meditate upon), is that the conversation is always one-sided and has one aim: one person (the customer) is always talking about *his* or *her* needs to the rep with the expectation of having the rep take care of/fix/listen to/ address/give satisfaction/delight etc. etc. to the customer.
>
> This is not bad or undesirable or unreasonable. But the true challenge of a call center agent is being able to deal with this call after call. It is this aspect that should guide the hiring decisions (i.e., can you somehow make an assessment regarding the candidate's capacity for fielding pleas for help).

He has come to believe there is also a responsibility on the part of the customer in the interaction:

> Technology will not replace humans' need and desire to speak to one of their own kind—i.e. not a machine. The

upshot is that we need each other in our daily transactions. We want to make a phone call, or send an email, and have a genuine human interaction in which a genuine human helps us out.

But I believe, contrary to the "have it your way" consumer culture that has become standard, that we (customers) have a responsibility to behave in the same manner that we expect from those who answer our calls. Making unreasonable demands, treating a call center rep poorly, using degrading and abusive language is not right or acceptable. Sometimes, the customer, contrary to "have it your way" culture, is *not* right.

Another supervisor blog, "The Supervisor of Customer Service Hell," is more charged. This supervisor describes himself as "the company's wage-slave, my manager's gofer, the puppet of the upper brass, the faceless representative of 'The Man'—the one that's responsible for shepherding over all of this misery that you see." He goes on: "I'm a supervisor working in a customer service call center owned by a huge multi-national corporation. I like to write about my observations—or, more often, about amusing or horrifying episodes at work." In an entry entitled "Apathy," he says:

> I feel a strange lassitude about [my job]. My anger and rage has started to even out to general depression and despair about management, but genuine pleasure as well in dealing with my core group. I guess, now that I think about it, I really don't feel bad at all. I've gotten hugged this week. I've been told that I was the best boss someone ever had. I've been told that I've made this job better than anything else in their life for someone, and I'm happy about that. I guess I've found that little spark that made me like being a supervisor to begin with.
>
> So, you know what? I'll always get mad about the stu-

pid corporate policies, ridiculous management types who can't walk the talk, useless employees that I can never seem to get permission to fire, and endless turnover. I may move to another job. But, in a moment of extreme anger, I took a step back and realized that I need to find happiness in what I'm doing—the "Zen of supervising," if you will.

That's what I try to tell myself, anyway. Stress, it'll kill you.

—⁂—

While the telephone is still the main communication line between customers and companies, the use of other channels such as text messaging, instant messaging, and e-mails is becoming more prevalent. In recognition of that expansion, the term *call center* has been replaced by, or at least is being used interchangeably with, the term *contact center* within the industry. As companies steer more customers to self-service channels such as the Web and IVRs to take care of the simple transactions that were once some of the telephone customer service agent's most basic functions, the perception among customers is that anything but live phone help is cheaper for companies. That is true, except for e-mail, which is the most time-consuming and therefore most expensive channel for a company to offer. Instant messaging is cheaper than the phone or e-mails because agents can take care of more than one IM or text message at a time. But as newer channels are adopted in the customer's world, such as social networking, video messaging on cell phones and computer phone lines, and phone calls migrating to the Internet, contact centers are having to keep up with how their customers prefer to communicate. In the not-too-distant future, live video interactions with agents on the Internet will likely become common in contact centers.

But for all the Internet and self-service innovations, studies show that customers still prefer a live phone conversation. The Internet and consumer technology consulting firm Jupiter Research predicts that while the use of the Web for customer service will increase in the next few years, it will make up only 14 percent of the more than 50 billion contacts between customers and companies predicted to occur in 2012. That apparently unflagging demand for live phone contact is what led the call center industry to turn to outsourcing in the past decade. To meet demand and reduce the time customers spend on hold, the reasoning went, hiring more people at a lower cost without sacrificing quality was a promise many in the industry couldn't resist.

Outsourcing comes in many forms. A company can set up its own call centers in a foreign country to take advantage of lower labor costs. Or a company can contract with an outsourcing supplier to set up and run call centers for it domestically or in foreign countries, or both. Technological advances have spurred outsourcing as the migration of telephone communication to the Internet and the worldwide spread of high-speed Web networks mean all the agents don't have to be in one place to do their work. So contact centers no longer have to be on site at a company, as they generally did until at least the late 1990s.

A report on customer service outsourcing by the International Customer Management Institute surveyed contact center managers, primarily in North America, and found that nearly 30 percent of call centers outsource some portion of their company's customer contacts. The most common outsourced functions were the most basic requests, as well as overflow during peak times, after-hours inquiries, and contacts in a foreign language. Saving money was the main reason for outsourcing contact center work, cited by 65 percent of the managers surveyed. Some said they also outsourced to "tap into the overall experience and expertise" of the companies that specialize in handling the customer service contacts of their client companies.

India has gotten most of the attention for being a contact center destination. Large Indian outsourcing companies such as Tata Consultancy Services, Infosys, and Wipro have grown exponentially during the country's boom. But one of the largest contact center outsourcing companies in the world is Cincinnati-based Convergys, which has contact centers in the United States and internationally, including in India. The company says that more than half of the top fifty companies on the

Fortune 500 list are clients. Other outsourcing companies based in the United States and abroad are also major players in the business and run contact centers all over the world as well. Those include French-based Teleperformance and U.S.-based Sitel, among many others. Annual revenues for every one of these largest outsourcing companies are in the billions of dollars. They all operate multilingual contact centers worldwide, and each has more than fifty thousand employees.

Despite all the promises, foreign contact centers have gotten a reputation for bad service among American customers, who have repeatedly expressed dismay at speaking to agents whose accents they found hard to understand, especially from India. In response, more emphasis has been placed on training at many foreign call centers. But some call center jobs have also migrated back to the United States, even though salaries for American employees are exponentially higher than those of workers in the countries where work is most often outsourced. In addition, some state and federal laws now specify that government contracts must be filled by workers in the United States, so outsourcing to India or beyond is not always an option. These factors have left companies searching again for other lower-cost possibilities.

The concept of work-at-home agents, pioneered by companies like JetBlue, has become one of the fastest-growing and most promising such trends in contact center outsourcing. The *Wall Street Journal* reported in 2006 that the number of home-based agents in the United States had tripled since 2000. A survey in 2006 of U.S. and Canadian centers found that 24 percent of all agents were based in their homes. Homesourcing, as it is sometimes called, appeals to working parents, semiretired workers, and disabled workers in particular. Seventy to 80 percent have college degrees, compared to 30 to 40 percent of contact center workers. And most home-based workers are in their thirties and forties, older than average call center employees. Agents are generally given strict rules about keeping the noise of dogs and children off the lines, and their calls are recorded and monitored just as closely as in a traditional call center setting.

Homesourcing saves companies money on the overhead of running a call center, especially real estate and utility costs. It also saves money by cutting attrition and absenteeism rates, since at-home workers are generally happier. And it attracts more educated agents who would not normally want to work in a call center setting. Without commuting, agents working from home also reduce a company's carbon footprint.

Most of the major multinational outsourcing companies have created work-at-home programs. But during the past decade or so, new domestic outsourcing companies have also formed that exclusively supply work-at-home agents. Some of the first include Arise, LiveOps, Working Solutions, and Alpine Access. And more are on the way.

It was the urge for a change of lifestyle that led Sean Erickson to start a work-at-home outsourcing company called Cloud 10 in 2005. For more than twenty years, he had moved up in customer service management at major companies, including Dell, MCI, and the large Denver-based outsourcer TeleTech. He had helped set up call center operations for companies all over North America and in the Philippines. But in his early forties, he came to a crossroads and took some time to figure out what to do next with his life. At first, he just spent time with his three daughters. "Never having taken off more than seven days consecutively, I took four months off. I just did stuff with my kids, and didn't think about working." After being so driven for so many years, it took a while for him to adjust to being at home more, to the change of pace that allowed him to enjoy other parts of his life besides work. "I was not used to checking out like that, so it didn't feel like a luxury for a long time." He would wake up and say, "I don't have to go to work tomorrow. I don't have to be boss. I don't have to put on that executive armor." That was the subtle beginning of a revelation that showed him what his next move would be.

"I had been watching this whole work-at-home call center thing evolve," he said, "ever since I did a pilot work-at-home agent program for MCI in about 1993. We did it back then because we were exploding in growth, and every call center you build, with the technology and the real estate commitments, the infrastructure, it's a $10-million-plus investment. So we were looking for another way. People were starting to talk about work at home, but nobody was really doing it. So we did a test. I think eight or twelve agents were allowed to work at home for three months. What we found was that their job satisfaction was higher. Their customer satisfaction scores were better than anybody else's. Their work quality was better. But at that time the technology for it was not very good. Then fast-forward to where we are today. Broadband really allows us to connect to the agents' homes with speed. And the overall call center infrastructure has evolved where we can deliver those calls and manage those agents much like we do in a call center."

Toward the end of his four-month hiatus, Erickson was asked to lunch by an investor in Alpine Access, one of the largest of the work-at-home agent companies based just outside Denver, where Erickson lives. This investor wanted to pick Erickson's brain about the call center industry. "Then he started talking about the work-at-home business and how bullish he was about it, and where he thought it was going to go." Erickson's growing fondness for the less corporate lifestyle he was living came together with his memories of the experiment from his MCI days. The path seemed clear. "Somewhere between lunch and dessert, I thought, *Why don't I just do that? I know the industry. I've got great contacts. I can go do that.*"

He also believed that this part of the customer service industry was still new enough that there was room for two or three companies to set themselves apart from what he was sure would be many entrants into the field in coming years. Plus, Erickson always liked being a part of global contact center outsourcing. "It's very exciting, because you really get to be a part of many different industries. You're supporting clients across a broad range of industries. So if you're intellectually curious about these kinds of things, you can become very well versed in what drives financial services industries, what drives telecommunications, or what drives transportation." Cloud 10 is backed by the Danish call center outsourcing firm Transcom. By its third year of operations, Cloud 10 employed a thousand agents and was recruiting in twenty-nine states.

In less ambitious forms, the work-at-home idea is also being used to give job options to other groups of workers, such as disabled military veterans, including those injured in combat in the wars in Iraq and Afghanistan. A program to train veterans to do call center work from their homes was implemented by the Military Order of the Purple Heart in 2005.

Another unexpected niche for work-at-home agents is in the fast food industry. When customers drive up to a McDonald's or Wendy's in many cities, their orders are no longer taken by an employee a few feet away. Instead they could be answered by someone working from home in a small town in North Dakota. A company called Verety has hired more than 250 at-home workers to take the drive-through orders at more than fifty McDonald's restaurants and relay them back to the on-site workers making the Big Macs, fries, Happy Meals, and other food. Since it shaves precious seconds off each order and thereby saves money, many fast food companies have instituted this kind of remote order taking for their drive-throughs. But most use workers based in call centers run by outsourcing companies. Verety is one of the few outsourcers that uses at-home workers to handle the orders. Verety's CEO, John Jasper, told the Associated Press that fast food customers from Florida to Washington State are "talking to moms and grandmoms working out of their basements in rural North Dakota. It's going to take a few years, but this could be a big income source for people in rural communities."

At-home agents aren't the only way U.S. businesses are trying to backtrack on foreign outsourcing. Alternative call centers have shown up in other unique environments. UNICOR, a branch of the Federal Bureau of Prisons, is operating call centers in prisons, employing about two thousand inmates around the country to take directory assistance calls and phone inquiries for government agencies. Agents tend to be minimum- and medium-security prisoners, and mostly female. They don't handle any personal or financial customer information, and pay has been reported to range from as low as 8 cents to as much as $1.25 an hour. A percentage of their wages goes to victim assistance funds. UNICOR sees itself as competing with international outsourcers. On its website, it calls itself "the best kept secret in outsourcing! All the benefits of domestic outsourcing at offshore prices." UNICOR then touts its "low labor rates, native English and Spanish language skills, high security," and "locations throughout the country." State prisons have also gotten into the act. Katey Grabenhorst, an inmate at an Oregon women's prison, had finished serving her five-year sentence for attempted murder when she told *USA Today* that the customer service job she held at the Oregon Department of Motor Vehicles during her imprisonment had "brought self-esteem, order, skills and a stable income" to her life.

Another alternative kind of call center is being pioneered in eastern Oregon by the global consulting and outsourcing firm Accenture, formerly Andersen Consulting. Accenture is teaming with the Umatilla Native American tribe to create Cayuse Technologies, a call center and information technology outsourcing company within the United States. The idea came from Randy Willis, a senior consultant in Accenture's government group who is from the Lakota Sioux tribe in South Dakota. Driven by a growing client demand for low-cost, U.S.-based outsourcing options, Willis had been researching the prospect of creating such a company on a Native American reservation. He knew he had to find the right place for a pilot program. The tribes don't pay corporate income taxes, which helps them provide a lower-cost alternative than many other U.S.-based outsourcers. Among the tribes Willis researched, the Umatilla reservation had an unemployment rate of 17 percent, which, while high, is lower than that among many other Native American tribes. That meant the tribe had a relatively stable workforce. In addition, since Willis's wife is from the Umatilla tribe, he had good connections with them. So, during a family visit, Willis presented the idea to the chief, who embraced it. In 2006 Accenture entered into a five-year contract to train employees in call center and technology jobs. It was the first time a major international outsourcer had teamed with a Native American tribe to create such a company.

BusinessWeek ran an article about Cayuse's pilot program with the headline "The Other Indian Outsourcer," which was not only a clever twist on that singular partnership, but also encapsulated the circuitous route that all contact center outsourcing has taken in the past ten to fifteen years as the boundaries between being at work and at home, and between national and multinational identities, have grown less distinct.

6.   The Next Available Agent: John, Juan, Sean, or Sanjay

An unwritten law of telephone customer service, especially when it is outsourced overseas, is that customers and agents will never meet face-to-face and never speak to each other again in their lives. Therefore, neither is personally accountable to the other for what is said or done during a particular phone interaction. I managed to break through that invisible but rigid barrier when I flew all the way to a Buenos Aires call center to meet Pablo, a supervisor who had helped me six months earlier when I phoned Office Depot's U.S. 800 number about a delivery problem.

The serendipity of the route that led me to Argentina—involving an offhand comment of mine, an odds-defying coincidence, and a smart public relations executive—was topped only by the concrete payoff I found on arrival. Spending time at the call center with Pablo and his colleagues offered a rare glimpse into the lives of people who answer our calls abroad, as well as insight into what they really think of us.

It all started on the day—a Tuesday—that Office Depot promised me free next-day home delivery of the paper and toner I bought for my printer on its website. But the order didn't come Wednesday. By Thursday afternoon, I was talking to Pablo, after the agent I spoke with first, Nick, couldn't guarantee when my order would be delivered. At first, Pablo told me the same things Nick had. Then, in an effort to loosen Pablo up, I asked where he lived, and he said Argentina. Since my college-age niece, Isabel, was spending the year studying there, I jokingly said, "My niece lives in Buenos Aires. I hope I don't have to send her down there after you." Pablo paused, and in a wary tone replied, "I'm not afraid of your niece, ma'am."

I backed off and restated my case logically, without any more facetious threats. Pablo warmed up eventually and promised the toner and paper would be delivered by noon the next day. For my trouble, he gave me the $116 order for free. The tenor of the conversation became even friendlier when Pablo offered a little joke of his own. He said, "Your niece isn't going to come down here with a gun, is she?" I assured him that not all Americans carried guns and that my niece was especially nonviolent. We laughed and talked a bit more. He said he was a college student in Buenos Aires. In the end, he gave me his employee number and told me if I had any more problems to call back. Then I promptly e-mailed Isabel in Buenos Aires with the whole story.

My order arrived about two hours later. The driver said the person who was supposed to deliver it the day before had called in sick and they were only then catching up with his Wednesday deliveries. I told him I wasn't too upset because of the credit I had just received. The next day, Friday, the same driver came to my door with another delivery of the same order. I signed a delivery slip verifying I was refusing it. After he left, I realized the one I had just rejected was the free order from Pablo, and the one I accepted the day before was the original order. I tried to reach Pablo again, to explain what happened and make sure I wasn't going to be charged.

I dialed the same 800 number I had called before. Someone named Michelle answered. She was in the Philippines and wanted to help me. But instead of repeating the whole story to her, I said I would rather talk to Pablo. Michelle asked and found out there was no way to transfer me to Argentina.

So I decided to make an exercise of it and see if I could keep calling the same 800 number and eventually reach Argentina. Over the next few minutes, I spoke to Natalie in the Dominican Republic, Andrea in the Philippines, then to Jen in the Philippines, and to Stephen in the Dominican Republic. No Argentina. But every time I called Office Depot, I was connected quickly to agents who were professional, smart, and eager to help. They all said they were college students and had been in their jobs for a few months. Realizing I probably wouldn't be connected to Argentina, I dialed the number one more time and was connected to Sarah in the Philippines. I explained what Pablo and I had agreed. And because I had so much information, including a supervisor's employee number, she said she could credit the original order right away, without having to wait for a manager's approval. "It was our fault. You were promised," said Sarah. Sure enough, the $116 credit showed up in my account within the week.

A few days later, my niece Isabel e-mailed that she had shared the story of her role in my Office Depot phone odyssey at dinner one night with a group of friends from her study-abroad program in Buenos Aires. It turned out one of the other American women was dating a guy named Eduardo, who was also a friend of Isabel, and who answered customer service lines for Office Depot. When the woman asked the name of the supervisor, Isabel told her it was Pablo. At that, the woman gasped in amazement: "Pablo is Eduardo's boss."

In a city of 12 million people, a continent away, I had managed to talk to someone on a customer service phone line who had one degree of separation from my niece—the very niece about whom he and I had joked during the call. I found out that Eduardo and Pablo worked for one of the larger U.S.-based outsourcing companies, TeleTech, located in Denver. The agents I spoke with in the Dominican Republic worked for another U.S.-based call center outsourcing company, Stream, which also answers calls for Office Depot. Stream's main offices are in Texas, with call center locations worldwide. Often a company like Office Depot uses a few different call center providers to get the right mix of price and personnel.

I called the head of public relations for TeleTech in Denver and told her my story. She explained that much of Office Depot's account is handled jointly by its call centers in Argentina and the Philippines. The different time zones allow it to operate around the clock. Tapping into the resources of both countries means the company can supply enough agents to fill clients' needs. She invited me to visit the Buenos Aires call center, which she said would be a window into its operations world-wide. TeleTech works hard to make sure that the way its agents sound and the quality of service they provide is identical, no matter where in the world the call is answered. And of course, she said, by visiting their Buenos Aires offices, I could meet Pablo in person.

A few months later I arrived in Argentina, which has become a stylish tourist destination. Many guidebooks call Buenos Aires the most European of Latin American cities. Indeed, at certain fashionable points around town, Buenos Aires feels variously like Paris, London, or even Rome. The cultural influences of a large influx of Italian immigrants about a century ago are particularly evident. At other points, Buenos Aires evokes New York's tony Upper East Side and the urban sprawl of Los Angeles. But pockets of extreme poverty, worse than even the most desperate parts of the United States, and streets clogged by mostly late-model cars with drivers who ignore lane markers, are undeniable reminders that Buenos Aires is one of the larger cities in the developing world.

Still, its historic and commercial center is full of cafés, upscale shopping districts, parks, and grand boulevards that intersect narrow, almost alley-like side streets. Visitors seek out Argentina's superior steakhouses or *parrillas*, its tango clubs, its robust wines, and its inexpensive leather goods, all made more appealing by a favorable exchange rate even when the U.S. dollar is weak. Many of the prominent buildings in downtown Buenos Aires were designed by French architects, commissioned in the late nineteenth and early twentieth centuries when Argentina was one of the richest countries in the world. The city's original main square, the Plaza de Mayo, dates back to the late sixteenth century and contains the famous presidential palace, the Casa Rosada (Pink House), where Eva Perón—and, years later, Madonna playing Evita in the film version of her life—stood on the balcony and addressed the Argentinean people.

Every Thursday afternoon since the mid-1970s, the well-known Madres de Plaza de Mayo have marched in the square to call attention to the abduction of their children by the military regime that ruled Argentina then. These mothers and grandmothers of the tens of thousands of people who disappeared in the 1970s wear white head scarves and hang photos of their missing children around their necks. As the government has changed and some of the people responsible for the disappearances have been brought to justice, the group has also changed. The more left-wing mothers in the group have continued the weekly marches and have expanded their mission to protest trade agreements with the United States and demand an end to what they see as U.S. interference in Latin America.

Just a few blocks away from the Plaza de Mayo, with its reminders of how Argentina's economic and political tides have ebbed and flowed, are TeleTech's main offices—a hub of the U.S. outsourcing that has been helped along in recent years by various trade agreements with, and incentives from, developing nations around the globe. TeleTech's headquarters are located in the heart of Microcentro, the financial and governmental district of downtown Buenos Aires. One of the two TeleTech buildings on Chacabuco Street was converted from a large, graceful mansion. At the main entrance of the company, a perpetual line of trendy-looking college-age people—many smoking cigarettes, talking and texting on cell phones, or listening to their iPods—spills out onto the narrow street and snakes around the corner. In the time before and after I visited, TeleTech was hiring about 350 new call center agents a month. Buses, trains, and subways all converge near the offices, making them accessible for most potential employees. Radio ads recruiting bilingual workers target the young and well educated, and posters and billboards touting jobs at TeleTech are positioned near universities and at other strategic locations around Buenos Aires.

I was escorted up to the main conference room on the third floor of the building, where eight official-looking men, standing around a long, elegant, wooden table, greeted me warmly. The head of all Latin American operations for TeleTech had flown down from Denver to oversee my visit. The head of the Argentinean branch of TeleTech, Martin Sucari, welcomed me to his country and his offices. I met the men who headed up the Office Depot account and those who ran the call center for TeleTech.

Then I spotted a nice-looking younger man with dark, curly hair, and a five-o'clock shadow, wearing a suit and tie. It was Pablo. Everyone grinned as they introduced us. Smiling wide, I greeted him like an old friend.

For him, I must have personified every distant American he had ever helped in his two and a half years taking calls from Office Depot customers. As we shook hands, his eyes lit up, and he appeared to be a little bit in awe. He received me as if I were a celebrity, and his first words to me in that conference room were "This is amazing. I've never met a customer before."

Of course he hadn't. But every day he had spoken to us, helped us, been yelled at by us, and even laughed with some of us. He knew more about us than we did about him. And when I finally got to sit down, look Pablo in the eye, and have a real conversation with him, it was an odd feeling. He was no longer just some supervisor at the end of a customer service line. And I think for him, I became more than just some pushy American who wanted her order yesterday.

I asked Pablo if he knew I was joking about my niece during our initial phone call. "At first, I really thought you were serious," he told me. "But when you started laughing, I knew you were not." I understood then that he would have had to take me seriously at first, since they hear all kinds of strange things from callers. "After we hung up," Pablo said, "I told everyone that you had threatened me. It was actually funny."

Pablo, who was twenty-three, told me he had worked his way up from agent to supervisor at TeleTech while getting a degree in psychology at the University of Buenos Aires. As a supervisor, he takes only ten to fifteen calls a day; agents working on his team take about a hundred. He has been to Europe and would like to go to the United States someday, but since the September 11 attacks, it has been harder for Argentineans to get a visa. He initially learned English from watching the Sony television network, which plays lots of American sitcoms. *Seinfeld* and *Friends* are his favorites. He became so adept at English that someone suggested he apply for a job at an American call center in his hometown of Buenos Aires. He didn't think he could do it at first. "I said, 'No way. I do speak English, but I am not capable of holding a conversation with a native speaker.'" Yet he applied and got the job. And once he began working, he surprised himself. Talking to native speakers every day helped him build quickly on what he already knew and become fluent enough to handle the job. "All those years of television eventually paid off," Pablo joked.

In fact, the language was not Pablo's biggest hurdle. Comprehending the ground rules Americans take for granted when interacting with companies was more of a challenge. "I tend to be interested a lot in how people think and feel and perceive the world through a culture. I thought I understood American culture and that it was not so different from Argentinean culture. But it is. We Argentineans are not so expectant of private companies. Our rights are not so supported by the government and laws. We are very used to not having our deliveries on time. We're very used to being overcharged. Since we're used to that and Americans are not, then it is very hard to understand how a person can get so upset and make a call because they are charged one cent or one dollar more than they expected. But then I understood that it's not about the dollar. It's about them having the right to be charged the right price."

Calls like mine used to baffle Pablo as well. "At first it was really hard for me to understand why someone would call to say, 'My order was delivered half an hour late and that is very inconvenient.' Because when we order something, we know it's going to be late. So we are already expecting it to be late, and we don't complain. We are starting to have higher expectations here as Argentineans. But we still have a long way to go. I admire that in American people. Because they demand what they think is right, and we don't. It's unfortunate."

Pablo believes the higher expectations come from the fact that Americans are used to having more options than most of the rest of the world. "The environment is so competitive today. OfficeMax and Staples usually have the same prices as Office Depot. What makes the difference between one company and the other is customer service.

If you don't get good customer service at Staples, you're going to go to Office Depot, because that is the only difference you'll find. All that's left is customer service."

When Pablo started at TeleTech, his main motivation was to improve his English. He wanted to be a psychiatrist, and the call center hours were flexible enough that he could work while he went to school. But Pablo was good at the job. And after he became a supervisor, he found his knowledge of psychology helped him stay attuned to his team of about fifteen to twenty agents and support them in doing their best work. "You have to be very aware of how each one responds, every day. You have to notice their emotions by the way they move or the way they speak." Turnover is an issue at foreign call centers, just as it is in the United States, so Pablo is mindful of trying to keep employees for as long as possible. "You see when their faces are indicating that this is not a good day for them. That is an alarm bell ringing. You have to sit down with that person and discuss it, and make sure that person is comfortable enough to be working. Because if you don't pay attention to that, they will eventually resign."

Now, instead of becoming a psychiatrist, Pablo is considering a career in human resources because of the satisfaction he gets from his work at TeleTech. He sees the agents he supervises as his customers and tries to treat them with the same consideration he asks them to use with Office Depot's customers. "We have to be there for them all the time, be available. We cannot say, 'No, I'm busy,' or 'I can't.' That's something that we have to take out of our vocabulary. Because they are really our customers. They are choosing us. We have to be the employer of choice."

Pablo doesn't use that phrase by accident. Being the employer of choice is a theme at TeleTech. Martin Sucari, who runs TeleTech in Argentina, says attracting the best agents is an ongoing process. One of TeleTech's main competitors in Argentina, and around the rest of the world, is Teleperformance, which also runs major call centers in Buenos Aires and provides services to many companies in the United States. Teleperformance has a Utah-based headquarters and operates globally under its parent company in France. Teleperformance,

TeleTech, and other multinational outsourcing companies compete for corporate clients, but perhaps even more pressing is their competition for employees.

In Argentina, about 90 percent of TeleTech's workers either have college degrees or are in the process of getting them. Public university education in Argentina is free, but most TeleTech workers have attended language schools beyond their standard education. Those schools are private and expensive, so people who are bilingual in Argentina generally come from the middle and upper classes, Sucari knows that very few of them will be with TeleTech for long. "We don't see someone joining here and retiring, or being twenty years in the same place. We don't expect that. We don't want that." Instead he expects them to stay for two or three years until they complete their college degrees. But a few find that they like working for an American-based multinational company. For instance, Sucari sees Pablo moving up in the ranks and gives much credit to the business skills he is developing. "He leads a team of associates he needs to motivate. I always say he is no longer a supervisor; he is the manager of a small company. Because when you take the revenues coming out of his team, they are larger than the entire revenues of many small companies in Argentina."

It was after enduring its worst-ever economic meltdown, from late 2001 into 2002, that Argentina turned into a viable call center outsourcing destination. During that time, which most people call "the crisis," Argentina's peso plummeted. The poverty rate skyrocketed to almost 60 percent, and Sucari said many companies either collapsed or barely made it through. "The exchange rate had been tied to the U.S. dollar for ten years, one to one. Then all of a sudden, overnight, it went one to four. We had five different presidents of the country in ten days. The banks literally closed the doors. You couldn't even withdraw money markets, your deposits, your account, nothing. After a couple of weeks, they only let us withdraw a hundred dollars a week, so we would not starve. All these kidnappings and insecurities in the streets came out. Savings were closed. People were starting riots and assaulting supermarkets. It was really a mess."

Since then, outsourcing from the United States and other countries, along with a rise in tourism and exports, has helped the country recover. In fact, from 2002 to 2007, Argentina increased its revenues by 25 percent and reduced its debt significantly. Poverty rates dropped but still hover between 20 and 25 percent.

TeleTech had established itself in Argentina before the crisis by buying a local call center company in 1998 that mostly answered calls within the country. After the crisis, business inside Argentina was drying up, but instead of folding, Sucari saw a way out by showing the U.S. headquarters that it had the personnel and the technology and could provide the quality of service to take on international business. "In the very beginning, we did some work with Mexico. We did some work with Spain. But the majority of our work went to the U.S. We were able to prove the English-speaking capabilities in the country. We were able to prove that the IT was in place. And we showed that the human resources were able and available to deploy service to American companies."

The fact that Argentina has one of the highest percentages of university-educated people in Latin America also helped. In addition to answering calls, the Argentinean branch of TeleTech also develops most of the software for the company worldwide. With the company's business thriving in Argentina, everyone in that Buenos Aires conference room displayed a fierce determination not to let a downturn happen again. Sucari says that is what drives most Argentineans these days to keep improving and growing. "We went through the other situation. And nobody wants to go back to that again. We like this."

Worldwide, TeleTech's annual revenues have exceeded $1 billion. The 2,500 agents at TeleTech in Argentina handle about 3 million calls per month, mostly from American customers. But they also take calls in German, Italian, Portuguese, French, and of course Spanish. Agents start out at the equivalent of about $2.70 an hour. The company also runs call centers around the United States, as well as in Brazil, Mexico, and Costa Rica, and elsewhere globally, including in the Philippines, India, Ireland, Spain, Australia, South Africa, and Hong Kong. Generally the foreign call centers are located in cities with large university populations that include multilingual workers.

Brian Delaney, TeleTech's executive vice president of global operations and international sales, says, "To properly focus our employees, regardless of where they are in the world, it's important to understand their cultural nuance—what makes each of them happy and a good employee rather than forcing a specific corporate monologue on them all. We are a centralized company. We've got common platforms and processes, so 85 to 90 percent of what we do is the same. When you walk into a center in Argentina or in the Philippines, they've got a common feel. But there's local nuance."

Delaney, who is based at the company's sleek Denver corporate campus, didn't start out with the intention of becoming a global business process outsourcing executive. He was an English major at the University of California, Santa Barbara, and moved to New York City to become a journalist in the 1980s. He ended up teaching for a few years in a public high school for troubled students on Manhattan's West Side after getting a master's in English education from New York University. He says teaching was "a great foundation" for his work at TeleTech because he already had a "comfort in dealing with a younger workforce." Also, in his teaching, he developed sensitivities he still uses in managing nearly forty thousand customer care workers from diverse cultural and economic backgrounds. He has had to balance similarities and differences in college-age employees' needs, goals, and worldviews in Latin America, North America, Asia, Europe, Africa, and Australia. "The most exciting and challenging part of my work is inspiring our employees with the desire to resolve customers' problems. That's a very subtle, hard thing to do—to get a large, global workforce in a frame of mind where they really, truly care on every interaction. It's a neverending process. And it's important that we do it better than all of our competitors."

For many of the young agents TeleTech employs, the call center job is their first foray into office work, much less the global corporate world. Pablo says he keeps that in mind as he helps newly hired agents adjust to coming onto the call center floor and beginning to answer the phones. "We do have people on the first day who cry because they're afraid of the customer's response. Or they anticipate that a customer might not feel comfortable with them on the phone, because it's a different language. But they realize that they should act naturally. They usually adapt in the first two weeks and become pretty at ease with taking phone calls. But at first, for most people, not really having talked to anyone in the United States before, it is frightening to be on the phone with an American person."

—

In the basement of TeleTech's Buenos Aires call center, approximately sixty customer service agents are stationed at their computers in four rows of gray cubicles. A steady hum of conversation—the sound of everyday, intercontinental commerce taking place—resonates through the large, pleasant room as they sit in red office chairs, under fluorescent lights, with their headsets on, talking to Office Depot customers in the United States. This is just one account among the many familiar American brands whose calls are answered in these clusters of agents throughout the four floors of the call center. Argentineans pride themselves on their warmth, a quality that Martin Sucari says makes them especially good at customer service work. Indeed, as Sucari walks around the call center, his employees—both male and female—greet him with a hug and kisses on both cheeks, as they do with each other and with all visitors, even those they have never met before. In Argentina, though, the greetings are somehow more effusive than in other countries with the same custom.

Hernan, one of the top-performing agents on the Office Depot account, sits at his workstation talking to customers. Supervisors like Pablo wear suits, but Hernan and most of his colleagues working the phones are dressed casually, though it is Argentinean casual—with more of an affinity for relaxed Italian chic than for, say, casual Fridays in corporate America. Hernan is a lanky twenty-five-year-old with tousled light-brown hair, a well-trimmed goatee, tasteful green-plastic-rimmed glasses, and a silver ring on his middle finger. He wears jeans with the cuffs rolled up once, a short-sleeved plaid shirt unbuttoned three-quarters of the way down, a white tank shirt underneath, and beige Converse sneakers.

As he deftly maneuvers callers through the process of ordering supplies or lodging complaints about delivery problems, Hernan always starts by saying, "Hi. Thank you for calling Office Depot. My name is Mark. How may I help you today?" He and all his colleagues use pseudonyms, though supervisors like Pablo do not. Most people in the United States would not be able to understand Hernan's name over the phone, with its silent H at the beginning. A more American name helps keep things moving. Hernan is finishing his degree in communications at the University of Buenos Aires. He has been at TeleTech for about eight months and hopes to go into corporate public relations when he graduates. He took the name Mark from a character in a French film he saw the night before he started the job, but can't remember the film's name.

Mary from Orlando, Florida, calls to say that she faxed an order for pens recently but has not received them yet. Hernan says, "I'll be more than happy to assist you, Mary. Would you provide me please with the confirmation number?" As he talks, he is pulling up screens on his computer that show her account history. Mary doesn't have a confirmation number. Hernan's computer shows no pen order. So even though Mary might think she had completed her order, she probably did not. Nevertheless, when Hernan takes over, he is careful to assume responsibility and to give Mary the benefit of the doubt on whether the order was placed correctly. "I really do apologize for this inconvenience. But I don't have any order here placed over the fax. That means that the order was never placed. What I can offer is for you to resend the fax, or I can offer you to place the order over the phone right now." Mary chooses to order from Hernan. It takes a few more minutes. All the while, he never allows much silence on the line, as he politely cues Mary to progress through her order. He says things like, "Whenever you are ready, you can give me the next part of your order." Or, "And the next item, Mary?" Then he ends by giving her the final price and the delivery details.

Hernan explains how the pacing of what he says as an agent is as important as the tone and content. "If you stay quiet, that makes the call really boring, and it never ends. You need to get a constant feedback with the customer. The trick is not to rush them. For instance, when you are reading the total, you need to read it easy and quiet and real slow. Because that is the only part they really hear from you, the price. If you say it very slow the first time, you won't have to repeat yourself, and that will make the call quicker. Sometimes you get a call from someone who needs extra attention. They start to ask about the weather. You can talk for just a little bit. But you need to take more calls, so you can't go too far with that."

Hernan has gotten some aggressive customers. "There are days when you have calls that make you want to throw the headset and run. Because it is customer service, you deal with a lot of complaints, and when they have a problem, they vent it with you. Also they are venting frustration for other things in their lives, and they take it out on you. But I notice that if I don't put anything in their way, anything that makes the call hard, they will be smiling by the end." Hernan says that working in customer service has helped him better handle his own calls for service. "Now when I call somewhere if I'm having a problem, for instance, with a cell phone, I don't yell to the person on the other side of the line. I say, 'Okay, I understand. What can you do for me?'"

Hernan emphasizes that 90 to 95 percent of the customers he talks to are "pretty easygoing. When they realize you are in Argentina, they like that. Some of them are interested. Then, sometimes, they have a problem because English is not our native language and they hang up on us." Though Hernan has never been to the United States, he is interested in American and British pop culture. His favorite band is Queen, and his favorite singer is Madonna. Like Pablo, he watches *Friends*, *Seinfeld*, and *Scrubs* on the Sony network, which helps him with his accent.

But TeleTech doesn't rely solely on American television sitcoms to help agents learn how to talk to their customers. Walking around the call center floor is a twenty-one-year-old woman named Mariella. She is what the industry calls an ACE trainer, which stands for Accent and Conversational English. Born in the city of Mendoza, northwest of Buenos Aires near the border with Chile, Mariella lived in Alexandria, Virginia, for two years in high school. She has a more American-sounding accent than most of her colleagues. Mariella studies English translation at the University of Buenos Aires and started at TeleTech answering phones when she was nineteen. After about a year and a half, she was promoted and now teaches newly hired agents how to "neutralize" their accents. She also listens to recorded calls of agents already working on the phones and coaches them on areas for improvement. She says the two things she has to work on most are their pronunciation of vowels and their inclination to translate directly from Spanish into English. For instance, instead of saying "I am twenty-one years old," they might say, "I have twenty-one years," the literal translation from Spanish.

Some idioms don't translate well either. Mariella remembers one agent who used a common saying in Argentina that translates literally to English as "take it with soda," and means "take it easy." When a customer called, upset because his printer wasn't working, the agent said to him, "Sir, take it with soda." The customer was confused, and Mariella had to explain to the agent that the saying didn't work in English. These are the kinds of problems she has to follow up on continuously, so no misunderstandings fall through the cracks.

Mariella also deals with what she calls the culture shock that agents go through when they first begin to speak to Americans. For instance, the fact that many in the United States don't know much about Argentina really bothers some of the agents. Customers often cannot place Argentina on a map. Some even believe that Argentina is a city in Brazil. Or they talk about Carnival, a Brazilian tradition that is not part of Argentina's culture. Those misperceptions are particularly insulting to the famously patriotic Argentineans for whom Brazil is a neighborly rival in Latin America. Mariella says agents often don't know what to make of that sort of ignorance, especially since they are trained to know so much about the United States. "It's a shock to them. It's like, 'I'm in Argentina and they don't know that Argentina exists, or where we are.'" Mariella does the best she can to explain it to her co-workers. But usually she tries to encourage them just to let it roll off their backs, or perhaps to take it with soda. "I always tell them it's a culture thing. It's not like they have something against us as a country, or you personally. It's just their culture."

While outsourcing of manufacturing jobs to foreign countries had already been a touchy subject for many years in the United States, the outsourcing of call centers and information technology jobs to India was just becoming a major trend when it emerged as an issue in the 2004 presidential race. The Democratic nominee, John Kerry, adopted a protectionist stance, campaigning against what he called "Benedict Arnold companies and CEO's" that sent American jobs abroad. The *Times of India* called *outsourcing* the "swear word" of the elections that year. And when George W. Bush won reelection in November 2004, a *New York Times* article with the headline "An Industry in India Cheers Bush's Victory" reported that "the tone of some campaign comments criticizing outsourcing was noted with some concern in India," and "thousands of workers in India's technology centers like Bangalore and Hyderabad closely followed the campaign." When they found out Bush had won, "India's outsourcing companies were jubilant." The head of India's National Association of Software and Service Companies, Kiran S. Karnik, told the paper it was because President Bush had a "track record" of "recognizing the advantages of free trade."

American companies like General Electric led the way on call center outsourcing to India in the 1990s by setting up call centers there to take advantage of cheaper labor and the large number of educated English speakers. In fact, India has a greater number of English speakers than the United States, even if it isn't always spoken as a first language. Soon India was growing into the place to go for what is known in business jargon as business process outsourcing, or BPO. The term is a catch-all that encompasses contact centers, as well as computer programming, other information technology work, and back office work like accounting. By the dawn of this century, India had become the off-shore BPO epicenter for most English-speaking countries in the developed world.

The circumstances within India that made it so ripe for that role have as much to do with the country's weaknesses as its strengths. With upward of 1.1 billion people, India is the second largest country in the world, after China. Its poverty rate is also staggering. About 275 million people live below the poverty line, almost equal to the entire U.S. population of approximately 300 million. India's literacy rate is only about 60 percent, compared to 99 percent in the United States, and its per capita income is around $1,000 a year. Yet the top 10 to 20 percent of Indians are generally well educated, and at least bilingual. English is widespread because of years of British rule. So a call center worker in India, who usually has a college degree and is proficient in English, can earn a starting salary of $4,500 a year answering customer service calls from American customers. A call center worker in the United States with only a high school diploma would start at about five times that to answer the very same calls.

Though outsourced workers account for a relatively small percentage of India's workforce, the residuals from that commerce have helped establish India's business credentials and led to more advanced work, all of which has begun to make a dent in the country's economic woes. In addition to American companies with branches in India and large American and European outsourcing companies, three home-grown companies are at the top of India's outsourcing world: Tata, Wipro, and Infosys. Some other Indian companies have become major players as well. But the landscape is fast growing and ever changing. In 2004 an estimated 300,000 people were working in outsourcing in India. By 2007, estimates were around 600,000 workers, and analysts predicted that number would top 1 million in 2010.

The November 2004 *New York Times* article about Bush winning the American election observed that "in spite of some strong American sentiment against offshoring, Indian outsourcing companies have been growing robustly recently. In the quarter that ended in September, Infosys Technologies announced a 49 percent rise in profit, and added more than 5,000 employees. Its rival Wipro had a 65 percent increase in quarterly profit, and hired 5,500 more workers."

Just weeks later, some highly publicized incidents of agent abuse by American callers were making big news in India. In January 2005, the *Times of India* reported, "In the last few months, and particularly since the U.S. presidential elections, people working in call centers in the country say that they are receiving more abusive and racist phone calls than ever before. 'Earlier, people would get abusive if we didn't answer their questions satisfactorily. Now, I get calls—on some days up to five a shift—from people who are calling only to abuse,' says a 22-year-old engineering graduate who works in a major call centre in Madad.'"

The newspaper went on to report: "While earlier, abusive calls would come from drunken callers, now they come from sober people who are calling only to vent their feeling about their jobs being off-shored, or 'Bangalored' as it is now called, says a Mumbai call centre executive." The title of the article was " 'I Made an Indian Girl Cry, You Can Do It Too!'" and it reported on "thousands of messages in cyberspace calling for a campaign to harass Indian call centre operators, to put an end to the offshoring of jobs." It quoted an unidentified website on which an American described how he made a sport of calling Indian call center workers to harangue them and invited others to join him in doing the same. "I made an Indian woman cry and promise to quit her job in 60 seconds. I've been doing this about 20 minutes a day. It's great fun! The usual response is confusion. I get the impression these are not the brightest bulbs in India's chandeliers." Another post quoted in the paper referred to the same tactics and said, "All of this will have a cumulative effect. If 100 people across the U.S. would commit to spending 10 minutes a day, we could cripple them, and bring those jobs back to the U.S."

A month later, in February 2005, a *Washington Post* article, "India

Call Centers Suffer Storm of 4-Letter Words," reported more vitriol from American customers outraged by outsourcing. The article ended with an Indian call center agent who worked for an American Internet company in Bangalore showing some empathy with the callers' bitter sentiments. " 'I would be mad too if somebody took away my job,' said Vidya Ramathas, 24, 'I love my job. It has brought me freedom. I moved out of my parents' home. I don't ask them for money anymore. I do what I want to. I don't ask for their permission.' Ramathas, who uses 'Amanda' as her phone name, added: 'In that sense, I am like an American.'"

By January 2006, such accounts were common in the United States and India. But another article, this one in *New York Newsday*, reported on particular consternation in India and among Indian Americans about the abuse of call center workers by American customers. "Debalina Das, a computer help-line agent in the southern India city of Hyderabad, punched the button last winter for a call from the United States. 'You Indian slut,' came the man's voice, the 22-year-old recounted, 'in some Third World country, roaming about naked without food and clothes, what do you know about computers? Have you seen one? This company is just saving money by outsourcing to Third World countries like yours.'

"Das, who quit after four months, said she learned to dislike Americans. 'Rarely there are people who are good,' she said, 'but then others remind me that all they believe in is cursing and they don't have respect for others.'"

Call center workers and their abusive American (and British) customers ended up becoming a fixture in Indian popular culture. A television sitcom launched on Indian TV in 2006, *The Call Centre*, depicted Indian agents dealing with arrogant and rude Western callers. Another fictional account, a book by Indian author Chetan Bhagat, *One Night at the Call Center*, struck a chord with the hundreds of thousands of young Indian workers in the information technology and call center outsourcing industry. It became a big bestseller in India and was even made into a movie by Bollywood, India's film industry. It follows twenty-four hours in the lives of six call center workers who answer phones for an American appliance retailer. In one scene in the book, a particularly bitter agent gets a harassing call from an American customer complaining that his vacuum cleaner doesn't work. The agent figures out he merely needs to change the dust bag. Problem solved. But the customer can't leave it at that. He starts swearing and insulting the agent:

> You're some kid in India, ain't you?
>
> Sir, I'm afraid I can't disclose my location.
>
> You're from India. Tell me, boy?
>
> Yes sir. I am in India.

The man shouts obscenities at him, as the agent tries to steer the conversation back to the vacuum cleaner dust bags. The man screams:

> Yeah, I'll change the dust bag. What about you guys?
> When will you change your dusty country?
>
> Excuse me, sir, but I want you to stop talking like that.
>
> Oh really, now some brown kid's telling me what to do.

At that, the agent cut off the call and began seething. "His whole body trembled and he was breathing heavily, then he placed his elbows on the table and covered his face with his hands." Later he ranted to his co-workers: "Why do some fat-ass, dim-witted Americans get to act superior to us? Do you know why? I'll tell you why. Not because they are smarter. Not because they are better people. But because their country is rich and ours is poor. That is the only damn reason. Because the losers who have run our country for the last fifty years couldn't do better than make India one of the poorest countries on earth."

Around the same time all this backlash from the United States permeated through India, the country was starting to show signs of outgrowing the call center part of the business process outsourcing industry. More lucrative types of outsourcing began to hold stronger appeal for the most qualified college graduates in India. By October 2007, a *Time* magazine article, "India's Call-Center Jobs Go Begging," reported that a few colleges in India banned call center recruiters from their campuses after complaints from students who didn't want to be bothered with them. "Young people say it is no longer worthwhile going through sleepless nights serving customers halfway around the world. They have better job opportunities in other fields. The work is tiring and stressful and offers few career advancement opportunities." The article quoted students at a college in New Delhi. "Earlier it was considered cool to work at a call center," said one nineteen-year-old. "That died out quite quickly." His friend, also nineteen, added, "If you work at a call center today people will think you don't have anything else to do or were a bad student."

But India's growing pains yielded opportunities for growth in other countries eager to step into the fray and reap some of the benefits that India's call centers had shown were possible. The Philippines became the next major destination of outsourced U.S. call centers. In mid-2007, the Business Process Outsourcing Association of the Philippines announced that call centers employed 229,000 Filipinos, which was equivalent to the number employed in India just a few years before. The association also promoted the idea that with the support of government training programs to prepare more workers, the call center industry would employ more than half a million Filipinos by 2010.

It could be taken as a bad sign when a country possesses some of the elements that multinational corporations look for when deciding where to locate outsourced call centers. After all, it probably means the country is a developing nation with high unemployment and high poverty rates, since wages in outsourcing locations have to be low compared to those in the developed world. It also usually means that a country was once colonized by a European power or occupied by the United States at some point in its history and left with a legacy of language skills and cultural understanding important to building a successful outsourcing workforce. For instance, India was ruled by Great Britain, and the Philippines was occupied by Spain and the United States at different times.

But there are also good signs in being ripe for outsourcing. It means there is a reasonable expectation of a country's ongoing economic and political stability. There also has to be government support of the industry, so business can be conducted with minimal cost and bureaucratic hassle. And there has to be a solid technological infrastructure, ensuring that phone lines work and the power will stay on. In addition, there has to be a consistent supply of educated, multilingual workers with technological know-how.

After India and the Philippines, some Latin American countries emerged with the right combination of these elements. In addition to Argentina, Mexico, Brazil, Uruguay, Chile, and parts of Central America all stepped up. Even Nicaragua put some of its development eggs in the call center basket.

A May 2006 ribbon-cutting ceremony at a new $4 million call center in Managua, Nicaragua, signaled that customer service outsourcing had hit the second poorest country in the Western Hemisphere (after Haiti). With it came the fervent hope among many in attendance that it would help provide their beleaguered country a clear way out of that dismal position. Juan Carlos Pereira was there. Twenty-five years earlier, Pereira had been in elementary school when his family fled their home in Nicaragua for America to get away from the Soviet-backed Sandinistas, led by Daniel Ortega, who took control of the country in 1979. Pereira grew up in Washington, D.C., eventually got an MBA from Harvard, and worked in telecommunications in the United States. About a decade after Ortega lost power in the early 1990s, Pereira went back to his native country to found a public-private venture, ProNicaragua, dedicated to attracting foreign investment to help Nicaragua dig out of its economic isolation. This call center was one of his first projects.

Ricardo Terán was at the ribbon-cutting too. He is the head of a conglomerate his father started in Nicaragua in 1936, Corporación Roberto Terán G, with stores all over the country and the rest of Central America, selling electronic and photographic equipment, Internet and satellite access, construction equipment, food, and automobiles.

During the first Sandinista government, his family left the country, and their family business dropped from thirty-eight stores nationwide to just one. Ricardo Terán, who attended business school at Georgetown University, is also part of ProNicaragua. His family moved back to Nicaragua in the 1990s and rebuilt and diversified. Now the company is at work on a new venture, Press Two—as in "press two for Spanish," hoping to become a premier provider of Spanish-speaking customer service for North American customers. "We're planning large alliances," Terán said, "so that, for example, when you call American Airlines, you'll press two for Spanish and they'll answer in Nicaragua." Press Two is also backed by Danish investors and has two contact centers in Managua near its international airport. When Nicaragua was connected to North America in 2005 by the Arcos-1 submarine fiber-optic cable, the country suddenly had the same connectivity as call centers in Miami to anywhere in the United States. But employees in Nicaragua were paid about $2.35 an hour, and there was no tax on businesses that are based in Nicaragua but providing services outside the country, so the savings compared to American call centers were immense.

These former exiles, and many like them with similar American college degrees, mostly from the Ivy League, went back home to try to turn the tide in their country. They all supported the Central American Free Trade Agreement (CAFTA) that went into effect in January 2006 and hoped it would help Nicaragua become a hot investment and outsourcing haven for American businesses. Projections seemed to back up that hope. The market research firm Datamonitor said the number of call center workstations in Latin America would rise to 730,000 by the end of 2008, up from 336,000 in 2004. And according to a 2010 Central American contact center report published by the Zagada Institute, a Miami research firm, the number of customer service phone agent positions in Central America doubled from more than 21,000 in 2006 to 42,000 by the end of 2008.

The argument from some advocates for the poor, reportedly including current president Daniel Ortega (who was reelected in 2007), was that these jobs, which require educated, multilingual workers, will do nothing for people in the rural areas, where poverty is so entrenched, and will increase the country's dependence on the United States and Europe. But when he came to power again, Ortega signaled he would not stand in the way of the economic development that ProNicaragua advocated.

ProNicaragua kept betting that the country could attract call center jobs and promoted Nicaragua's low cost of living. In a country where economists estimate that 78 percent of the population lives on less than two dollars a day, the wages offered by call centers seemed great. ProNicaragua also promoted its proximity to the United States—just a two-hour flight from Miami—as opposed to days to India and back. That is why the U.S.–Latin American outsourcing alliances are called "nearshoring." ProNicaragua also touted what it said are the softer accents of Nicaraguan Spanish and English over accents of other Latin Americans and over the Indian accents that are less familiar to people in the United States. ProNicaragua ran a training program to improve the English skills of 7,500 workers. Its new call center was designed to act as an incubation center for foreign companies considering setting up shop in Nicaragua.

The gamble seems to be working. In 2007, ProNicaragua helped negotiate the contract between Press Two and the Danish outsourcing company T26 A/S to operate a call center in Managua. And in 2008, Sitel, one of the largest U.S. call center outsourcers, opened a 14,000-square-foot call center in Managua. "Latin America is a key part of the growing near-shore horizon to support English and Spanish bilingual customers in North America," said Dave Garner, CEO of Nashville-based Sitel, in the press release announcing the expansion. "Nicaragua offers a talented bilingual workforce to support our clients. We're proud to expand Sitel's presence in the region."

ProNicaragua even negotiated with some Indian outsourcing companies to provide Spanish-speaking operators for contracts with multinational corporations. Other Latin American countries are already providing outsourcing services to Indian outsourcers. Tata Consultancy Services, Wipro, and Infosys have opened offices in Latin American countries, as well as in the Philippines, parts of China, Africa, eastern Europe, and even a few in the United States. Not all of those operations are call centers, but many are. And in August 2008, eTelecare, a Philippines-based outsourcing company, opened a five-hundred-employee call center in Managua to provide bilingual call center services to the United States.

Now another emerging outsourcing hub offers opportunities for call centers that provide not just English, but other much-used European and Middle Eastern languages: North Africa, especially Tunisia and Morocco, as well as the largest country in the region, Egypt.

—❦—

About ten miles from the famous ancient pyramids and Sphinx at Giza, on the edge of Cairo, lies one of Egypt's most ambitious forays into the modern world of high-tech global outsourcing. Rising out of the dusty poverty-laced landscape, just off the desert road to Alexandria, is a vast 450-acre gated oasis of green grass and sleek office buildings constructed from blue glass, gray metal, and white concrete. It is a corporate office park called Smart Village—a mecca of Egypt's budding information technology and contact center industries. Cars have to be searched for bombs by the stern guards at its entrance before anyone is permitted into the fenced enclave. But once inside, by design, the Smart Village resembles any other well-heeled office park in California, Texas, Europe, or India. It is meant to feel safe and familiar to a Western businessperson or one from Dubai. Its buildings are four or five stories high and flanked by serene man-made ponds, fountains, palm trees, and lush, manicured lawns. The government ministries of communications and information technology are there. The Cairo and Alexandria Stock Exchange is there. So are many software development outposts and call centers of familiar American and European multinational technology companies, including Microsoft, IBM, Intel, HP, Oracle, Vodafone, and Orange.

The Smart Village also houses the largest home-grown call center in Egypt: Xceed Contact Center. Started in 2001 as a division of Egyptian

Telecom, it first answered calls from Egyptian customers. But Xceed expanded in 2003 and began to take calls for foreign companies. By 2007 it had more than 1,600 call center stations and employed about 2,100 agents. Its employees answer phones for the European and Middle Eastern customers of Microsoft, Intel, and other companies.

The head of sales and marketing for Xceed is particularly well suited for his main responsibility of persuading multinational companies to buy into the company's call center services. He was born and raised in Egypt, earned an MBA at the University of Texas, El Paso, and worked for many years at the corporate level for McDonald's. He even attended McDonald's Hamburger University in Illinois for some executive training. But despite all his affinity with American people and his understanding of Western business and culture, the thing most Americans notice before all else about Ossama Nazmi is his first name. At least that's been the case ever since September 11, 2001, when he and his wife were living in Monroe, Louisiana, and he was working as director of operations for a group of McDonald's restaurants throughout the southern United States.

"We had never been harassed or anything, but after 9/11, it started to get a little bit uncomfortable." Nazmi says he would hear colleagues calling him Osama bin Laden, and when he asked them what they meant by it, they would tell him they were just joking. But he could feel their wariness. "Because of the name and the stereotyping that was going on, they would take me as a Muslim. But I'm not Muslim, I'm Christian. They put that name to that profile and hence they decide how to treat you. All the stereotyping and misconceptions and so forth, they form a big cloud and that puts an actual barrier between our two worlds." Nazmi was raised as a Coptic Christian, one of the first Christian religions, making him part of the 5 percent of Egyptians who are not Muslim.

Ossama and Joyce Nazmi had wanted to stay in the United States for a few more years to be near her parents, who emigrated from Egypt twenty-five years before and were living in Albuquerque. But about six months after 9/11, they decided to head back to their native Cairo. In

2002, Ossama was hired by Xceed. Fluent in English, French, and Arabic, he started learning Italian in the 1990s but says he hasn't mastered it yet. He can also speak a little Spanish, which he picked up during his time in El Paso.

When Nazmi makes the case for corporations to bring their call center business to Egypt, he has a few major selling points. Since Egypt's thousands of years of history include periods of occupation by almost all Western European nations, as well as Turkey and other Middle Eastern nations, influences remain from many different places, as do schools left behind to teach all their languages. So Xceed can set up call centers to speak to customers in at least nine languages: Arabic, English, French, Italian, Spanish, Greek, German, Portuguese, and even Hebrew. The country turns out about 250,000 new college graduates a year, and about 10 percent are multilingual. Also, since tourism is Egypt's number one industry, and with its five thousand years of experience in it, the culture of hospitality meshes well with the mind-set needed to perform customer service. During the past few years, the government has invested in building infrastructure to support the call center and IT outsourcing industries. The Smart Village is the best showcase of that.

Still, Nazmi encounters resistance, especially from American and Canadian executives. He says a few interrelated concerns usually top their lists. Companies are worried about geopolitical risks, which lead to concerns about the safety of corporate employees who will travel to Egypt. Those questions bring up more pointed concerns about the conditions for women in Egypt—both Egyptian women working in companies and Western women doing business in Egypt. Nazmi has answers for all that.

He recounts how Westerners who aren't aware of geography have asked if he can hear the bombing in Iraq. He reminds them that technically, Egypt is in North Africa, not the Middle East, and is a few countries away from Iraq. Others worry about violence at the border with Israel, but Nazmi is quick to point out that Egypt is the only Arab nation that has a peace treaty with Israel. And Xceed answers calls from Israeli customers in Hebrew.

Foreign confidence in the safety of employees who will travel to Egypt was shaken in 2005 by two high-profile terrorist bombings at Egyptian resorts. Nazmi says such attacks are not commonplace and that because tourism is its leading industry, the government has become more vigilant in preventing such attacks. "There is no country in the world that doesn't have problems," he says, pointing to school and university shootings in the United States, as well as high murder rates, 9/11, and home-grown terrorism like the Oklahoma City bombing. "In Paris you've had two major strikes that actually turned into violence in the street, and a lot of people got hurt. Plus a bombing happened at one of the embassies—in the middle of Paris." He says many executives are more willing to overlook similar threats in their own countries, or in countries with established business ties, than they are in Egypt.

"See what I'm saying? When you sit with big clients in the United States and they already have clients in India and they ask you about our geopolitical risks, I ask about geopolitical risks in India. Look at the nuclear threat between India and Pakistan—that's obvious." Nazmi also points out other things about India that many Westerners don't always take into account, including that it has a larger Muslim population than Egypt, even if it is not the predominant religion in the country. "Look at the monsoon—every year. It cuts a lot of fiber optic lines—marine cable, electricity. In the Philippines as well, they have those sorts of problems. I've been fortunate to have been to many countries—the U.S., the Philippines, India, Mexico—and I am telling you, honestly speaking, Egypt is one of the countries where I feel the very safest. In other places people don't walk after midnight in some neighborhoods— we don't have this here. If you want to take a walk after one o'clock in the morning, it's going to be busy."

Perhaps the most culturally jarring issue for some clients is the question of women's status in Egypt. Companies are concerned not only about the women employed in the call centers, but also about the conditions their Western female employees will encounter when they visit Egypt for business. Nazmi says a potential Canadian client "had a list of questions to go through on the very first conference call before they came here." They were very apologetic when they approached the subject. "They said, 'Please don't be offended,' but 'what is the ratio between male and female?' I said, 'Sixty percent female and 40 percent male.' They were surprised and asked, 'So you have women who work?' I said, 'Yes.' They said they heard about oppression of women here and so forth, and asked if the women get paid the same as men. I said sometimes higher."

At times Nazmi's arguments can sound like whitewashing to Westerners, but he is more forthcoming than most other Egyptian business or government officials on the subject of women's status. He says a French potential client asked him about Muslim women workers and their headscarves, or the *hijab*, as it is called. In the past decade or so, wearing of the hijab has increased considerably in Egypt, often attributed to the growing influence of hard-line Muslim groups, such as the Muslim Brotherhood. Guidebooks warn Western women traveling or doing business in Egypt to dress conservatively, covering arms and legs, and not even to wear V-necks. While it is not necessary to wear a veil, 90 to 95 percent of the women in the country, and in the call centers, do wear the hijab. Nazmi says he addressed the French concern about "the veil"—referring to all of the variations of Muslim women's religious attire, including the hijab—by saying that "the veil here is a way of dress, not a way of thinking. You will find some fundamentalists, or fanatics, that will definitely wear a veil. But it doesn't mean that every veiled woman is actually part of that."

Still, women not wearing at least a hijab, especially if they are Western looking, do face harassment on Cairo's streets. And discriminatory treatment of women is sanctioned by the Egyptian government as well. Egyptian marriage and divorce laws, for example, allow men great leeway, including polygamy, while women have practically no right even to seek divorce. The law in general and the almost totally male-run court system are weighted heavily against women's rights, including the ability to gain child custody and receive child support and alimony. Also, genital mutilation of women is a widespread practice in Egypt, as it is in many other African countries, but not in most Muslim nations. In 2005, a reported 96 percent of Egyptian women had undergone the procedure, in which their clitoris is cut off when they are somewhere between the ages of about seven and fourteen.

The call center industry in isolation cannot directly control or change these issues of women's status and human rights. But presumably the issues will continue to be a thorn in the side of Egypt and other African or Middle Eastern nations as they continue hoping to become players in the outsourcing game with Western nations. Yet some look to India, and see that disparities with the West in the status of women has not stopped the industry from booming there.

Nazmi and many other leaders of the Egyptian outsourcing industry are working on all fronts to overcome these real cultural barriers to business and the Western misconceptions about their country. To that end, the government and those in the industry have mounted a concerted campaign to brand Egypt as a smart outsourcing choice for European and American companies. "From day one," says Khaled Shash, the CEO of Raya Contact Center, another large Egyptian outsourcing company, "the most important point was to sell Egypt. Because Egypt was not on the map of outsourcing when we started."

Raya's offices are not in the Smart Village but in a neighborhood about twenty minutes away. Its modern call center building sits on a residential street next to a mosque. The call to prayer that resonates through the city five times a day from every mosque's minaret wafts through Shash's office window. But on the call center floors above, their sounds cannot be heard. That is where Raya's approximately fourteen hundred agents answer phones for companies like Dell, General Motors, Barclays Bank, Microsoft, Coca-Cola, and Cisco. It is only when Raya's contact center employees take time out that the differences between them and their Western counterparts emerge. Instead of coffee breaks, Raya's workers plan their work around prayer breaks. The office building provides two prayer rooms just outside the work area—one for men and one for women. (There is also a prayer area and a minaret from which the call to prayer goes out five times a day at the

Smart Village, right next to Xceed's headquarters.) Shash explains that it is more efficient to incorporate the prayer rooms into the design of his call center building than to have his employees go to the mosque next door. If they had to leave the building and come back through its security, they would need more than their fifteen-minute breaks.

Shash's cross-cultural experience helps him be an ambassador for his company and his country. A native of Cairo, he has worked in IT for multinational corporations such as Compaq and HP. He has been based in the United Kingdom and France, as well as Cairo. He has taught at the university level and is fluent in French, Arabic, and English. For the past decade, he has helped build Egypt's profile as it tries to become an outsourcing player on the world stage. "We put forth effort to convince these companies about the quality of our people, the stability of the country, the language quality, everything. We had to convince a company like Microsoft, like Dell, like Orange, like Oracle. These companies don't move without a lot of thought. Of course, India is number one. It is branded for outsourcing. And we have to respect that. But being a global player, that is our vision. Not just to win an account here or an account there. We need to be perceived as a global player in the world."

Back at the Smart Village, officials echo Shash's sentiments at the two government entities that oversee the industry: the Ministry of Communications and Information Technology (MCIT) and the Information Technology Industry Development Agency (ITIDA). But the support extends up to the highest levels of government. Egypt's prime minister, Ahmed Nazif, is an ally to industry leaders. As the former MCIT minister, he does not need to be persuaded of the value of the industry to Egypt and advocates for it regularly.

The CEO of ITIDA, Mohamed Omran, says of Egypt's quest, "The idea is to do exactly what India has done. Very smartly. And then learn from India's mistakes." Those mistakes have to do with the way some of India's call centers have alienated Western customers. Yet Omran and most others in the Egyptian government and the outsourcing industry are very careful not to criticize India directly since it is Egypt's third largest trading partner. "We consider India as a partner nation; they are not competitors. We are in peace. Indians and Egyptians have wonderful relations. Don't ask me why. I don't know. Since Nasser and Nehru's days, when they had the nonalliance movement, we became close. We like their food. They like ours. Some of our people love the Indian movies so much."

Omran says there is room in the call center outsourcing market for more countries. He stresses that Egypt is not a threat to India but instead is a good complement, as India moves into other business processing outsourcing areas and yet still needs to address their clients' basic call center and IT needs. "The Indian government cannot develop 1.1 billion souls in India, all at the same time. But they can certainly develop some of these industries to relay the country into prosperity. We can help them in achieving this, and in the process help ourselves."

On the second floor of Xceed's main building at the Smart Village is the call center for some of Microsoft's European, Middle Eastern, and African customers. The large room looks like a United Nations of cubicles, because after every few rows, a new flag planted on a cubicle wall signifies the language in which new groups of agents are answering phones. Hamade Henrique works under a Portuguese flag. He came to Egypt from Mozambique to attend college in 1997 and has been answering calls at Xceed since 2005. Fluent in Portuguese, Arabic, and English, he got the job when the Mozambique embassy in Cairo contacted him telling him that Xceed was looking for Portuguese speakers. They contacted the Portuguese and Brazilian embassies as well.

From just about all over the world, whenever customers call the Portuguese-speaking number for Microsoft, Henrique says, their calls will be routed to Xceed in Cairo. "We receive calls from Portugal. We receive calls from Mozambique. We also receive calls from Japan, because there are some Brazilians living there. But calls from Brazil go to a different call center in Brazil itself. Also we have English calls from Saudi Arabia and Dubai, mainly from people who speak English living in the Gulf area." He answers the phone with his last name, Henrique, rather than his first name, Hamade, since it is easier for people to understand. His high level of education and sophisticated language skills seem fairly common among the agents answering Microsoft's calls at Xceed. He says most callers assume he is based in Portugal, but if they ask, he tells them he is in Egypt. Most customers don't get angry that he is not in their country. There was one customer, however, who got really upset, and no amount of listening would calm him down. "The man was not just calling me names," says Henrique, "but he was insulting everybody else, and the product, and Microsoft too. He wanted to talk to Bill Gates himself."

If that customer had called in 2003, such a connection might have been possible. That is when Bill Gates first visited the Smart Village, a moment many people dedicated to promoting Egypt's viability in this arena, especially the promoters of the Smart Village, speak of with pride. For them, that was the greatest validation they could receive. The visit is well documented on most websites emanating from the Smart Village. Everyone at Xceed, and government ministers as well, are quick to point out that Gates didn't visit just once. He was there twice. And Microsoft moved some of its operations there, a fact they believe continues to help soothe anxious prospective clients. The visit was such a well-known event in Egypt that Henrique remembers it even though he didn't meet Gates then. "I wasn't here at that time. But I saw that on TV."

A few rows away from Henrique, agents answer calls in Spanish. Farther down the aisle, the Israeli flag signifies the section where calls are answered from Hebrew speakers around the world. The tower of Babel din continues in sections designated by the French, German, Greek, and Egyptian flags. Around the corner in the back of the room is the section marked with a British flag, denoting the English speakers. People in this section get calls mostly from British customers and from Americans living or working in Europe who use Microsoft's Xbox.

Mohammed Ghazoy is one of the star agents in this section. He is in his mid-twenties and has been working at Xceed for seven months.

Ghazoy grew up in Cairo but attended one year of high school in the United Kingdom, then returned to Egypt and completed college in Cairo. He uses the name Richard to answer calls because the name Mohammed would stir up too many questions. "Sometimes people aren't always accepting of a foreigner," Ghazoy says. "Sometimes they feel more comfortable speaking to someone from the same country. Sometimes we get customers who want to speak to agents with a British accent." They will ask him if he is in India, and he says, "No. I'm not Indian." Often that is enough to calm them down. But he doesn't tell customers he is in Egypt. Instead he says, "Unfortunately, we're unable to say exactly where we are, but we are somewhere near."

In the time leading up to Ramadan, Ghazoy hung seasonal decorations from the ceiling all over the call center. He thought it was a good way to create a feeling of cohesiveness among his co-workers since, during the month of daytime fasting and nights of festivities that their families will be experiencing at home, they will still have to be at work taking calls that come in twenty-four hours a day. In small ways like this, Ghazoy and many other people in the industry work at making sure that the rush to bridge cultural gaps and adapt to customers' Western ways does not cause them to lose their connection with their own traditions.

Management efforts to create a hospitable environment for workers extend beyond the call center. They also include arrangements for getting workers to and from work. In a city like Cairo, transportation can be a challenge. Instead of relying on public transportation, Xceed, like many other companies in large Indian cities, provides shuttle buses.

While commuting in any large city involves delays and tedium, not many Westerners could relate to what an agent they might speak with would see during a daily commute to and from the Smart Village on Xceed's minibuses. The 4:00 p.m. fleet of shuttles to take day shift workers home rolls out of the Smart Village on time. About a mile or two down the Cairo-Alexandria Desert Road is the entrance ramp for the Ring Road that takes riders back to central Cairo. Getting onto the Ring Road by an on-ramp would take about twenty seconds in light traffic and fifteen minutes on the worst American commute. In Cairo, it isn't unusual for it to take thirty minutes. The modern Xceed company buses are air-conditioned against the brutal summer heat, unlike the dilapidated city buses that travel alongside. During such a wait, people in those public buses nearby can be seen throwing juice cartons, empty cigarette packs, and entire lunch bags of trash out the open windows onto the road below. Trash is heaped all around the on-ramp. Crowds of men wearing turbans and loose clothing, and women dressed in long black robes and veils despite the 96-degree desert temperatures, walk on the expressways and on-ramps to get where they need to go, weaving in and out of traffic that is sometimes barely moving, and often at a standstill.

Once on the main expressway, there are few, if any, barriers, trees, or even billboards between the road and the city to camouflage each from the other, as is customary in the West. Right beside the clogged freeways, people go in and out of ramshackle high-rises, more decrepit than some of the worst American urban public housing. Only the satellite dishes that crowd the roofs of almost every residential building in Cairo signal the Egyptians' intrepid connection to the outside world. But fields of crops are interspersed between the buildings. In each field is at least one shack made from what looks like cardboard at best—often without any kind of roof—where people live. It all denotes the isolation and crippling poverty that qualifies Egypt as a developing country.

On the Xceed bus, all the men are dressed in Western clothing. Most of the women are wearing colorful headscarves, but the rest of their dress is Western style. Only one young woman is wearing the traditional Muslim dress, covering her head, neck, and entire body. The workers read newspapers, and some chat with each other as the trip back into central Cairo that should take about thirty minutes lengthens to almost two hours. Cairo's roads were built for half a million cars, but handle more than 2 million each day. A three-lane road is made into six lanes as cars, trucks, and buses squeeze perilously close in between and around each other.

Back at Xceed's call center, Reem Fahmy answers calls from Microsoft Xbox's English-speaking customers. Fahmy was born and grew up in New Jersey, before her family moved back to her parents' homeland of Egypt. She completed her degree in business administration in Cairo and immediately started working as a customer support agent. She has been at Xceed for eight months and is what is called a tier-two support agent, meaning she handles the more complicated calls the first-tier agents send her. Fahmy says that the cultural differences between many of her customers and her colleagues do occasionally get in the way of communication.

But Fahmy says she doesn't believe the disparities are as wide as they might appear. More frustrating and alienating to her and her colleagues than economic or cultural differences, she says, is the ignorance about Egyptian culture on the part of Westerners. "I've met people who still think that Egypt is all sand, and we are all walking around with camels." Fahmy thinks the same sort of uninformed attitude also applies to the way that Westerners see Muslim women. While she acknowledges that many women in Egypt wear headscarves and might look different from many Westerners because of that, she doesn't think the differences go much deeper and points out that the whole issue has little to do with the quality of anyone's work in a call center. She doesn't wear a hijab, but her sister does. "A veiled girl is exactly like an unveiled one. It's just a way of showing part of your religion, of respecting religion. Not all of them wear veils. Most of them, yes. But we never talk about that on the phone with customers. It never comes up. As long as you're doing your job well, I don't think there is a difference."

Fahmy is more concerned with helping her colleagues get their accents right and understand the differences between speaking to American and British customers. She coaches other agents on their pronunciation and on cultural references. She speaks Arabic and some French, and of course her English is spoken with an American accent. Many Western callers think she is in the United States. "They say, 'Thank God we got someone who understands us.' Three-fourths of the people who call are UK customers, so an American is okay to them. Except sometimes I'm too fast for them. They don't like that either.

They are so precise. With a British person it's like you have to take care of everything you say, and you don't want to sound abrupt. But Americans want everything to be done quickly. At the end of the day, as long as you give them the service and support they're looking for, as human beings, when they sense that someone's helping, that kind of overcomes everything else."

Arabic speakers can get closer to native pronunciation when learning languages, Fahmy says, than people whose first language is something else. "Arabic has a way of teaching and pronouncing every single letter, so it helps you in English and in French. In India and in America, we have a way of eating off letters. So sometimes only other Indians can understand Indians, and only other Americans can understand Americans. British people speak more precisely, except when you get a heavy Scottish accent or something. Tempo makes a lot of difference too. If I pronounce a word in a way that native people would not pronounce it, that causes a barrier to start, where the customer doesn't understand what I am saying. Or the agent might not understand what the customer is saying. We're trying to get close to native. So I tell the agents to slow down the tempo of their talk and try again if they don't understand the customer, or if the customer doesn't understand them."

Fahmy sits only a few cubicles away from Mohammed Ghazoy. He says he finds American customers a little easier to handle than British ones. He thinks it is because the Americans he speaks to are not living in their own country. "Since we provide customer support for an American product, they think they are speaking to an American call center and that they are speaking with a voice from home, so they take a different attitude psychologically. When you say *Microsoft*, people just think America. It makes it easier." Although Ghazoy has never been to the United States, he believes, from what he has heard and from his experience at Xceed, that Americans are more used to hearing English speakers with accents than British people are, because, he says, America is a "melting of nationalities."

The main difference Ghazoy sees between American and British customers is in the kinds of answers they want. He takes a call from an

American mechanical engineer working in Germany. There are issues with the Xbox he bought in the United States and plug converters in Germany. Ghazoy conveys all of the three possible alternatives to the customer, and the man chooses the one he wants. If it had been a British customer, Ghazoy says, he would have just presented the simplest solution. "Americans want options, and then they will think about the alternatives. British people are more serious. They are not looking for options. They just want you to tell them a solution."

Kevin Gatens can't stand it when he hears people in Great Britain refer to call centers as "the coal mines of the twenty-first century." Gatens is the head of a big call center in Sunderland, in northeastern England, an area where, until a few years ago, coal had been mined since Roman times. Gatens grew up between Newcastle and Sunderland, a little south of the border with Scotland. Much of the coal that fueled the British-born Industrial Revolution came from the area, and it was where some of the first labor unions in the world were formed during the 1800s. Galvanized by the coal mine owners' brutality to their employees through the years, unions organized against the kinds of cruel conditions that, as an 1842 government report said, sent entire families, including children as young as four, into the mines. They were made to drag tubs of coal attached to their bodies by chains up mine shafts on their hands and knees. Wages, hours, and working conditions were unfair and unregulated. Children were not schooled, and never learned to read or write. Poor ventilation in the mines meant workers were sickened or died from toxic gases, sparks from improper lighting caused deadly explosions, and structural inadequacies meant fatal cave-ins.

But coal was king and a chief employer in Sunderland, Newcastle, Durham, and the entire area for almost four hundred years until changes in energy consumption, cheaper coal imports, and Prime Minister Margaret Thatcher's fights with the unions broke the back of the industry in the 1980s. By then, industrialization was giving way to the service economy in many developed nations, and most of the last coal mines in Britain's northeast closed in the mid-1990s. Unemployment in the industrialized regions of the country climbed. Around that same time, Gatens says, call centers began to spring up in the area and "helped close the gap where the heavy industry had been." It was also when Gatens graduated from Sunderland University and took a job with London Electricity as a call center agent in 1996. The company had just moved from London to become one of the original tenants in Sunderland's Doxford International Business Park, a 125-acre site built to create a hub for technology and call center work that was supposed to help pull the northeast of England out of its unemployment slump.

Joy Thompson also began working for London Electricity when it arrived at the Doxford site. She was returning to the workforce after taking time off to raise her children and had worked in the insurance industry before that. London Electricity was subsequently bought by the French power company EDF Energy, but the call center stayed in the same location, where Thompson is a team manager today. "I think this industry put Sunderland back on the map. I mean, previously we were a mining and ship-building area. But call centers, or customer contact centers, as I would prefer to call them, gave people from different backgrounds the opportunity to actually work, and get paid a good wage. It has dramatically reduced unemployment in this area. Also it's a growth industry."

Not everyone sees it that way, though. In the summer of 2007, Gatens, Thompson, and EDF found themselves in the midst of a controversy that tapped into the varied perceptions of call centers today and of northeastern England's economic past, present, and future. The head of Sunderland's branch of the National Union of Teachers was quoted in national newspapers criticizing a vocational program set up with help from EDF's call center workers at a secondary school in a low-income neighborhood. The Hylton Red House school began offering a class for credit toward graduation that would teach fifteen- and sixteen-year-old students how to sell mobile phone contracts and handle customer complaints in a hypothetical call center. Howard Brown, the union's regional head, heard of the scheme and told the *Daily Mail,* "Children, particularly in this area, must be taught that there is more to life than working in a call centre. By introducing this course, all they are doing is lowering their aspirations."

Stirring up negative historical images that many people in Great Britain, and particularly in the northeast, had learned from a young age, Brown told the *Guardian:* "We do have to equip our children for a variety of different jobs, but I think this is a step too far. It seems that this is going back to the old days when we told children round here that they had to go straight down the mines when they left [school]. Now the mines have gone and we are saying they have to go and work in a call centre. We have an obligation to give them a bit more than that."

Joy Thompson and members of her team helped set up the mock call center at the Hylton Red House school, with equipment and computers that EDF Energy donated. They had been working with the school for more than three years, teaching how to develop business plans for other ventures, including a hair-styling service. The idea for the call center training course, says Thompson, came from the teacher in charge of the program, who said the students had come to her with the idea. "For me, personally," says Thompson, "I'm really proud of the partnership that we built, quite proud of what we achieved together. I think it's really important for companies to work within schools. And I certainly don't think that it was in any way detrimental or pushing people into call centers. I think it just gives kids the opportunity to build up skills that they're going to need in life, regardless of where they work."

Hylton Red House students who went through the program were quoted in the *Guardian* article echoing that sentiment. "Angela Bryan, 15, said the call centre course had already proved popular with pupils and at the school. 'A lot of people want to do it because it teaches us how to use computers better and about getting used to dealing with people on the telephone.' Another pupil, Vicky Ward, said: 'It's like proper work experience and that means it is useful, which makes it more popular.'"

Kevin Gatens was taken aback, even insulted, by the teachers' union criticism. "There has been a stigma attached to the contact center industry. I think in the UK, in particular, the industry has a reputation that it's low-scale, highly repetitive work. It's as if we wheel them in. We stick them on a chair. And then they go back out again at the end of their shift. It is totally incorrect. Personally, I think some of the bad impression comes from people who've never been in a call center. What people see when they come inside a call center isn't what they expected. It isn't about sitting on the telephones for eight hours a day. The working conditions aren't what people expected, and the opportunities aren't what people expected. It's not just a job. Careers exist within the contact centers. This can be a career."

To be sure, the offices of EDF Energy's call center in Sunderland are as comfortable and professional looking as any modern corporate location. The twelve hundred agents who work to keep the center open twenty-four hours a day, seven days a week, divide their daily work so they don't spend all their time on the phones. They take time each day to handle administrative work and coach or train newer employees. The campus has an on-site cafeteria, a gym, several lounge areas with televisions where employees can relax, and quiet areas where those attending college can study. "It's not the sweatshop that people make it out to be," says Joy Thompson.

In the northeast, call centers are estimated to employ upward of 10 percent of the working population. Other parts of the United Kingdom, many of them formerly industrial areas, are also hubs of domestic call centers, including parts of Northern Ireland, Scotland, and Wales. These areas have embraced call centers for the same benefits they produce in other parts of the developed world and in the developing world: to stem high unemployment by offering educated workers at relatively low wages. The situation in the northeast and other parts of the United Kingdom is reflective of areas in other developed countries as well. But perhaps because the UK learned from the early pitfalls of American towns that embraced call centers before them, northeastern England has had more luck in fostering its call center industry than some similar areas in the United States.

Just as the backlash against call center outsourcing had taken hold in the United States, and as India was taking note of the resentment it had engendered in American callers, the *Times of India* reported in February 2004 on Clintwood, a small former coal mining town in Virginia, where industrialization had gone bust:

> For the past three years, Clintwood rejoiced at having struck a small economic bonanza. In 2001, the Internet company Travelocity decided to locate a call centre here. Nothing big. It began with a 250-seat customer service centre, but it provided a way out of the hardscrabble existence for a community that for years depended on employment in the area's dying coal mines and disappearing apparel industry. In time, the call centre was to grow to a 500-seater, making Travelocity the largest private employer in Dickenson County, where Clintwood is located. The county went out of its way to embrace the newbie online firm, proud to become even a minor techno blip in an America hooked on the internet. It gave tax breaks to Travelocity.
>
> It forked out a $250,000 loan to expand the facility. The local congressman rounded up $1.4 million in federal funding for a child care centre next to the call centre, with 45 of 107 slots promised to Travelocity. For 30 months, Clintwood and its Dickenson County Technology Park thrived. Travelocity was the showpiece of white collar employment in blue collar boonies. Young men and women of backwoods U.S.A. found work answering calls from all over the country in their sweet southern accents. Life was good.
>
> On Wednesday morning, it all ended quite unexpectedly. A senior Travelocity executive informed them the call centre was being closed by December. Travelocity lost $55 million last year and was falling behind rivals such as Expedia, which were outsourcing such jobs

abroad to cut costs. Travelocity had to follow suit, and send the jobs to India.

The 2004 article went on to explain to its Indian audience: "It's not just Wall Street and Silicon Valley which are stung by outsourcing. Middle America is hurting too and that is why politicians are upset."

The British may not actually have stronger feelings against Indian call centers than Americans do, but they express their disdain more publicly. Recent advertising campaigns from some British companies touted the fact that they had brought all their call centers back home from abroad. The bank NatWest, in particular, ran ads promising that all its customer calls would be answered in UK call centers. That stirred up accusations of xenophobia, but the ads continued. And while some British people, like some people in the United States, complain about outsourced foreign call centers taking their jobs away, many other British and American customers had another complaint: that the quality of Indian call center service is not good.

A *BusinessWeek* article in 2007, "Luring Customers with Local Call Centers," reported that many companies were finding that their initial savings from offshore outsourcing were often outweighed by drops in customer satisfaction. "A growing number of British companies are warming to the idea that paying higher wages to local call center employees pays off. 'Foreign call centers feed into the perception that companies aren't interested in their customers,' says Rita Clifton, chairman of London-based brand consultancy Interbrand. 'Firms will have to spend more money on UK centers so customers feel taken care of.'" The article said the cost of attracting new customers can be up to five times as high as keeping the customers a company already has. "British call centers can thus be cost-effective if taken as part of a company's overall business strategy. For instance, total global spending on call centers last year amounted to $34 billion, compared to $434 billion spent on advertising worldwide, according to media consultants Zenith Optimedia. Yet money shifted from advertising to improve call center operations can be a more efficient way of attracting and holding on to customers, thanks in part to word of mouth."

This is where Gatens sees the advantage that call centers in his region have in the British marketplace. "There are lots of surveys which tout the accent and the friendliness of the people within the northeast. The workforce is available, and they have the right skills and the right attitude to deliver the service that customers are looking for."

But after all the talk of the merits and pitfalls of customer service being globalized, outsourced, local, or multinational, Gatens believes the key equation for good customer service remains quite simple: "If you have bad service it is down to one of two things," he explains. "It is either the individual person you're dealing with, in which case it is a coaching issue," meaning an agent needs more or better training. "Or, it is the process, in which case the system is breaking down, and that is a management issue." Because once all is said and done on the front lines, good or bad customer service always is a direct reflection of the management.

7.   The Solution
Is the Problem

Halloween night in 2003 must have been particularly scary for many employees of AT&T Wireless—and not because of the trick-or-treaters coming to their homes. In fact, most of the workers were still at the office, since that was the evening the company, then based in Seattle, had picked to launch a new software system, designed to streamline and simplify all of its customer service operations. But when the switch was flipped on the new system, it crashed.

"It went down and stayed down," said a former worker. There were so many glitches that even after three days straight trying to rescue it, the tech people charged with getting the new system up and running declared they would not be able to make it work for weeks, or possibly months. And the old system had not been adequately backed up, so most of the information about current customers was unavailable to anyone in the company.

The timing could not have been worse. Three weeks later, on November 24, a new Federal Communications Commission (FCC) rule went into effect allowing cell phone customers to take their phone numbers with them if they switched wireless carriers. Then, just when the tech people at AT&T Wireless finally cobbled together the downed customer service system, a second software system, this one designed to handle the transitions among phone numbers coming into and out of their network, crashed as well. Customer service agents were in the dark again. At the very point when call volumes were at their highest in years, agents could barely access customers' accounts. And even if they could, there was little agents could do to close them out, activate new service, or integrate phone numbers customers brought with them from other carriers. The same AT&T Wireless workers who had just endured such a fraught Halloween were probably also a little less grateful than usual as they sat down to Thanksgiving dinner that week.

"The mood here is bad and getting worse all the time. The problems were both pretty disastrous," one AT&T Wireless customer service representative told the *Seattle Post-Intelligencer*. "You have lots of people complaining to you, including my own father, who'd been a customer since 1996." Indeed, the FCC later reported that nearly half of the 4,734 complaints it received in the weeks after the number portability rule went into effect were against AT&T Wireless, which had split from its parent company, AT&T Corporation, in 1997 and had once boasted the most subscribers of any wireless provider.

But it had seen customers steadily defect during the first years of the 2000s, making it number three at the time of the new FCC rule in 2003, behind Verizon and Cingular. The AT&T Wireless customers who wanted to leave couldn't because of the problems agents had accessing their accounts in the new customer service system. Those troubles appeared to be more of the same kind of customer service woes that had plagued the company leading up to the system breakdown and had made customers so desperate to get out in the first place. New subscribers who wanted to switch to AT&T Wireless couldn't do that either. Reportedly, workers at AT&T Wireless retail stores who couldn't activate new accounts resorted to steering customers to other wireless carriers instead.

In the last quarter of 2003, AT&T Wireless added only 128,000 new customers, while industry leader Verizon picked up 1.5 million new subscribers. In January 2004, amid rumors that there was nothing left to do but sell the hobbled company, the AT&T Wireless CEO at the time, John Zeglis, admitted to analysts that the company had failed. "Frankly," he said, "our customer service went pretty far south." In February 2004, the company announced its sale to Cingular Wireless for $41 billion, or $15 a share. It was the largest such buyout ever at the time, even though the value of shares was just less than half their value when the company went public in April 2000. And if all that were not enough, in August 2004, two months before the sale to Cingular was finalized, the wireless carrier's birth parent, AT&T Corporation, notified the Securities and Exchange Commission that it wanted to take back the wireless company's right to use its name, forever. AT&T Corporation believed that AT&T Wireless's confirmed reputation for such poor customer service was ruining the value of the larger AT&T brand.

The wireless company never actually had to give up rights to its maiden name, but the circumstances that caused the threat could have been enough to make Theodore N. Vail turn in his grave. He was the early president of AT&T, and a contemporary of Alexander Graham Bell, who left the company back in 1887 because he felt the financiers were running AT&T's reputation into the ground. Vail said he couldn't work with the money men, who, in his view, were more concerned with the short-term bottom line than with the good of AT&T's customers. Vail was asked back to the helm twenty years later to restore customer confidence in the company after his criticisms were proven true.

And in 2006, the story came full circle again as mergers and acquisitions meant the original AT&T, SBC, Bell South, and Cingular (which had bought the ill-fated AT&T Wireless in 2004) were all gathered into one company that, it was decided, would do business under the AT&T name. By 2008, the new AT&T, as it called itself, was the largest cell phone provider. But Verizon was nipping at its heels, and surpassed it in 2009, after completing an acquisition of Alltel.

If the nerdy and maniacal telephone operator Ernestine—created and portrayed by comedienne Lily Tomlin on the TV show *Laugh-In* in the 1970s—had heard about these twenty-first-century telecom twists and turns, she might have let out a few of her signature chortles and snorts in recognition. After all, Ernestine is the one who laid out what everyone believed was AT&T's attitude toward customer service back then, when it had a monopoly on providing telephone access:

Here at the phone company, we handle 84 billion calls a year, serving everyone from presidents and kings to the scum of the earth. We realize that every so often you can't get an operator. For no apparent reason your phone goes out of order, perhaps you've been charged for a call you didn't make. We don't care. . . . You see, this phone system consists of a multi-billion-dollar matrix of space age technology that is so sophisticated, even we can't handle it. But that's your problem, isn't it? Next time you complain about your phone service, why don't you try using two Dixie cups with a string? We don't care. We don't have to. We're the phone company.

The software system that failed at AT&T Wireless in 2003 was a product from a multibillion-dollar subindustry of the customer service industry called customer relationship management, or CRM. It is just one of the many cottage industries that have grown up around the customer service industry. According to Gartner, a technology consulting firm, in 2008 the CRM industry had revenues of $9.15 billion.

CRM started as a business strategy. As technology began to enable companies to amass more and more information about their customers, the systems for managing that information were lagging. The history of a customer's transactions might have been documented, and customers might have indicated their preferences and their reactions to products and services to the company in earlier transactions, but companies did not always save that information. Or if they did they usually did not share it between or even within departments. So agents might have no access to a customer's billing or sales data or to records of previous calls to customer service, even when customers were calling with problems regarding those previous interactions. Or agents would have to navigate among many cumbersome databases to ferret out any such information. That took too much time, especially when customers were waiting impatiently on the line for answers.

So a great need arose for more streamlined means of managing customer information and making it accessible and useful within companies. The CRM strategy was designed to coordinate the corporate functions of marketing, customer service, and sales. Companies hoped that by doing that, they would enable agents to help customers more effectively and efficiently than before. And marketing and sales could keep track of their customers' needs in real time. CRM software would bring all that rich customer information into one uniform database. CRM initiatives were also touted as a way for companies to cut costs, even as CRM made life better for their customers. It promised the best for all worlds. The concept took hold, and a cadre of CRM software producers and consultants sprang up. In the 1990s the CRM industry grew at phenomenal rates.

Yet by the early 2000s, according to analysts, anywhere from 50 to 85 percent of CRM initiatives turned out to be costly failures. The AT&T Wireless debacle was just one example. A main reason analysts cited for the failures was that companies focused more on the short-term cost-saving promise of installing CRM technology than on implementing the original mind-set–changing and corporate culture–changing philosophy of integration and cooperation.

"CRM emphasized the importance of getting the sales, marketing and customer service organizations to work together," said Donna Fluss, president of New Jersey–based DMG Consulting, in 2004, "a goal that has continued to elude many companies." Fluss was vice president and director of research at Gartner, a major information technology consulting firm, before heading up her own consulting company. "The technology is just an enabler of the strategy. It is much more difficult to change people, processes and culture than a system. If organizations do not adapt their processes and people, the best technology in the world is not going to make a difference. Too many companies continue to miss this step."

In 2004, telecom industry analyst Jeff Kagan commented to the trade publication *Wireless Week* that the AT&T Wireless CRM failure illustrated how "we as customers don't mind automation if it makes our lives easier," but, he said, we do mind "if it only benefits the company at the expense of the user." The magazine continued, "Kagan also says the incident indicates that CRM systems will become more, not less, important in the years ahead. The technology will become tuned more finely."

Indeed, by 2006, the CRM industry had regained some of its ground, informed by past failures, and fueled by the ongoing need companies have to manage and make the pertinent information they collect about their customers accessible to key employees throughout a company. By that time, the industry was also having to factor in the new power that customers were gaining through the Internet. Dick Lee is a consultant and author of a 2006 study, "Customers Say What Companies Don't Want to Hear." He wrote in a trade publication, after the study came out, that "CRM has become a vestige of traditional, internally focused business—instead of the leading edge of customer centricity it promised to be."

Lee's study found that two factors had the greatest influence on customers' choices of where to buy: product quality and empowered employees. Lee joined a chorus of many others who had been calling for the CRM industry to move toward that focus or fade away. "CRM has to become less about consultants and software vendors maximizing sales of goods and services to companies—and much more focused on helping companies meet customer expectations. CRM has to be about changing the whole company, down to its roots—not about doing what's easy for companies."

Talk of impending doom periodically comes up within the CRM industry and is evident at the many industry trade shows and conventions. One, called destinationCRM, has been held for the past few years at the Marriott Marquis hotel in New York City's Times Square. The chairman of the conference, Barton Goldenberg, a consultant and *CRM* magazine columnist, gave a keynote address in 2007, "The State of the CRM Union." Putting the industry's present and future in its most positive light, he said the CRM industry was in what he called "a healthy transition." Then he outlined the past as he saw it. "We had a great ten- to 15-year period in the 80s and 90s, of 20, 30, and 40 percent growth rates. We became accustomed to this." He said the emergence of the Internet hurt the CRM industry, and "we went into actual negative growth rates in the early 2000s." Vendors went out of business. Others "tucked their tail between their legs and acknowledged that perhaps they had over-promised and under-delivered." He said the industry then came to see that CRM was not a technology business but was instead "about getting good policies in place that would drive the customer experience," and that the technology was just there to reinforce that. By 2004, he said, the growth began to pick up again.

Around that time, the Internet provided one boon to CRM, as access to CRM software and updates through the Web simplified the process of installing CRM systems in companies. Individual agents could download their own software and updates, simply and frequently, with software systems like Salesforce.com, one leader in such cutting-edge CRM technology. In fact, the ticker name for Salesforce on the New York Stock Exchange is CRM.

In recent years, the uses of CRM have gone beyond corporations into other areas where communicating with masses of people, particularly on the Internet, has become essential. For example, in the 2008 presidential election, all the campaigns had some sort of CRM technology on their websites. Most notably, Mitt Romney used Salesforce technology for fund-raising. But it was universally agreed that Barack Obama's campaign used CRM technology most effectively. The Obama campaign's record-breaking fundraising efforts and embrace of younger voters were at least partially fueled by its successful use of various types of CRM technology from many different vendors. In April 2008, a CRM trade magazine published an article, "Barack Obama: First CRM President?" noting the campaign's extensive use of CRM and how it would end up with information that could also keep voters informed and connected after the election. That same month, a CRM industry blogger, Brent Leary, posted a piece with the headline "Barack and the Audacity of CRM." Leary commented: "The 'C' in CRM can stand for many things, including: customer, client, congregation and of course

CONSTITUENT. But if most politicians didn't understand it before, I think they know it now after seeing Obama raise tens of millions of dollars via the web . . . thanks to Cash Relationship Management."

Since the 2003 AT&T Wireless CRM debacle, the need that spurred the rise of CRM has not gone away. A spokesperson for Gartner said in 2008, "Many buyers have experienced multiple CRM implementations and are more knowledgeable of their requirements for the next phase. Expect buyers to be more discriminating and focus on more targeted solutions moving forward."

But as Goldenberg pointed out in his keynote speech at the destinationCRM conference, the CRM industry has a public relations problem. "We still have a lot of people who think of CRM as an industry term that was big and important in the 90s, and has clearly dropped off the map and is being replaced with such things as 'customer experience,' and 'customer centricity,' et cetera. So what we have is this baggage that we have to deal with."

Goldenberg then turned to corporate culture issues that he said continue to affect the success of CRM. Without naming names, he cited the case of one of his clients as an example of the kinds of obstacles that persist when implementing CRM strategies. "There are four divisions that are trying to become one, and brand themselves as a unified offering. But the infighting between the four divisions—the differences in how they approach business between the four divisions—has led to some resistance. I look at this as a cultural barrier inside corporations. Different departments, and different individuals are not necessarily always willing to play along with the team. And that's a challenge that we'll have to work through."

Goldenberg said another cultural barrier "to the future of the industry" was the rise of new channels of communication between customers and companies on the Internet, often referred to as Web 2.0, especially social networking. "It's something that John Chambers, the head of Cisco Systems, says is the future of business. But it's something that a lot of corporations are not necessarily welcoming at this time." Goldenberg said when he goes to some in management and asks them what they are doing to prepare for new Internet opportunities, "a lot of the executives look at me in a strange way. So we also have a challenge to address there as we move through this transition."

That sentiment reverberated in an exhibit hall at the destination-CRM conference, where representatives from most of the cottage industries supporting the customer service industry had set up booths, including software vendors and consultants, as well as people selling call center equipment, customer satisfaction measuring services, and tools for data mining and call recording. None was promoting a product. Instead, each was "providing a solution." True to that lingo, the convention's exhibit hall was full of banners on booths variously trumpeting "speech solutions," "call center solutions," "software solutions," and "care solutions." No one said much about exactly what the problems were. Apparently those were questions better left for the conference itself. But a clue could be found in the trepidation about the future, resignation about the past, and odd dehumanization of the whole equation that was implicit in the message on one of the banners in the hall. It asked: "Are You Ready for a Care 2.0 World?"

It is tempting for customers to blame many of the problems with customer service on the billion-dollar call center industry and its surrounding cottage industries—often billion-dollar offshoots themselves—such as the CRM industry, outsourcers, and the speech technology industry. After all, the call center is the place where customers experience the bad encounters, and it is full of the people who seem to cause them. But most people who seriously examine and try to address the issues that customers have with customer service tend to believe trouble with contact centers and their supporting players is just a symptom of a larger management problem in corporations. The way companies view their call centers within their whole corporate infrastructure is what many point to as the greater culprit. The status of a call center within a company, or the lack of status, is widely seen as one of the best barometers of how a company truly regards and values its customers—and therefore of how good its customer service turns out to be.

Keith Dawson worked on the editorial end of customer service trade publications and websites for about two decades. In 1990 he started following the changes in the industry, and he wrote about them for an online industry news service he ran and also for *Call Center* magazine, where he was a senior writer and then editor-in-chief. In 2007, he left the magazine, which changed its name to *Customer Insight Management*, to become an analyst at the research and consulting firm Frost & Sullivan. Dawson was an English major in college and after graduation in the 1980s moved to New York to get into journalism. While he never thought he was going to become a pundit of the customer service industry, during his tenure in that realm he has developed some well-informed and relatively objective views on the challenges and who is to blame when it comes to customer service gone wrong.

He doesn't see the cottage industries as the problem. "They are responding to what these companies say they want. The real disconnect is not between the company and the cottage industry. It's between the company and the call center because call centers grew up on their own, without being required to give much feedback to the rest of the company about what the hell was going on in the customer base. They tell the corporate management what's going on in the call center: 'We're handling many, many calls and we're doing it well.'" But they have not traditionally been required to tell the company what is going on with their customers.

"The call center—the customer service infrastructure—is used to talking about customers through the framework of activity: How many calls did we answer? How long did the calls take? How long did the person wait on hold? End of story. So companies have blind spots. They don't see relationships between the big problems, and the small, individual problems that are happening among their customers. They don't see patterns that emerge—how individual problems add up to large-scale problems—often until it's too late. The people who hear the problems from the customers are not the ones who are also responsible for fixing them. And people aren't used to sharing different perspectives and viewpoints internally at companies, or to giving executives a holistic view of what is going on in dealing with the customer."

Dawson continues: "So the people who run the call centers go to the cottage industries and say, 'We need tools to help us answer calls faster'; or 'We need tools to make our agents more efficient'; or 'We need tools to control costs because that's what we are being measured on.' The company looks at the call center as a cost center. It looks at it as technical and operational. It doesn't look at it as strategic and revenue producing.

"The company doesn't see the call center as a place where human relationships are nurtured. Instead, the call center is traditionally seen as a place where interactions have to be managed," says Dawson. "Every interaction has a component that is easily measured. And every interaction also has a component that's impossible to parse, the human part of it, the nuance side of the interaction. Most companies reduce the customer relationship to its most easily parsable, which is the economic side. Then they just try to mitigate the most egregious, human side, such as an irate customer."

Yet Dawson also points out that as customers have been able to make their voices heard more publicly through the Internet and as those voices increasingly are driving buying decisions and the reputation of companies, the value of the contact center is growing in many companies. "Slowly, people in other departments, outside the contact center, are starting to see that the contact center is more than just a place where calls go to die."

Still, many in top management aren't there yet. And the measures they regard as paramount in contact centers still aren't always clearly aligned to what customers want and need. So as long as the people running the contact centers are meeting the cost-related goals of the top corporate management, they often believe they are doing their jobs well, even if customers do not share that belief. A study of North American contact center managers, agents, and their customers confirmed that. The 2005 Aspect Contact Center Satisfaction Index said, "Overall, contact center managers overestimate their performance, with 90 percent believing call centers meet or exceed consumer expectations." But among customers, 77 percent felt that way, with only 31 percent saying that contact centers had exceeded their expectations.

Those expectations have gotten lower as more people experience bad service. "Overall, contact center professionals are underestimating consumer expectations, while also not satisfying them. The gaps are greatest in the areas that we found most important to consumers. In particular, consumers want to speak directly with a person, with minimized wait times, and they don't want automation to impede personal interactions. Once connected with an agent, consumers expect to speak with someone who is knowledgeable, patient, and informed and who speaks clearly and intelligibly. Conversely, contact centers perceive criteria such as consistent company image and providing followup to make sure an issue is resolved as more important than consumers report."

In 2007, another study, this one by Accenture, compared the impressions of executives at global technology companies and their customers. "There's considerable disparity," the study reported, "between how companies and customers perceive the state of customer service, as well as in the service priorities expressed by each group. When looking at the service agendas for companies and their customers, it's apparent that the two groups aren't even close to being on the same page. For instance, consumers' two most important wishes when it comes to customer service are to have their problem solved completely and quickly. Conversely, the top service agenda item for companies—increasing revenue opportunities from service and support—is completely company-centric and has little to do with what customers want. Similarly, while only 11 percent of consumers said they value the ability to solve a problem themselves with online tools, nearly 40 percent of high-tech executives said increasing customer self-help capabilities via the Web was a top agenda item for them in the coming year (good enough for second place on their list). In sum, companies have a long way to go before their customer service capabilities provide the experience customers seek."

The Accenture study went on to say that "many companies delude themselves into thinking that their service experiences truly please their customers—when, in fact, customers as a group are more angry than ever about their encounters. While companies applaud themselves for the 'improvements' they have made in their service capabilities, their customers are desperately seeking—and often finding—alternative providers."

Accenture started to prescribe a remedy. "Creating a superior customer service experience requires companies to shift their thinking from service starts after the sale, to service sells the product; from service is elective—the customer has to ask for it—to service is embedded in the product or solution; and from service is operated as a cost center (with 'call avoidance' being a key metric) to service is operated as a profit center (with customer intimacy being a differentiating feature)."

Cormac Twomey is the director of UK operations for Denver-based call center outsourcing company TeleTech. He also oversees TeleTech's operations in the rest of Europe, the Middle East, and Africa. In his many years in global customer service management, at TeleTech and other companies worldwide, he has seen the industry evolve. Twomey has witnessed firsthand the gap between customer needs and corporate priorities. Like many others, he believes the problems in customer service come down to management and what is measured by managers. "Most organizations aren't tracking the important things. They've always tracked what I would call the inputs to the process: how much does it cost; how many calls did we get; how long were you on the phone for; all those kind of things. Whereas, in reality the important things to be measuring are the outputs of that process: How happy are my customers? How often do I get it right the first time? How many of my customers have chronic issues? How often do I fix those chronic issues?"

Twomey gives an example of a company in the United Kingdom that wanted to reduce costs by reducing the number of calls coming in. "So they invested quite heavily in improving their business processes—eradicating the breakages in the system. And they were really successful. But the hidden—or the intangible—effect of all of that was they made it easier to interact with them. So call volumes went up. The objective of the process was to reduce the calls. So the perception within this organization was that the process failed—even though, to their customers, it became an easier service to use. To them, this thing didn't work because they spent all this money and it didn't reduce call volumes. It doesn't matter that it improved the customer satisfaction. They weren't measuring that.

"It's a hearts-and-minds conversation as opposed to a financially driven one. The way we have industrialized the process and siloed it, looked for economy to scale, mass produced—for lack of a better word—creates an environment whereby we actually precipitate this type of behavior. So, fundamentally, how we structure our business is actually creating a lot of the issues. It's customer dissatisfaction and anger, and agent disenchantment—disempowerment. Everybody's unhappy. And if you talk to agents—one of the prevailing issues they have is the anger they have to deal with all the time. And that begets things like attrition and absence—another cost of the industry.

"By going industrial," Twomey continues, "we kind of lose sight that there's a person at the other end of the process, the customer. And behind the company facade, the agent is a human being as well. If the company has horrible policies which they're asking the agent to enforce, the agent is just a mouthpiece. So customers should be angry with the company, not the agent."

Twomey believes the changes have to happen at the highest corporate levels. "It needs leadership from the top. It's not something people in middle management or even senior management roles will take on, because you put your head above the parapet. It's becoming an executive level discussion," as well as a shareholder issue.

In the summer of 2007, Sprint sent out letters to about a thousand of its 53 million wireless phone subscribers at the time that read:

> Our records indicate that over the past year, we have received frequent calls from you regarding your billing or other general account information. While we have worked to resolve your issues and questions to the best of

our ability, the number of inquiries you have made during this time has led us to determine that we are unable to meet your current wireless needs.

Therefore, after careful consideration, the decision has been made to terminate your wireless service agreement. This will allow you to pursue and engage with another wireless carrier.

In effect, Sprint fired customers it felt were too needy, and therefore too expensive to serve. The letter went on to explain that the people at Sprint "understand that having to switch to another wireless carrier may be an inconvenience." So in order to help with the "transition" they said they would credit any remaining balances on the accounts and waive any termination fee.

Immediately, the story was all over the Internet. Many comments on all sorts of sites ran along the same lines:

> Unbelievable . . . Sprint canceling my service! Just got a letter and it's due to too many billing calls—which were due to THEIR MISTAKES. I've paid early every month for the past 7+ years! —Comment on a SprintUsers.com forum

> Damn. I wish Sprint would send me that letter. I would be thrilled! It is disturbing that they would do that, but it doesn't surprise me at all. It's a totally typical Sprint reaction. You will be better off in the long run. The service from Sprint has hit an all-time low and I have a feeling they will be losing a lot more customers with or without their "customer firings." —Comment on PlanetFeedback.com

> So all I have to do to get out of my Sprint contract is call them all the time? Count me in. —Comment on Gizmodo.com

Earlier in 2007, MSN Money had posted "The Customer Service Hall of Shame," in which it conducted a poll with Zogby International to find the companies whose service was "most often rated 'poor' by consumers." The results showed one company ranked "below all the rest: Sprint Nextel. A remarkable 40% of people who had an opinion of Sprint's customer service said it was poor."

A few months after MSN Money's verdict, in the summer of 2007, Sprint was rated last in customer service among wireless providers for the fourth consecutive time in an annual study by J. D. Power and Associates. A Sprint spokesperson responded to that ranking in an article in *BusinessWeek*: "We know that customer service is a challenge for us." The spokesperson said Sprint wanted to assure subscribers "that we are working really hard to enhance their customer experience. We really are committed. We've certainly enhanced certain tools for customers, like self-service tools, so they can get the answers to their questions quicker."

By the fall of 2007, Sprint shareholders couldn't ignore the losses in customers and stock value any longer, so they forced CEO Gary Forsee to resign. He had been hired away from his number two position at Bell South in 2003 to save the already sinking Sprint. His biggest accomplishment during his Sprint tenure was the 2005 acquisition of Nextel, which was proving to be a big failure.

In December 2007, Sprint named a new CEO, Dan Hesse, who had been CEO of AT&T Wireless back when it was still in Seattle in the 1990s, but before the final problems with customer service there. *BusinessWeek*'s Spencer E. Ante, who had written about his own problems with Sprint customer service a few months before, interviewed Hesse in 2008 after Hesse was in the job for two months. Ante reported that Hesse was "increasing investments in customer care, adding service technicians in retail stores, and reversing many management practices in customer call centers. Hesse is convinced that restoring Sprint's reputation with customers is the key to its future."

A former employee, who worked in a Temple, Texas, call center that had previously been run by Nextel, told Ante how a few months after the 2005 merger with Sprint, management changed. Everything in the call center became driven by numbers; even the employees' bathroom trips were counted. Her managers began monitoring what she was doing on her computer. At Nextel, which had a reputation for good customer service before the merger, she had been authorized to spend more time on a call if a particularly difficult customer problem arose. But after Sprint took over, managers pressured agents to keep their customer calls short, above all else. "They would micromanage us like children." She said she was fired in 2007 after taking time off when her father died.

Ante said that Forsee had overpromised on savings projections to analysts after the merger, which put pressure on everyone in the company to cut costs. Sprint's more quantitative management techniques were imported to Nextel. "In particular, call centers began to be measured and viewed primarily as cost centers, rather than opportunities for strategic advantage. Customer service ended up a secondary priority, say former executives." The corporate culture differences in the two companies were not well factored into the merger. Ante reported that Nextel board members told him how previously they had "talked at every board meeting about 'churn,' the industry term for the percentage of existing customers who leave each month. The directors felt churn was a good shorthand way to understand the quality of customer service, and they prided themselves on Nextel having the lowest in the industry. But after the merger closed, the combined board paid little attention to churn."

Hesse noticed a similar thing when he came to his first operations meeting just after taking over the company in late 2007. Customer service wasn't even on the agenda. Immediately he changed that and made it the first topic they talked about at every meeting. He discussed the switch in February 2008, on his first conference call with analysts after reporting dismal fourth-quarter results for 2007, including the loss of nearly 700,000 subscribers, or 2.3 percent of customers, in the last three months of the year. "Most important to our brand is delivering a good customer experience across all touch points. We have not done this. Improving the customer experience is job one at Sprint. We now begin every week's operations reviews with a discussion of the customer experience and a review of the specific projects we're putting in place."

One of Hesse's early moves at the helm was to cut four thousand jobs and close 125 underperforming retail locations. In his February 2008 *BusinessWeek* article, Ante concluded that many of Hesse's first actions, especially in regard to service, were focused on "reversing course on several fronts, hoping to salvage what he can from the troubled merger. He and his lieutenants aren't eliminating the quantitative approach entirely, but they're changing many of the old metrics to now emphasize service over efficiency." So instead of measuring how long each call took, they adopted Nextel's original approach of measuring whether a caller's problems are resolved on the first call, even if the call takes longer. In the industry, that is called "first call resolution," and Hesse said it was becoming Sprint's "number one performance metric."

But the fallout from the past was not over yet. Just after the 2007 fourth-quarter earnings were released, the final details of former CEO Gary Forsee's departure were reported. In accordance with the agreement Forsee made on being hired, it was announced in spring 2008 that his total compensation in 2007, including severance from Sprint, was $40 million.

In Sprint's hometown of Kansas City, the details of Forsee's severance provoked immediate outrage. The town was still reeling from Hesse's recent job cuts in January 2008, as well as from cuts in early 2007 when Sprint, under Forsee's management, had laid off at least five thousand workers, many of them from customer service, because the company was losing money. Diane Stafford, a workplace columnist for the *Kansas City Star*, said in her blog just after Forsee's severance was announced, "The latest disclosure, from Sprint Nextel, is just another in a long line of inexplicable CEO pay packages. In heaven's name: How much is enough? And how many of the former Sprint Nextel workers that I meet at job loss support groups might still have their comparatively puny paychecks if executive pay wasn't so outlandishly excessive? The disparity overwhelms me."

Stafford's readers agreed in comments on her blog. "Absolutely inexcusable," said one. "We don't reward failure at any level of employment . . . except the executive level. Here we have a person who history has judged to be unqualified for the job, yet he has no shame in accepting payment for failure that ethical business leaders would be embarrassed to receive for success. To say the system is broken and needs overhaul is to put it mildly."

Another reader, who said she was a former Sprint employee, added, "The daily fear for their livelihoods that Sprint employees live with is palpable as one walks across the Sprint campus. This latest news revealing Forsee's platinum parachute unquestionably adds insult to injury to the thousands of hard-working Sprint employees who were informed late last year that they would be receiving neither annual raises nor bonuses in the foreseeable future."

And another reader said, "It's immoral and absolutely obscene for any one person to be paid so much—especially when he drives the company into the ditch. And don't call it 'compensation'—there's no way Forsee (or any of his predecessors) did enough to EARN what they're being given. This is the main reason I will NEVER do business with Sprint. Forsee should have to not only forfeit his Golden Parachute, but also pay back all that he has collected. Further, the Board of Directors should be held financially accountable for such ridiculous actions. Sprint and other companies that run as Sprint does are setting this society up for class wars. It's disgusting!"

A March 2008 editorial in the *Kansas City Star* echoed those sentiments. "Talk about eye-popping. Gary Forsee's compensation from Sprint Nextel last year came to a cool $40 million. What's wrong with this picture? Forsee was forced out last October amid mounting displeasure from shareholders and board members. Sprint's merger with Nextel has failed to deliver many of the hoped-for synergies. The company is hemorrhaging customers and its stock price has plummeted by nearly 65 percent since last fall."

In April 2008, an ABC News *Nightline* story about executive pay started out saying, "CEOs have advantages that the average American worker does not, that might allow them to get paid for failure." The story pointed to figures showing that in 1980, CEO pay averaged forty times that of an average worker. By 2008, CEO pay was up to more than four hundred times that of the average worker. Then the story turned to Sprint. "When Gary Forsee, the CEO of Sprint, was fired he got $40 million, an $84,000-a-month pension for life." And he got help finding a $400,000-a-year job as the president of the University of Missouri. The *Nightline* story continued: "Critics say that all too often, boards of directors, which set CEO pay, are filled with the CEO's cronies."

Hesse had his work cut out for him after taking over the helm of Sprint. In addition to ironing out all the fallout from Forsee's tenure and the corporate culture gap with Nextel, technical considerations were getting in the way of change. Not only were the driving technologies on the Sprint and Nextel networks different, causing problems for technicians, but the billing systems were different, so agents often had to navigate between at least two separate systems when handling customers. In the May 2008 earnings conference call for the first quarter of the year, Hesse said, "The conversion to a single billing system" had just been completed, "and we are getting positive feedback from the front lines on how using one system is making it easier to care for our customers."

In that conference call with analysts, Hesse kept returning to the issue of customer churn. "Of all of the metrics that govern this business, churn is by far the most important. Because of the customer experience we provided last year, churn is accelerating. As you may know, we have performed poorly in customer surveys that were taken last year. This has hurt our brand. We have done much to improve the network and [customer] care issues which drive customer dissatisfaction, but there is much more that still needs to be done. We have rolled out a unified company culture which is focused, among other things, on improving the customer experience, creating a sense of urgency, and increasing accountability. There is also a lag period between the time when we make improvements and when the marketplace recognizes these improvements. This can take many quarters. It takes hard work and time to regain a reputation."

—⁓—

Hundreds of the people who design and build the automated phone systems that so many customers have come to revile settled into a large banquet hall at the Marriott Marquis Hotel in the heart of Times Square in New York City. These main players in the speech technology industry were gathering for the opening morning of their largest annual conference, SpeechTEK. The three-day meeting was sponsored by Information Today, which owns the trade magazines *Speech Technology* and *CRM* magazine. And SpeechTEK was taking place simultaneously with the destinationCRM conference, the smaller yearly gathering of CRM professionals. That meant that the two conferences shared some resources, including the opening morning's keynote speaker, Malcolm Gladwell, a *New Yorker* contributor and the bestselling author of *The Tipping Point, Blink*, and *Outliers*. Gladwell, a particularly popular speaker at business conventions, has spoken to many gatherings of customer service professionals, including groups such as this with members who work in the cottage industries that support the customer service industry. His talk on this day was entitled "Speech Technology at the Tipping Point."

Gladwell started with the story of how broadcasting pioneer David Sarnoff's airing of one of the first major radio sportscasts, a 1921 prizefight, showed the world that this new technology, radio, had the potential to be used in innovative ways by delivering something other than just news. Gladwell drew a parallel to the SpeechTEK and destination-CRM audience's challenge of proving the utility and value of their new technology, speech recognition systems and CRM software, to potential users in the general public today.

Then Gladwell talked about Paul Revere and the fact that people acted on his message that the British were coming because Revere was such a trusted messenger or, as Gladwell called him, a connector. "Now I think that social role, the role played by the connector, is extraordinarily important in the world we live in now. Because we live in a world that is marked by the rise of social isolation."

Relating it all to people in the meeting hall, he said, "When you construct these speech technology systems, when you think about how to reach out and connect with your customers, you need to ask yourself a very basic question. And that is, 'Am I feeding into social isolation or am I combating social isolation?' If you are perceived by your customers as linking them and connecting them in a real way, you will succeed because you will be answering a deeply felt psychological need of the American public right now. If you are seen by them as enhancing social isolation, as preventing them from making that connection, you will not succeed. Because you will be feeding into one of the most powerful and divisive psychological circumstances of the present day."

In a broad sense, Gladwell touched on an issue that seems to plague many in the cottage industries that surround customer service. Both SpeechTEK and destinationCRM conventioneers, in many of their breakout sessions after the keynote address, kept referring to their public relations problem—with their buyers in corporations and with customers at the other end of a customer service line. But the convention goers displayed a surprisingly passionate devotion to overcoming the bad rap and getting their work right. At SpeechTEK in particular, that fervor made many of the sessions livelier than might be expected at a typical industry convention.

One hour-long panel, "Is Paul English Right?" focused on English's GetHuman efforts to thwart the speech technology industry by listing on his website the codes for avoiding the IVR systems these Speech-TEK attendees design and reaching human operators at most large companies. English had been the keynote speaker at SpeechTEK the year before, and his campaign was still a hot topic. When English, Nuance Communications, and Microsoft came up with the GetHuman standards in late 2006, many in the industry were skeptical, and the standards were not adopted widely.

One of the panelists, Michael Zirngibl, the CEO of leading IVR application developer Angel.com, said he agreed in principle with English's idea of more thoughtful design of IVR systems, but didn't take too kindly to his tactics. Zirngibl brought up a point from Gladwell's keynote speech to bolster his argument. "When Malcolm Gladwell was asked by an audience member, 'What can we do to create this idea of ours that automation is good?' Gladwell answered, 'Well, I don't have really specific recommendations but I think you, as an industry, need to educate the consumers to become more patient.' Now think about this," said Zirngibl, "the entire notion of GetHuman.com was, 'Don't be patient. Hit the zero button right away. Do not even listen to the first prompt.' I think that is very dangerous because that takes away a lot of the business benefits of using automation. If somebody calls an 800 number to get customer service and hits zero in the first second, it costs you a lot of money. You have no benefit out of it; the customer doesn't get any benefit out of it. It's routed to a generic queue. He's going to wait even longer. He gets even more frustrated. Zeroing out is not the solution to the problem."

Zirngibl continued, "There's probably not a single person in this room who will disagree with the GetHuman standard. It is fantastic. If every IVR system could follow the GetHuman standard, the world would be a better place. But it's idealistic; it's not reality."

An audience member chimed in. "The very systems that are the poorest—the hardest to get out of—are the ones that are probably the worst built and the worst designed. And that's a function of somebody—an organization—that didn't provide enough budget. Or maybe it's older technology. Maybe it hasn't provided all of the options that are available in today's world. If one system is bad, all of a sudden everybody's complaining about that one system. There could be a lot of really good systems out there, but we're not hearing about those nearly so much. I just happen to believe that we, as a collective group in this industry, have to proselytize why self-service is a good thing. Because if we aren't doing that, then those complainers are going to drown out the benefits that this technology can provide."

Zirngibl responded. "I think we have a tremendous PR problem. It has had a negative impact on our chances, as an industry, to be successful in providing better systems."

Another panelist, Walter Rolandi, a consultant on IVR design who was also involved in the creation of GetHuman, mentioned the public relations problem too. As evidence, he cited the many parodies of the industry in the mainstream media, including the *Saturday Night Live* skit making fun of Amtrak Julie. "When an industry or its products become the fodder of jokes and spoofing like this, you've got to wonder if everything is okay."

Rolandi said many people's sense of a lack of control and choice are at the root of their objections to IVR systems. "Based on my personal experience, and observing thousands of these calls over the years, I'm saying give them a choice. We are not against automation. Anytime you can do something with a machine faster than you can do it with a person, they're going to prefer to do it with automation. It's that simple. But let them be the one who decides whether or not they need a person. Let them be the decision maker. Without giving people choices, you take away some degree of their dignity."

Throughout the SpeechTEK conference, there were a lot of specifics about how to perfect the systems and what could be done to address negative public perceptions of them. In one session, "Worst Practices," Jason Tepper, of Cisco's contact center business unit, said: "You may not realize it, but you're being really tough on your callers. It's time to turn the tides a bit. It's time to make things simpler for your customer. It's time to get into their shoes and understand the caller experience. Don't ask them to repeat themselves. Give them some choices. Handle errors courteously. Don't have robotic prompts repeating themselves over and over again. Don't disconnect on errors. That's just unacceptable. As an industry—let's not make things so complex. Let's get out of our world of looking at it from the business point of view and start getting into the shoes of our customer."

—⁂—

In the 1985 book *Service America: Doing Business in the New Economy*, business consultants Karl Albrecht and Ron Zemke argued that the shift from a manufacturing to a service economy would make an emphasis on customer service more essential to success in business:

Organizations concerned with honing a competitive edge for the 1980s, 90s, and beyond must develop two new capacities. The first is the ability to think strategically about service and to build a strong service orientation around and into the vision of their strategic future. The second capacity, which is perhaps more difficult to develop, is the ability to effectively and efficiently manage the design, development, and delivery of a service.

In our view, the ability to manage the production and delivery of a service differs from the ability to manage the production and delivery of a commodity. It requires a familiarity with the idea of an intangible having economic value, and a deftness in conceptualizing intangible outcomes. It requires a tolerance for ambiguity, an ease in dealing with lack of direct control over every key process, and a finely tuned appreciation of the notion that the organization is equally dependent on soft (or people-related) skills and hard (or production-related) skills. Last but not least, it requires a tolerance for—perhaps even an enjoyment of—sudden and sometimes dramatic change. The only constant in service is change.

In their book's second chapter, "What We Can Learn About Service from Scandinavia," Albrecht and Zemke turned to Sweden, which they referred to as a bellwether country because of a business approach developed there called service management. Pointing to the dramatic turnaround of SAS, the Swedish airline company, as a template, they outlined the strategy that was "characterized by an almost obsessive commitment to managing the customer's experience at all points in the cycle of service." They said that "word spread" in the region "of this new approach to the management of service organizations, and a new business theory was born: service management. Books, articles, master's theses, doctoral dissertations, and seminars began to appear. Service management was the new wave in Scandinavia. The term and the concept became so popular" that Scandinavian business schools began offering concentrations in it. Albrecht and Zemke urged American companies to heed the idea. Many did, for a while.

More than twenty years later, Karl Albrecht reflected on that time on his website. Albrecht said that in the mid-1980s, "The business world embraced the concept of service management with remarkable enthusiasm." It seemed at the time that everyone was "making 'customer focus' a critical and permanent part of Western management thinking. Even the established management gurus, who had made their names on other topics, were moved to declare the primacy of customer value. Yet the wave didn't last. The service revolution got hijacked somewhere along the road to victory. Like most other management movements before it, customer focus became the object of intense flirtation by many firms, but ultimately the infatuation faded."

Albrecht, who is now also called a "futurist" in addition to being a consultant, gave a hindsight perspective on the industry's dalliance in the 1980s with the Swedish model: "The service revolution Ron Zemke and I predicted so confidently in our book published in 1985 has turned out to be a service evolution, and a slow one at that. Looking beyond all the slogans, campaigns, and hoopla we've been through, it seems that real lasting change in Western management practice has been agonizingly slow."

Cormac Twomey, of TeleTech in the United Kingdom, agrees that changes have been slow. "Rome wasn't built in a day. These things are hard. And as consumers, we're kind of difficult. We're willful and whimsical and hard to pin down, and we move around. And these organizations are big beasts. They're like supertankers; they take a couple of days to turn. You know, it's not as if you can spin on a top and away you go.

"But the customer *does* care about how they're being treated. When they're interacting with companies, whether it's face-to-face, over the phone, via e-mail, or whatever the case may be, the tone of the conversation and the impact that makes on the person is critical, and it's an absolutely personal thing. You cannot measure the customer's perception of that by making assumptions. You have to listen to the customer and understand what they mean.

"Those things are now beginning to be seen as very important. And that means the equation is now changing. So what organizations are measuring now is moving away from, 'How much is it costing to service a customer?' to 'What's a customer's perception of the service?' The challenge which a lot of organizations are facing today is: How do I create that feeling of ownership again, at the individual level for a customer, without disenfranchising the agent, and without losing some of the advantages of scale that I have? Brands around the world are beginning to see that there has to be a different way to play this game."

Keith Dawson, former editor of *Call Center* magazine and senior analyst at Frost & Sullivan, sees one change in the way companies are looking at the people who run call centers. "If you go back to 1990, when I first started talking about this and observing it, the job of a person running a call center was as deeply enmeshed with managing the technology as it was with managing the people, if not more so. The people who were managing contact centers tended to come out of telecom, or came up from being an agent supervisor. And in neither case were they particularly highly regarded by overall corporate management. I mean, you don't pick your CEO from the head of the call center. You pick somebody from sales management, or you pick somebody from a lot of other channels, but the call center wasn't one of them.

"During the last ten to fifteen years, I've seen a change in the kind of person who's interested in managing contact centers. They're no longer technology managers, exclusively. It is often where they come from, but it's not where they succeed and move up. Those who are making higher profiles for themselves are younger, but also much more diverse. I see a lot more racial, ethnic, and gender diversity in contact center management than I used to.

"For example, there have always been a lot of women in contact centers. It was always common to see women in real positions of authority in contact centers. But the centers themselves were somewhat marginalized. Now, I'm seeing a lot more women at much higher levels than I used to, and the centers are less marginalized. And they are headed by women who themselves are less marginalized. The call center managers have become much more creative actors within their companies."

Dawson continues: "You don't have to be a technician to run a contact center anymore. What you have to be is a much better manager of human resources, of customer issues, of communications issues. If you can get the marketing department and the finance department to understand the value of the contact center, then the contact center manager will become more highly appreciated as well.

"So a smart manager will go to other executives and say, 'Well, yes, we've been calculating all this activity-based stuff, and we've been very good at it and we're the most finely honed machine functioning at peak efficiency,' which they really are. When you look at call centers, they are perfectly tuned machines. Yet the successful, interesting contact center manager is one who can say, 'But look beyond these activity metrics. Because we're the contact center, we also happen to know that customers are unhappy because of X, Y, and Z.' Or that 'the customers who are unhappy because of X, Y, and Z go to our competitors A, B, and C.'"

Dawson believes that contact center managers are "starting to show that they can explain deeper patterns of customer behavior to people in other parts of the company who think they understand deeper patterns of customer behavior because they have marketing departments and focus groups. That's why we're starting to see customer satisfaction and first-call-resolution metrics becoming more important. Other parts of the company are starting to look at the call center as one of the sources of more subtle complex patterns of information, which can be translated into more nuanced meaning and understanding, and therefore can lead to prescriptions for action."

—⚏—

The way Beth Thomas-Kim sees it, customer service managers traditionally have been stuck in or relegated to such fallow roles inside most companies that everyone—the company, its customers, the managers, and their workers—has missed out on the call center's potential for making things better all around. But Thomas-Kim, the head of consumer services at Nestlé USA and president of the Society of Consumer Affairs Professionals (SOCAP), feels it is up to her and her colleagues to change that, and not to continue letting the opportunities pass everyone by.

"We have been too passive," Thomas-Kim says. "We are defined by the four walls of our contact center, and we wait for customers to come and talk to us. That's a very controlled environment, where we can say we're open and available to take your call at certain hours." But she notes that customers have found other outlets for getting information about the company, such as social networks. And by not being more proactive about that too, she says companies are missing another opportunity. "We have to blow out the four walls of our contact center and realize this is not the only way. Now companies need to go out there and find out where customers are, to connect with them where they're talking, and try to address their issues."

Thomas-Kim is referred to as the head of "consumer affairs" instead of "customer service" because she works at a consumer goods manufacturer, which uses lingo different from that of other kinds of companies. Nestlé USA's "customers" are those who buy the products directly from Nestlé to sell in their own grocery stores and other venues. The people who buy their products from those stores and use them are their "consumers." But Thomas-Kim recognizes that whatever the name for her work within her company's sector of the economy, her own success and status defy conventional career path wisdom. They also qualify her to give a history lesson on how customer service, or consumer affairs, has evolved and why it hasn't always put the customer at the center of the equation. "Oftentimes companies will promote the receptionist—and by the way, I came from a receptionist background so I'm not speaking out of turn here. But here's the problem. If these individuals have grown up with the company, and they've done a good job and kept the complainers out of the hair of the management—which, historically, has been their role—then that person is not necessarily able to go sit down in front of an executive. They are not the ones to make a case, and communicate on a true business level, and get executives to see the missed value, the missed potential. A big miss right now, in our profession as customer service people, is sometimes we don't think big enough, broadly enough, in the true business sense. We've been so marginalized for so long that it sort of bred itself in."

But no matter whether customer service managers get the message across to top management, Thomas-Kim says that eventually companies will have to recognize the value of their function and bond it more closely to other corporate functions: "Think about who we're talking to and the rich opportunity to learn and to connect." At Nestlé USA, Thomas-Kim's staff talks to about 880,000 callers each year. From Baby Ruth bars to Coffee-Mate, to Alpo, to Lean Cuisine, each product has a toll-free number printed on its package. Thomas-Kim says that only a "minuscule number" of those calls are people calling with problems. The majority are calling with questions, or comments, or asking for recipes. But agents get a valuable glimpse at how customers feel and think about the company's products. That is why Thomas-Kim has worked hard to make sure the rest of the company understands the resonance of the information her team gathers.

"We should absolutely be aligned with quality assurance," she says, "because we should be able to give them actionable information, so they can deliver a better product. We should be aligned with marketing because this is an incredibly important touch point with the consumers. We're talking to them. We're listening to them. We're hearing what they have to say. We hear how they are responding emotionally to the products. We should be aligned with the PR department because it's important for us to understand what's happening in the external world, the media world, that might be driving consumers to contact us with questions. All of this falls on our shoulders. In my group, we have to understand how manufacturing lines work, and supply chain logistics, and legal, and regulatory. It's a fabulous place to learn about the workings of a company. You have to know it all."

When Thomas-Kim first came to Nestlé USA, she said, there was not much interaction between customer service and other departments. "Marketing would launch a promotion, and we would have no knowledge of it. And then suddenly we would start getting calls from consumers. We looked like we didn't know what we were doing. And that had to stop." So Thomas-Kim and her team "started to connect with, and have lunch with, people in the marketing organization. And we would sit down and ask: 'Tell me what you do. Explain to me your biggest challenges.' We got to know them as people instead of them and us. And that changed everything."

While customer service is concerned with how agents interact with customers as representatives of the company, it is equally important for managers to be concerned with how agents and the department interact on behalf of the customers with other parts of the company, particularly with the marketing department. That is especially true now, says Thomas-Kim, as the dynamics of the customer-company equation are changing.

"I do feel that the power has shifted to the consumer. The shotgun marketing blasts of the past are no longer effective. And consumers are using the Internet to amplify their voice and to connect with others. And it has shifted the balance of power. Suddenly companies are reeling from this overnight change and they're now scrambling to figure out, 'How the heck do I respond to this?' Ultimately companies are recognizing that the consumer of the fifties is gone. There used to be three channels, and you could put your commercial on the television and the majority of the households in the United States saw it. And consumers were naïve at that point, and they were willing to listen to the message and then go out and buy the product.

"Well, the world has exploded and it's incredibly complicated and consumers recognize that they are individuals—first and foremost—and they want to be treated like an individual. But business has squeezed that pipeline so tightly in order to try and be more efficient and more cost effective—that consumers have just gone elsewhere to be heard. The consumer said, 'I don't need to be talking to you. I can get just as much satisfaction by going out and talking to other people on the Web who are willing to empathize with me and validate my thinking.' Well, that creates an enormous challenge for companies—one that everyone's struggling to try and figure out."

That could just be history repeating itself. Thomas-Kim points out that a similar phenomenon happened when 800 numbers first became a part of product packaging in the 1970s, thus prompting the creation of call centers to answer consumer questions. It took another decade or more for all consumer product manufacturers to fall in line. And Nestlé didn't offer toll-free numbers on all of its products until 1992. So Thomas-Kim recognizes that new technology has always had a way of changing the playing field every few years. "When e-mail suddenly became this new communication channel, which technically wasn't that long ago, companies were terrified. Like, 'Oh, my God. We're going to actually have to write things down and there will be a record of them.' We used to have letters. So the legal department was typically part of the process of reviewing all of the outbound letters to make sure everything was properly worded. Suddenly e-mail came and just blew that process out of the water. Companies were trying desperately to operationalize this new communication channel. They were slow to respond. Companies needed to absorb this as a new way of communicating.

"But technology has been going at bullet-speed forward, and we've just figured out how to get on top of e-mail. Now, blogging and text messaging, social networks, these are all the new e-mails. And by the way, there are companies out there that still don't offer e-mail, which is mind-bending. They're trying to control the environment. What they don't realize is, you've got to just move forward. You cannot remain where you are because if you stay where you are, life will pass you by. You can't stay static. You have to continuously innovate. You've got to continuously grow."

That, she says, is where contact centers come in. "Now, companies are saying, 'Whoa. The world has changed. My advertising strategy for putting a commercial on television is not having the same impact as it always had. And I now need to start to pay very close attention to our consumers.' Well, when this all happened, I raised my hand and said, 'Hi, everyone. Guess who I'm talking to? I'm talking to your customers every day.' So now marketing and advertising recognize this is a very rich environment. Customer service has always been marketing. It's just now the marketing people are beginning to see it. It has never been really used or recognized in that way. But the integration is happening more and more now."

As the business world moves forward in this new landscape, Thomas-Kim thinks executives "need to stop hiding behind the image of the company. They need to put themselves out there. There needs to be accountability. They need to rebuild trust and credibility and create transparency. If you don't do that, your competitor will. So it's the only way to survive. Ultimately the company-customer relationship is like a human relationship between any two people. You have to demonstrate your interest in them. You've got to nurture that relationship. Both sides have to be open and honest, and accepting, and willing to make changes as a result. There are going to be some companies that are going to be faster to adapt to that, that are going to be better at it than others. But fundamentally that's the direction we're going. And that's the direction we should go."

Keith Dawson, of Frost & Sullivan, sees a larger challenge in the relationship between customers and companies, having to do with the way we as customers view and treat those who serve us in our culture. "If you're going to somebody about a problem that you're having, or something that you want, you have to recognize their fundamental humanity. You have to recognize that they are consumers just like you, that they are workers just like you, that they are family members just like you are. That's step one. And that's where we have a problem as a culture. There's something fundamental in our culture that removes us from understanding or empathizing with the basic humanity of those who serve us. It's epidemic and it's beyond call centers, but call centers amplify it. And paradoxically, part of call center training is to teach people to be a paragon of empathy, in the face of people who are remarkably unempathetic."

Cormac Twomey of TeleTech UK says that equation works both ways. "The reality is we all know things don't work. We'd all love everything to be perfect. But how a company deals with me, as a customer, when it's not perfect is really important. It's about respect and empathy. And respect covers many things. Have respect for my time. Have respect for my life. In your tone, have respect for the fact that this is an issue for me, and by giving me the right person to fix it. Respect my dignity. Things are going to break. But what makes or breaks the relationship is what are you thinking about when a thing goes wrong? Are you thinking about your customers or are you thinking about yourself?

"To empathize is quite a fundamental change for companies. And perhaps some of the principles that are perceived as somewhat old-fashioned are a good starting point for them. People are deriding the lack of manners. People deride the lack of patience and respect. Maybe those are good places to start. How can we blend some of those old-fashioned principles with some modern-day working practices? Because then, it might work for us all."

Keith Dawson says the way a company treats its customers is closely aligned to how it treats its employees. "The agent is the pivot point. If a company is sympathetic, and human, and empathizes with its agents, then the agents will likely be the same with customers. Whereas, if a company treats their agents like a group of automatons, the agents will turn around and treat their customers in kind."

A paragraph from the 2007 Accenture study of executives in high-tech industries confirmed what Dawson, Twomey, and Thomas-Kim are seeing evolve in the way the art and science of customer service are applied in our world, and in the way some forward-thinking companies are putting this newly valued tool into practice for the benefit of all sides: "It's time for companies to recognize the critical role that service plays. Breaking out of the customer service morass requires an entirely new approach to designing, building and sustaining customer support and service. All the incremental improvement in the world won't create the capabilities necessary to keep customers in the fold in today's hyper-competitive environment. As we have seen time and again, service often spells the difference between mediocre companies, poor performers and market leaders. One could argue that many, if not most companies are failing the service test today. This is unfortunate because the tools, approaches and resources exist today for companies to create world-class customer service that lives up to customers' expectations while remaining fiscally sensible. Such capabilities may be considered by many companies to be an option today. But they will be a competitive necessity tomorrow—especially for those organizations seeking to build enduring customer loyalty and achieve high performance in an ever-changing world."

8.   Absolutely, Positively

Sheila Harrell began working as a part-time customer service agent at a Memphis Federal Express counter in 1979, when the express package delivery company was eight years old. In those days, the company still went by its longer, original name, not by the current, more succinct FedEx, which has also become a verb. And back then, the company's customer service agents performed myriad functions, the most public of which was receiving packages dropped off by customers at one of their "stations." Before today's multiple drop-off points, there was just one station in each of the cities the company served—usually located at or near the airport.

But Harrell's customer service agent job didn't end at the front counter. "I would take in a package, then run back and answer the phone—and I mean literally answer the old-fashioned phone—and accept a pick-up order. Then I might even go around the corner—same office—get on the radio, and become a dispatcher and relay the order to a courier, who would be out in the city going to various places picking up. After the cut-off time in each market, couriers would come back. And then we would all load the packages onto the plane. Before long, that little facility could not maintain all the packages that we had coming in."

So the company began to separate the various functions that Harrell and other early customer service agents performed. "It came down to efficiency," said Harrell, who had moved to Memphis, FedEx's hometown, with a degree in education from Mississippi University for Women. She came to get her master's degree in business at Memphis

State University. The part-time customer service job was merely meant to bring in extra money as she studied. But after her first six months on the job, she quit her graduate work and signed on full time. Her regional manager heard she had an education degree and tapped her to become one of the first employee trainers: "Our job was to help build out the network of couriers, service agents, management folks. So I trained various positions. Then one day, management decided it would be more efficient, both for customers and for FedEx, to merge all the calls coming in. That would take the work off of those stations, so that they could do the pickup and delivery, and handle walk-in customers more effectively. Call centers were becoming in vogue then, and we were one of the early adapters."

In 1981, Harrell began training call center agents in the first Federal Express call center, located in an office building on a street full of car dealerships in suburban Memphis. When that first center opened, Harrell says, "I do remember, as a trainer, walking around to the agents and asking, 'Have you got any calls yet?' We couldn't wait. Then somebody would shout out, 'Got one!' They would raise their hand, 'I got one, I got one.' And we would all come running to listen in. It was fun, because this was a new phenomenon in U.S. history." The novelty didn't last long. By the end of the first week, Harrell says, the Memphis call center was handling one thousand calls a day. By the end of that year, two more call centers opened—one in Somerset, New Jersey, and one in Sacramento, California—and approximately 175 reps were handling about twenty thousand calls a day. "We began to open more call centers because the volume was growing, and we needed to spread our staffing around so we could have contingency planning."

While telephone and computer communication had evolved, personal computers had not taken hold yet. The rise of cell phones and the Internet were at least a decade or two away. But the widespread use of toll-free numbers and mainframe computers made call centers possible. "The world was going through an evolution with technology and telecommunications at that time. We were not yet global, but we were becoming more nationalized."

At the start, customers, who were used to speaking to customer service agents in their own town, complained. "Because back then it was the first time you no longer spoke to Jane, who worked in the local station. Customers would say, 'But I liked talking to Jane. What happened to Jane?' So it was an education process for the customer, that now you're going to get Sheila in the call center. You no longer get Jane, who was in the station. But don't worry, I will take care of you—Sheila, the call center rep, will take care of you."

One of the first big issues the Memphis call center encountered, says Harrell, is that people from other parts of the country did not like talking to people from the South, partly because they didn't trust southerners to be efficient. Then when the call centers opened in New Jersey and Sacramento, people from the South didn't like talking to northerners (or Californians), because they didn't consider them to be polite enough.

Of course, today FedEx's customer service is a highly sophisticated, massive operation. In 2009, the company averaged 7.5 million shipments worldwide per day. The call centers handled about 650,000 calls per day. Seventy percent of those were fielded by the fifty-three company-run contact centers around the world, with twenty of those in the United States. Another 28 to 30 percent of the calls were handled at outsourced call centers.

FedEx's website now fulfills many of the basic functions that used to be handled by call center agents. The company pioneered package tracking in the 1980s, allowing customers to call in and find out where their packages were. Making the shipping process transparent to customers was a revolutionary concept at the time. Then in 1994, as the Internet was just becoming ubiquitous, customers could begin to track their own packages online. According to FedEx, in 2007, more than 3 million package tracking requests were handled online daily. And 15 million packages were shipped monthly using company-supplied software that allows account holders to complete shipments through the website without ever speaking to anyone in a call center.

Harrell has been part of the customer service evolution at FedEx every step of the way. She never finished her business master's degree because she was too busy working her way up the Fortune 100 company's executive ladder. By the mid-1990s, she had become head of global strategic planning for customer service. "There was so much opportunity to start looking at how we could change the call centers. For instance, we were doing online tracking, but at that point, it was run as a separate channel from the call center. So what if we could figure out a way to better integrate those channels and grow into the next millennium? We were sitting at a pivotal point to change the call center as it was going more global."

Around the same time—the mid- to late 1990s—FedEx began working on a customer relationship management strategy. "CRM was the buzzword," says Harrell. "Everybody was doing it. And it became interesting for sales and marketing too. Customer relationship management said we all need the same data about the customer. But the technology that was out there at that time was nowhere near what we needed as an enterprise. We knew we couldn't build the tool internally." So they turned to outside vendors to custom-build their early CRM tools. "Thank goodness, we thought through CRM before we implemented anything."

Always inherent in the strategy was a consideration of the needs of the customer. "We held a customer summit, in 1999 I believe, chaired by all the senior officers and the key players on the special team that worked on the CRM implementation. We listened to the customers. But we also became customers. As a part of this summit, each group was given various responsibilities and tasks to do. Some were calling the call center and asking for various capabilities. Some were to go on the Web and see the disconnects. And, yes, it did raise a lot of emotion— excitement, to-dos. Rightly so—that's what it was designed to do.

"We also brought in customers, small and medium," said Harrell, "and we talked with them about their ideas for the future. And it always came back to one thing: what we call 'one and done.' Once that FedEx brand goes on a company, or goes on a van, or is with that rep, there's an expectation that it's handled. I don't want to be passed around. I don't want to fill out more than one form. Just like the package is handled. Whatever it is, it's handled.

"So the question became: 'How can we do that within our cost structure?' Because customers in this environment, with fuel going at the price it's going, they're not really willing to continue to let us add expense. But more importantly, they really just want service. Because the customer is very, very busy. How do we have a balanced economic strategy within FedEx, and better serve the customer—in every channel? We need to know their preferences, know all the events that could happen to them, and be more proactive in those events. And we have to let them be the decision maker. And do it in the most time-efficient and cost-efficient manner possible. Because that's what the customers have said they are expecting. That's what I expect when I interact with a company. FedEx started the express business with 'absolutely, positively overnight.' You get that—we get that—it's simple. High expectations is the principle upon which FedEx was founded. That is our culture."

But managing those high expectations is always a balancing act, and it is where Harrell says many companies fall short today. "Customers are expecting companies to know everything about them, on every little infrastructure within the company—all the channels that are incorporated in customer service: IVR, the Web, texting, whatever new thing comes out, and telephone. Companies are having difficulty getting to all this at one time—because of time, energy, and just capacity, money. You're dealing with all the dynamics of changing out your infrastructures for communicating with customers, and it's global. Yet you've also got to keep your products going, and keep changing and enhancing them. It's very, very difficult. I am sympathetic to that. But I believe it starts at the very top."

Harrell says that "customer service in the good companies is viewed as an integral part of the business. It is the information hub for the company. And if you believe that, and you fund it accordingly, give it a voice accordingly, it will drive for you. Where customer service fails is when it's viewed as back office. Emphasis is put on product development, marketing, sales. And customer service is thought of much as it was in the seventies, as the complaint department. If the company views it that way, but I, as a customer, believe customer service is a more integral part of their business, that's a disconnect."

The key, she contends, to realigning with customers is a more serious approach to customer service. "The real leaders in customer service organizations will influence their companies to figure out how we move where society's going. Because society, technology, and human beings are constantly changing. We've got to change with them. In the past, leaders of call centers might have seen themselves as back office too, and not had the voice at the table to say, 'I need to have more integrated systems, more information, and here's how we go about doing it.' But the right leadership will change what the call center is."

To do that, Harrell says, "you've got to be an innovative company. If we don't move fast enough as a company and help reps give the customer what they want, then there's frustration. In call centers, we hear that frustration from the customer. Moving forward in customer service is no longer just about the telephone. It's about information and how do you get information to the customer and how do you be proactive with that information?" She stresses the role of the call center rep in that equation. "I need to have the right kind of personality type who wants to serve the customer. I need the kind of person who just naturally, by personality, will create their own frenzy from the bottom up on how to better serve the customer, just by who they are.

"At the same time, the company leadership has a responsibility of setting strategy and implementing tactics—real, tangible improvements—that will help move customer service forward, both within the company and the world, within society. I need to feel, as a call center rep, that my company is listening to me. And they're helping my customers, and helping me help my customers by improving and staying with what the world is doing. That turns into having plans where they'll spend dollars on the right technology and processes and programs. The moment you become stagnant, then that's when you have an issue.

"I'd love to say FedEx is always a step ahead, but we'll never be perfect." Harrell says, "And will we have a rep who may not respond right?

Yes. But we need to have the passion to correct that, and the right leadership and strategy to prevent that from happening again."

—⟋⟍—

By the time I visited the FedEx call center in Memphis, I was not sure I was going to see or hear anything much different than I had at the various contact centers I had already been to in Salt Lake City, Buenos Aires, Cairo, northern England, and a few other places. And I did find similarities, to be sure—especially to the JetBlue call center, another company-owned operation in the transportation business that is built on a strong ethic of customer service. But there were also some notable differences at FedEx's call center in Memphis.

I visited there during December, always the busiest month at FedEx because of holiday shipping. I was taken on a tour of the center, the largest among the fifty-four company-owned call centers worldwide, and met some of the 285 customer service representatives who work there. One of the first things that struck me as different from other places I had been was the length of time most of the call center workers had been in their jobs. At many call centers the employees are mostly in their twenties. But at the Memphis center the majority were in their thirties, forties, and fifties and had been with the company for ten to twenty-five years.

FedEx is the largest private employer in this city of about 1 million on the bluffs of the Mississippi River. I grew up in Memphis, moved away for many years, and then moved back more than a decade ago. After Elvis Presley, FedEx is probably Memphis's most famous global export. But because it is responsible for the livelihoods of so many residents and is integral to the city's economy, pride in the company runs much deeper among most residents than does any amusement or wonder at the continued posthumous notoriety, fame, and tourist dollars generated by the city's best-known musical son. Everyone here either works at FedEx, is related to someone who works at FedEx, or knows at least a couple of people who do.

Because of the 3.2 million FedEx packages that flow through its sorting hub each day, Memphis has the largest cargo airport in the world. Just off a street that runs alongside the airport on the southern side of town is the Memphis call center. It is nestled in a landscaped corporate campus that was the main headquarters for the company until the 1990s, when FedEx built bigger, fancier corporate offices in three separate locations in the suburbs.

Senior manager Kathy Anderson is the top executive at the Memphis center. She started as a customer service rep with FedEx at the Sacramento call center in 1984. She then moved to the Kansas City call center and worked there for seventeen and a half years, before moving to head up the Memphis call center in March 2004. In a field plagued by short-term employees, Anderson said proudly that FedEx's call centers have a low turnover rate compared to the rest of the industry and that "this call center has the lowest attrition in the FedEx customer service network." She acknowledged that some of the employee loyalty is because her center is in the company's hometown. But she believes the reasons go deeper too. "Attrition is management failure. Either we hired the wrong person in the beginning, or we didn't do a proper job of training and developing them and helping them to see the value in working for FedEx."

Originally from a small town in Louisiana, Anderson gets passionate about the larger importance of the skills needed to be good at customer service—skills she looks for and instills in her employees and skills she thinks the whole world could benefit from honing. "If you're dealing with a representative who does not seem to want to help you—maybe has a very canned type of response, isn't tailoring it to your needs, or treats you as though you're bothering him—then you're not getting good customer service. Sometimes it has nothing to do with the employee. It could be the company and how they train and teach a customer representative. I also think it has to do with our society. A lot of people don't have what I consider basic courtesy skills. They are not being taught in homes or in schools. If I were an educator, I would write a curriculum called 'Life 101' for junior high and high school students, just to teach how to communicate, how to be courteous, and how to build relationships with people. I think we're missing that. Everyone is in a hurry. They want to get it done now. It's all about me, and we're not a very giving and nurturing society anymore."

Back in the days when she was working the phones, Anderson developed her approach. "You have to make sure customers know that 'I've got this, and we'll take care of you.' Most customers want to know that you hear them, and you care about their situation, and you're going to do something. If you can help them to feel that assurance, most customers change their demeanor. If the customer knows you're going to fix their problem, most of the time that solves the problem."

But Anderson also realizes how hard it can be to maintain that deportment in the face of the pressures of the job. "We teach our employees that they manage the customer experience, and they cannot allow the customer to switch them off and on like a light. They have to be in control. They have to remain professional and deal with the situation, regardless of how the customer is acting toward them. If the customer is upset, they can't be upset. If customers are sarcastic, they can't give it back to them. It's human nature to want to give it back if someone is nasty. But you can't do that and be a professional in a service environment."

Not only does the workforce at this call center seem to skew a little older than at many others, it also has a greater percentage of African American workers than the others I visited. Anderson, who is African American, says race is just one of the issues that comes up in managing the workers and their dealings with the cross-section of customers they handle from around the world. "We hear some vulgar language from some customers. Sometimes it might be gender related. Sometimes it may be race related. Sometimes it might be someone is having a bad day and they just kind of let us have it. We've heard it all. And some people find it hard to accept. They're not accustomed to being spoken to that way. We teach our people to expect that, because they are dealing with the public. And it doesn't matter if it's the CEO of a company or someone who works on the dock, if the right thing goes wrong, it could make them become one of those customers who's off the chain.

And we just have to deal with them in a very professional manner. What used to work for me when I was a rep was to tell a customer, 'You know your language is really distracting me from assisting you.'" But agents are also told that if customers are too difficult, transfer them to a manager, or to a group in the call center specifically trained to handle especially challenging or time-consuming calls. That, says Anderson, is part of how they make sure to support their employees and make it possible for them to do their jobs well.

After my tour, I listened in on calls with Anita DeVall, an agent in the area where phones are answered for general domestic customers and who has been working at FedEx since 1986. Every time the tone sounded on her headset and computer, it meant another call was coming in. But DeVall had a few seconds before she was on, because her initial greeting is prerecorded, so she doesn't have to repeat one or two hundred times a day the words: "Thank you for calling FedEx. This is Anita DeVall. How can I assist you today?" That is just one of the small ways FedEx fosters efficiency and conserves its agents' energy for the real meat of the phone call.

On this particular morning, a huge snowstorm had shut down airports in Chicago and a few other midwestern cities, so callers were concerned about package delays. One woman in downtown Chicago called DeVall saying she had hired people to work on a project involving paperwork that was supposed to arrive by 10:30 that morning. It was 11:30, and she had tracked the packages to find they had gotten off the plane from Michigan on time, but the truck had not left the airport for some reason. DeVall checked into it. The truck was waiting to gather packages from other planes that had been delayed before venturing through the snowy streets to its appointed rounds in the downtown area. DeVall didn't tell the woman that. She just assured her of what she could guarantee: that her packages would arrive by 12:30. The woman griped, "I'm paying these people to just sit here while we all wait for you to deliver the packages." DeVall apologized again and then soothingly reassured her that the package would be there.

"Weather is the biggest thing people get upset about," said DeVall, a friendly blond mother of three who is in her forties. I asked why she didn't tell the woman the whole story. She said very sympathetically that it was clear to her the woman didn't want to hear it. The customer was so upset that DeVall's years of experience had taught her not to try to offer the explanation, even if it was a reasonable one, because she felt the customer would have taken it as an excuse, a shirking of FedEx's responsibility. DeVall opted instead to let the woman vent her anger and then to say she was sorry as much as was necessary and offer the best information she had on how FedEx would resolve her situation. "We do a lot of apologizing."

DeVall was born in Memphis and worked at FedEx the whole time she was raising her kids, who are all now adults. Her twenty-three-year-old son served in the Iraq war and has come back home to live with her and her husband, because he is suffering from posttraumatic stress syndrome. Working part-time means she has the flexibility to take more time with him, just as she did when she worked part-time while raising him, and his sister and brother.

The calls came in a steady stream the whole time I observed DeVall. It seemed relentless to me, but DeVall kept her cool no matter what. As a viewer of it, good customer service seems kind of like performance art. I remembered that Rolf DeVries had pointed that out when I listened in on some of his calls at JetBlue.

DeVall answered a call from a woman in Appleton, Wisconsin, whose husband had dropped off Christmas presents to be shipped the night before but didn't have the tracking numbers. Then a caller in Miami was asking for a pickup of packages that had been wrongly delivered to her. Another caller from Virginia wanted to ship a tear gas launcher. DeVall transferred him to a rep in a specialized group that deals with customers shipping dangerous goods, including firearms. "Besides cursing, I can handle just about anything," said DeVall. Next, a caller in Philadelphia was upset because her birthday was the next day and she was waiting for the delivery of a new dress that she was going to wear to her birthday party. But when the driver came, he rang only at the downstairs apartment. He didn't ring the bell to the second-floor apartment, where she was waiting. DeVall apologized again and managed to get the driver to redeliver it, telling the woman the package would be there by 4:30 that afternoon. The woman was relieved and grateful. As she ended that call, DeVall said, "Happy birthday." DeVall's job, in short, is to placate America.

A few rows over in the international section, I sat for a while with Karen Hobson. She kept up a brisk pace, answering customer questions about regulations on shipping to Santo Domingo, a delivery of organic candy to Australia, and a question (regarding a task that seemed a little redundant to me) about the best way to send hockey sticks to Canada. But there was no such editorializing by Hobson, who has been a FedEx call center agent since 1986. She was affable, kind, professional, and calm through it all.

In another part of the center, upstairs from domestic and international, is a section that handles calls from business clients who ship more than $1,500 worth of goods a day. I sat with David Stanley as he spoke to a client in Vermont. A shipment of five twenty-one-pound boxes of syrups, jams, and jellies had been delivered to the wrong hotel in Manhattan. Instead of the Hilton, they were meant to go to the Hudson. Stanley, who has been working in this part of the call center for two and a half years and whose wife also once worked at FedEx, took care of it and had the shipment redirected. Stanley talks to some of his clients many times in a week and has developed good working relationships with them. "In this area there is more follow-up, so we have more ownership of an issue" than in the domestic and international areas where DeVall and Hobson work.

Around the corner and down a few aisles from Stanley is the group that handles calls from agents with complicated questions, and "escalated" calls from particularly aggrieved customers whom other agents don't have the time or training to manage. The group is called CAT, for customer advocacy team. I sat with a CAT representative named Thalia Chalmers, who had started at FedEx loading planes in 1988. She left the company in 1991 and worked at a bank before returning to FedEx in 2001, and has been working in customer service since 2005. It is where she belongs. The caring spirit runs in her family, who all have jobs in health care, social work, and customer service. "I get a lot of satisfaction out of resolving something for a customer," she said.

It was just after noon when I plugged a spare headset into Chalmers's phone and began listening in on her calls. She told me the day had been fairly routine. And at first it continued that way. She mostly took questions from reps about special circumstances caused by the snowy delays. I joked with her that I wished she would get a more dramatic call so I could see how she would handle it. She told me those weren't very common. I remembered that Sheila Harrell, the head of customer service at FedEx, had pointed out that they aim for 100 percent satisfaction among their customers. But they know that is impossible. And since they ship 6.5 million packages a day, if they have dissatisfaction rates of 1 percent, that is still 65,000 customers a day—and even one-half of 1 percent would be about 32,500 problems a day, and more than 220,000 a week.

The beep went off on Chalmers's headset signaling another caller. It was a rep in New England dealing with a customer who went to pick up a package after she missed its delivery, only to find that it wasn't there as she had been told by an agent it would be. The customer called in to this rep in New England, who told her the station said the package was there. Understandably, the customer did not believe her. But when the New England rep told Chalmers the situation at hand, the rep was disparaging of the customer. After that, the rep immediately began to rant about one of Chalmers's colleagues. She said, "I hope you're not like your co-worker, Brenda. She made me look like a fool a few minutes ago."

Chalmers was polite and businesslike, gently interrupting the rep to remind her to go back to the customer on the line now and tell her she is working on the situation. Chalmers listened in. The rep told the customer that they were checking on the package again. The customer responded angrily. "And I'm just supposed to trust you? After all these missteps, I'm supposed to trust you that it's going to be there when my husband goes to pick it up?" The rep apologized while Chalmers called the station to find out where the package was. It was indeed there and ready to be picked up. Another rep had called and asked that the package be placed in the area for the next day's deliveries, so when the customer came to pick it up, it was not in the area for pickups. Chalmers told the rep to relay that information to the customer. She did. And the call was over.

But Chalmers remained on the line with the rep, who was complaining that a few minutes earlier, she had another customer on the phone who was crying and screaming. So she called the CAT department where Brenda took the call. But this rep had listened in as Brenda took care of the woman and heard her contradict what this rep had told the customer. "She made me look like a fool," the New England rep confided in Chalmers, who did her best to calm the rep before sending her back to work. But after she hung up, Chalmers started to get angry herself. Not only had the rep insulted her co-worker, who happened to be sitting in the next cubicle and was a friend of hers, but she had called with two upset customers in less than an hour.

Chalmers spoke to Brenda, and they compared notes. Brenda said the New England rep had said disparaging things to her as well about the other customer. The two decided that this qualified as an incident that needed to be documented formally and reported to their manager. Part of their job is to root out any reps who present what everyone in the call center euphemistically refers to as "a coaching opportunity."

Later that day, I spoke to Dante Williams, the manager of the CAT team, which consists of about eighteen agents on rotating shifts from early in the morning to late evening, seven days a week. The case with Chalmers and the rep in New England was a classic example of the practical use of the recording that callers are warned about by the familiar phrase, "Your call may be monitored for quality purposes." Chalmers and her colleague formally reported the incident to Williams, and he allowed me to sit in with him as he reviewed the calls, which are all recorded. Williams merely had to find the logs of calls for the agents involved and search on his computer for the approximate time the calls occurred. Then he could listen to the whole situation unfold.

He decided to start with the first call that prompted the rep in New England to call the CAT team and speak to Brenda in the first place.

Williams listened to the beginning of the conversation when a woman in New York calmly explained how she had been out for only ten minutes when a delivery came. The minute she got home and found the tag on the door indicating FedEx had tried to deliver her package, she called. She said the person she spoke to told her they would try to redeliver it that day. But she hadn't heard anything and was getting anxious. The agent immediately told her that FedEx doesn't do reattempts. The customer repeated that she had called earlier and someone at FedEx had told her they could reattempt delivery.

Williams stopped the recording and commented, "In my opinion the domestic rep should have immediately apologized for the inconvenience, which she didn't do. Secondly, with what the customer said about her conversation with someone about the reattempt—that would clue me in to check with the terminal to see if someone has called to make those arrangements or to contact someone in the CAT department to see if they had been working on it. With my CAT reps I always stress 'no' is not the first response. 'Let me check on it' would be the proper response. I think that's what first caused the customer to get upset. All the rep had to do was take a breath, pause, and assure the customer, 'Let me see what I can do for you.'"

As the call continued, the rep in New England kept arguing with the customer and telling her that the system didn't allow redeliveries. The implication was that the customer was lying by saying someone told her FedEx would redeliver it. Finally, the customer got so upset that she started to cry. She told the rep that the package contained a Chanukah present she was supposed to take to a celebration that night. The rep was unmoved. Angrily the customer said, "I bet if this were a Christmas present, you wouldn't do this." She then demanded to speak to someone else. That is when the rep transferred her to Brenda from the CAT team in Memphis.

While the customer was on hold, what she said was still being recorded. And she could be heard telling someone in the room with her, "I hate FedEx." Meanwhile, the New England rep got Brenda on another line and explained the situation. She told Brenda that the woman was a "crackpot" and was "screaming and crying." She relayed how she had explained that they can't redeliver and the customer got "so upset." The rep then told Brenda the customer was a "spoiled rotten brat in New York City." Brenda listened patiently and tried to calm the agent. Then she told her that she would take care of it. At that, the rep is supposed to connect the customer with the CAT rep, hang up, and go back to answering other calls. But Williams noted with dismay that the computer log showed that the agent stayed on the line and listened in as Brenda apologized to the customer and assured her that she could help her. Then Brenda politely asked the customer if she could put her on hold while she tried to get the package redelivered.

Williams stopped listening for a minute. He was extremely upset but tried to stay measured in his comments about the rep in New England. "In a professional way, I'll try to say what I want to say. To know that we have someone in the organization who obviously does not have the patience, the understanding, the sympathy—whatever the situation calls for—to handle the customer properly is disturbing. With all the training we send our reps through in understanding how to handle irate customers, how to resolve situations, it is bothersome to hear that. She doesn't have the right approach. You have to keep your personal emotion and thoughts out of it and focus on what the person needs. 'She needs her package. What can I do to help her get it?'"

He pointed to the way Brenda handled the customer as an example of the right thing to do. "She assured the customer that she was going to help resolve her issue. She apologized to her. She got her approval for every step. She knew exactly what to say and do, to assure the customer and to get the package delivered. Which she did." He then smiled and reported to me: "Brenda got it done. The package was delivered at 3:01 this afternoon."

Williams started at FedEx in 1989 in the Kansas City call center and came to Memphis in 2004. He has worked in customer service his whole career, and his dedication clearly wasn't forced for my benefit.

He naturally comes across as the kind of person most people would want as their manager or their customer service agent—smart, funny, and seemingly unflappable. He is also enthusiastic. He says of his work and his workers, "It's fun. It keeps me thinking. I wake up in the middle of the night with ideas about how I can get them motivated to do this or not say that, and to think this way or not." On his office wall, he has an inspirational quotation from Abraham Lincoln that reads: "Whatever you are, be a good one."

The way Williams sees it, "everyone wants respect—regardless of what position they hold in life, their financial status, whatever." But his team has to deal with what he sees as a fact. "Over the phone, people tend to say things that they wouldn't say face-to-face. I've had situations where reps have told me, 'That customer just asked to speak to somebody white or whatever. They don't want to talk to me because they assume that I'm black or whatever.' And I've had the reverse." He says on the phone people have assumed he is white, even though he is African American, and spoken to him about not wanting to talk to a black person. "We have things in place for that. If we have a customer who's using profanity, racial slurs, that kind of stuff, the rep escalates that call to a manager right away. Because it gets ugly and they need not have that stress. They have enough. They don't need that."

He obviously has spent a lot of time through the years thinking about the mission he feels in his job: "People tend to trust large companies less. So we, as FedEx, have to continue to build that trust. And the only way we can do it is to be honest and direct. If we can't get something done, say it. But say it after you've tried. Don't say initially, 'No, I can't do that.' See if you can work it out. Then you can say, 'I can't work it out to get it there today, but I can have it there tomorrow.' And work your best to keep that commitment. Because if you fail again they're going to be less likely to trust you. That's where the CAT reps come into play. They are the company's safety net. We try not to, but if we mess up the first time, they can do the right thing and make sure to get it right the second time."

After he listened to the calls, Williams said his next step was to notify the manager in New England about the problems they had encountered with the rep there. "I will send her an e-mail letting her know that there were two incidents that happened within thirty minutes or so of each other. I will tell her I've reviewed the calls, and I have them attached to the e-mail. I'll ask for feedback on what she will do. But I will let that manager handle her employee. Because I don't know what's going on, on that end."

He said the CAT reps got him involved in the incident because they are expected to "notify management when coaching opportunities are available." But Williams was still a little baffled, and even personally offended, by the whole thing. "Because of the training we offer and how we instruct and coach, I don't know how this person got to this point. And to get two calls within a half hour from the same rep with a bad attitude—this is severe. This is one that needs immediate action." Williams stressed again how pleased he was with the way the CAT reps handled it all: "Both were on target. They were not rude to the rep, even though she made disparaging comments about the customer and then about another CAT rep. They let her vent, and then they brought it to my attention, as they should have. There's no need for them to get into a combative situation with the rep. Let me handle that. I'll deal with it manager-to-manager and go forward, and hopefully we can get the person the coaching that she needs."

I asked Williams if he could find any sympathy for the rep in New England. He tried. "The only thing I can say is that the reps take maybe two hundred calls a day. And sometimes that gets difficult. They never know what's on the other end of the line or what's coming to them. They have to be able to think rather quickly about resolution—offer options. Customer service is not easy at all.

"But still, you need to have patience and understanding and remember who pays the bills: the customers. There's no excuse for it. That's the kind of thing that we don't need in this environment. We're built on our customer service. People expect not only excellent service from FedEx, but excellent customer service. They want the package delivered on time. And if it's not, they want us to be understanding, cordial, show some empathy, and above all, get it resolved for them. We try to coach the reps—not just my CAT reps but any rep—not to blame anyone for the situation, just resolve it."

—m—

The story of how founder and CEO Fred Smith started FedEx in 1971, and thereby created the overnight shipping industry, is legend. As a student at Yale in the 1960s, the story goes, Smith wrote a paper putting forth the idea for the company. He got a C. Then he went off to serve in the marines in Vietnam. He came back and started Federal Express in Little Rock, Arkansas. Then he moved the company to Memphis, and the first overnight deliveries began in 1973. Since then, the company has grown into the largest overnight shipper and the largest airline in the world, operating 661 aircraft in 375 airports, in 220 countries and territories. In 2009, FedEx had revenues of $35.5 billion. With worthy competition from UPS, a larger company overall, FedEx and the industry have remained at or near the top of the University of Michigan's American Customer Service Index for so many years that its presence there has just about become a foregone conclusion. In addition, in the past few years, when *Fortune* magazine polls global executives annually on the most-admired companies in the United States and the rest of the world, FedEx has always made it high up in the top ten on both lists.

In the early days of the tech revolution, FedEx was what would today be called a start-up. And Fred Smith was among the first young, Ivy League, founder-CEOs of the type of information-driven companies that dominate the current landscape. Smith has been quoted as saying that the story of the C paper is a bit of a myth. He does not remember what grade he got on it, and no academic assessment of his first theoretical rendering of FedEx went on his permanent record. But what did endure was the idea, present from the start, that the company could do what others thought impossible.

After spending time exploring the company's call center operation, I sat down with Smith in his Memphis office, two blocks from his home, and we talked about customer service. Everyone I had spoken to in the customer service industry so far had eventually come around to talking about how expectations were a big factor in driving most customer experiences. And it occurred to me that Smith and the existence of FedEx had done so much to change expectations about what was possible in the world. So I asked him if he thought he and his company's achievements, which might once have seemed to defy time and space, were at least partly responsible for fostering the impatience so many people complain about on both sides of the company-customer equation.

"When we started," he replied, "with the thought that you could get something shipped overnight—late in the day from any time zone in the United States to any address and have it delivered first thing the next morning—people said, 'You're out of your mind. It's impossible to do that. Maybe a week from some places to some place.' Others said, 'Maybe ten days. Maybe New York to Chicago in two or three days. But it's very expensive and hard to do.' Then we did it. And now we understand clearly that people think FedEx is capable of doing almost anything. Of course, we've created a lot of that expectation. We don't mind that. And if there is a problem, our view is if you can solve the problem heroically, that's an opportunity to cement your relationship with that customer forever."

It reminded me of my visit to the FedEx call center. So I told him the story of the caller and the Chanukah present that I had witnessed at the call center a few weeks earlier. I told him how the customer was out for only ten minutes, and that is when the delivery was attempted. "Of course," he said. "That's always the way it is."

I recounted how the customer was very upset because the agent she spoke to had told her they couldn't redeliver it. And when the customer was on hold, she could be heard saying, "I hate FedEx." But I also told Smith how it was ultimately handled well, and the customer ended up getting her package by three that afternoon.

"Now, that customer thinks," he said, "it's a very easy thing, 'You can come by with my package when I'm gone, so just bring it back.' But it's a big industrial choreography to put this show on every day—you're talking about millions of transactions, tens of thousands of team members. So there are lots of things that can happen. It doesn't happen very often, thank goodness, because to the best of our ability we engineer that out.

"But you're talking about millions of shipments a day, and tens of thousands of vehicles, and it's very difficult to do what that customer wanted us to do. But from her perspective, it should be a piece of cake, when it's just a big damn deal, and you have to escalate it to someone who has the authority to do that. And by the way, the cost of doing that is so big that it's incredibly unprofitable. So a lot of companies would simply say, 'We're not going to deliver it. You were out. That's your tough luck.' But we actually do try to do it. And in this case we did do it. Because it may be one of millions, and millions, and millions of packages that FedEx ships, but it's the most important thing that you've ever shipped. And it's not acceptable for our folks not to be empathetic simply because we should be commended for delivering so many millions of pieces. It's irrelevant to her. So I'd be interested to know, in retrospect, whether she still hates FedEx."

When I asked him how they have been able to maintain that attitude, grow, and make a profit, he said, "From the start, and carrying through to this day, the focus on customer service has been one of the critical success factors of FedEx. It was *baked* in from the earliest days." The metaphor was striking. So many companies seem to just sprinkle customer service on top after the whole thing is already cooked.

Smith went on to emphasize that baking customer service in means he has had to make his priorities clear from the start and has had to continue to do so through it all. "The commitment to customer service and outstanding customer experiences definitely has to come from the top management, and cascade to every area of the corporation. Because if it doesn't, it would be impossible to maintain it. And it's got to be completely reinforced, constantly. And the bar has to be consistently raised. Because as an organization gets bigger, some sort of law of thermodynamics comes into play that if you don't work hard against it in your management systems, a kind of entropy will happen, and the organization will get tired and become complacent."

A key aspect of avoiding that pitfall, he said, was to keep refocusing the company on what customers want and need. "We spend an inordinate amount of time asking our customers what constitutes an outstanding experience, what meets their expectations: from accepting packages, to dealing with a trace, to how they want their invoice presented, to how they would like our software to operate, to what they expect of our teammates. There are many, many things that go into having an outstanding customer experience and we probably don't know every single thing. But I bet you we know 99 percent of it, because we keep asking that question and refining it."

In the call centers, Smith said, keeping bad service at bay boils down to three main challenges that management has to address constantly. "You can define what gives rise to customer frustrations in call centers pretty clearly." The first problem, many times, "is that the person the customer is speaking to on the telephone simply does not have the information to deal with the problem. The second thing that can happen is that the person on the phone has the information. They see what's wrong. But they don't have the authority to do what needs to be done to fix the problem. And the third thing is that the person in the call center simply expresses no empathy for the person's situation: 'I hear you, but I don't care.' Problems usually come down to one of those three things."

That analysis made it all seem fairly simple. But the art of it, the complexity, is in the details. And, Smith said, "of all the three, the hardest part is number one: to make sure you can get all the information in the system, and slice and dice it any way the customer might present it to you" and through whatever channel or channels the customer chooses at any one time.

During the late 1990s and the early part of this decade, I had written about FedEx for the *New York Times* and a few other publications. And one thing most executives I interviewed stressed was that delivering information about the package was as much what FedEx was all about as delivering the package. That idea was always said to come from the top. When I brought that idea up to Smith, he took it a few steps further.

"It's not just the information about the package. It may be the information about the account, or some information about the recipient. It could be some information about how the package was delivered: Was it left on the front steps, or was it delivered to the neighbor next door? Both of those happen a thousand times a day, with the shipper's permission." That's an example of the courier being considerate. But if the customer service agent "doesn't have the information that the package is at the neighbor's, it can be extraordinarily contentious. So it is that synthesis of all the information about the customer, the recipient, the account, and so forth that you have got to have there at the customer service agent's fingertips."

In the end, Smith said, any company that hasn't worked on the first two root causes of bad customer service can't be very concerned with the third, empathy. "If they don't have the information to solve your problem or they haven't given the person who speaks to customers the power to solve your problem, it probably means that the organization really doesn't care."

—⁓—

Among those in the business world who keep their eyes out for new companies that are developing strong customer service reputations, Zappos.com is the latest darling. The Internet retailer started selling shoes online in 1998. It became profitable in 2006. And by 2008, it branched out into selling all sorts of clothing, as well as electronics and cookware. And its revenues were projected to hit $1 billion, with continued exponential growth.

In 2005, *BusinessWeek* said the company had "a near-fanatical devotion to customer service." In 2008, journalist and author Bill Taylor echoed that notion and added more praise at *Harvard Business Online*: "Part of the reason for Zappos's meteoric success is that it got the economics and operations right. But it's the emotional connection that seals the deal. The company is fanatical about great service—not just satisfying customers, but amazing them."

It's no coincidence that the word *fanatical* comes up so often when talking about this company's customer service ethic. It's hard to find a more apt description. The company has a 365-day return policy and free shipping both ways on returns. Its one call center is based at company headquarters in Las Vegas and staffed twenty-four hours every day. The company's only warehouse is open all night as well and is based in Kentucky, near a UPS hub, for instant shipping. It has an inventory of more than 4 million shoes. If a customer wants an item that is out of stock, Zappos customer service agents are trained to search at least three other competitor sites for the customer and direct them to where the item is more immediately available.

The company takes care of its workers too. It offers 100 percent medical and dental coverage. Lunches are free in the company cafeterias. Part of the four-week training of every employee, even executives, includes a week answering customer service calls and time working in the Kentucky warehouse filling orders. Sometime in the middle of the training period, the company offers newly hired workers a "bribe" to quit. It started out at $100 and has grown into a couple thousand dollars. That way, the theory goes, they can weed out the people who don't have the commitment to do the job early on. As Zappos CEO Tony Hsieh says, "If you're unhappy as an employee, it's pretty hard to give great customer service."

Hsieh (pronounced Shay) does things to keep his finger on the pulses of his workers and his customers and to care for them well. For instance, he works in a cubicle in the middle of his employees, not in a plush corner office. And he vows the company will never outsource its call centers. In 2004, when it found that running the call center from its former San Francisco corporate headquarters was too expensive because of the price of workers and real estate, it moved the whole company to Las Vegas. That was where the right labor pool for call center workers existed, and the company management wanted to stay connected to its frontline workers.

"Our call center is less efficient than most call centers," says Hsieh. "We don't measure call times. Someone can spend an hour on the phone with a customer and not have it result in a sale, and that's fine with us because we're not trying to minimize the cost of our call center. A lot of people say we're crazy. It just depends on what you want your company to stand for. If you don't care whether your company stands for customer service, then it might seem like an illogical choice." But the call center is run with the idea that good customer service fosters loyalty, which is more profitable in the long term. So they do all they do so that they can garner their customers' repeat business.

Hsieh, a Harvard graduate in his mid-thirties, sold his first start-up, an Internet advertising company called Link Exchange, to Microsoft for $265 million when he was twenty-four. He says his annual salary at Zappos is about $36,000. "I don't get a monetary bonus if we make our financial numbers each year, whereas I think most CEOs do, because I'm thinking of the long term." He is also thinking of the message he sends to his workers and customers. Hsieh says his own financial rewards are less important than what he does to contribute to the culture of the company, which he calls "the number one priority at Zappos. When a customer interacts with us, they feel like we care and we're trying to create the best experience for them. And if there is an issue then we want to resolve it, and we are capable of resolving it." He says "most businesses aren't thinking ten to twenty years down the line. So culture is not that important. But if you're thinking more about your financials ten or twenty years down the line than you are about the next quarter, then culture is going to make a difference."

A bulwark of the Zappos culture is a list of what the company calls its ten "core values." They include, "Be adventurous, creative, and openminded"; "Build a positive team and family spirit"; "Create fun and a little weirdness"; and "Be humble." Hsieh says, "We've always thought company culture was important but then that evolved into more formally defining our values."

Hsieh seems to take that core value about being humble particularly seriously. He is adamant that he sees his job not as dictating from above, but instead as making it possible for the company's nearly 1,800 workers to continue creating the company as it moves forward. "I think the spirit and the culture comes from the bottom up. But the permission to do that comes from the top."

Every year the company compiles and publishes what it calls the "culture book." Employees are asked to submit testimonials about what the company means to them. It reflects the decidedly relaxed, almost party-like atmosphere that visitors report after going to the Las Vegas offices. But excerpts from Zappos call center employees, in particular, also offer insights into the way the company nurtures its workers' camaraderie.

> After my last job, I never wanted to work at another call center. I had several options available when looking for a new job, but Zappos.com won me over. The interview was fun and the tour blew my mind. Other companies might throw meaningless pacifiers at their employees, to make them feel better about a job they don't really like. Zappos.com really is a family. The Zappos culture takes care of itself by taking care of the customers and the employees, which so few companies do these days. The catered lunches, expos, parties, discounts and gifts are only a few of the ways Zappos.com makes you feel important. I have never made so many friends so fast. I love how the entire company gets a chance to learn about every other department in the company. It really helps communication and answers all questions. I am so lucky to have found this job and to experience such a marvelous world! Zappos.com is not just a call center. I look forward to going into work, so I can help people and have fun doing it. I laugh every single day I am here.—Stacy H., customer loyalty department employee since 2006

> It's hard to write down what Zappos' culture really is. Living in Vegas, you get used to the fast pace—the no "Sorry," no "Hello," keep-to-yourself-and-hurry-on-your-way type

of lifestyle. Here at Zappos, it reminds me of home, the small-town feel. When walking around the office, everyone says, "Hello!" and asks you how you're doing. They actually care. When someone's arms are full, there's always a person there to help hold the door open. When the phones get busy during the holiday season, you look over and you see the CEO on the phone, answering the same calls that everyone else is! How is it that I wake up in the morning and WANT to go to work? For once in my life, I feel comfortable in my own skin. I don't need to hide who I am when I walk through the doors of Zappos. Even though I go to work and answer phones all day, I love it every day and wouldn't change a thing!—Stephanie B., customer loyalty department employee since 2006

My non-Zappos family and friends think that I work for some sort of cult. I am always comparing the high level of customer service that we provide to our customers to the service that I receive in my everyday life. I'm constantly saying, "This is not how we would do it at Zappos." There's a standard way that customer service is metered out to consumers, and then there's the Zappos way. I'm proud to work for a company that takes the term "customer service" so literally.—Terri A., customer loyalty department employee since 2004

But Hsieh is also careful to point out that Zappos is about more than the touchy-feely stuff. "We also need to make sure that everyone realizes this isn't just Disneyland. We actually have a business to run. I'm an investor and shareholder too. So while there is this kind of utopian dream of the best customer service here, we still have to make choices at the end of the day. We still have financial goals to make. We still have to look at P&L statements, and a balance sheet and figure out what are the best places to invest our resources in order to have the biggest return. I suppose the very best customer service would be if you order something, and it's delivered four hours later, no matter where you are in the country. But we can't afford to do that."

One gamble Zappos has taken is not to compete on price as much as on service. Hsieh says they hope one day not to have any sale items. "There will always be different consumers who will value low prices in some situations and customer service in others. So I think there's room for both. Walmart's not going away. But there is a lot of opportunity in the long term for companies that want to focus on great service. But the companies that don't focus on customer service aren't going to all go away either."

Another decision Zappos has made is not to have an elaborate IVR system. "My sense of IVR systems," says Hsieh, "is that they are basically a way to cut cost for the company and then push a lot of the work onto the consumer. I don't see the technology anytime soon being anywhere near where it needs to be to make it less work for the consumer. Maybe, I don't know, twenty years down the line, if you could have a normal conversation with a super high-tech system that understands what you're doing, then maybe."

In the meantime, callers to Zappos's 800 number are greeted by a simple routing system with three options. After that, there are two more, which they call "fun" options. By pressing 4, callers get a joke of the day, read by two employees. Press 5, and Zappos's "special guest," soul music legend Gladys Knight, reads the greeting menu again with her husband, laughing all the way. Then Tony Hsieh asks her to sing, and she belts out a few lines of her classic song, "Midnight Train to Georgia."

Thor Muller, the head of Get Satisfaction, is a fan of Zappos, which is also one of his clients. Muller's site helps companies and customers harness the latent powers of the Internet to connect with each other. "Zappos looks at every call as a branding opportunity. So for instance, they don't measure call times. They do measure how quickly their people answer the phone. They want it to be a very few number of rings. When you compare the cost of that to what a marketing department spends for a print ad or something like that—if you do the cost analysis on that basis—the numbers are completely different." That becomes an important new way of valuing customer service.

Like Muller, Hsieh has a background in the Silicon Valley tech world. Combine that with a younger workforce and the fact that Zappos exists only on the Internet. It means blogs and social networking figure heavily into the company culture as well. Hsieh, for instance, uses Twitter zealously. Anyone can follow his moves through the day. He doesn't see that as diminishing any kind of mystique he has as a CEO. In fact, it seems just to enhance it in the business world in which he operates.

It is all part of the transparency—a buzzword used a lot these days in the business-oriented social networking world—that Hsieh says the company seeks to cultivate. "The Internet has caused companies to become more and more transparent, whether they like it or not. That means they have to be truthful and not hide stuff, not try to project an image that's not real. We decided from the beginning we wanted to be transparent that way. One of our core values is to be open and honest. And so the fact that we were already committed to that plays very well into the fact that that transparency is going to happen whether you like it or not. What bigger, older corporations are struggling with is [that] fifty years ago, your brand was whatever you said your brand was. It was whatever your TV ads or billboards said it was. Whereas now, because of the Internet and transparency happening with blogging, or videos being captured, or whatever, your brand is what other people say it is. Definitely it seems there's a generational shift in attitude. Look at MySpace or Facebook—that's just about putting your life out there. I think fifty years ago that would have been a pretty weird thing."

Muller agrees, citing how companies are having to learn that in social networks, they must be accessible. For instance, their representatives usually give their full names on social sites, so they can't hide behind corporate identities as much as in the past. Muller is hopeful this will result in more individual responsibility in any dealings people from companies have with their customers. "Personal and professional reputations are getting blurred. And that's going to have an impact on how customer service is done over the long haul."

Hsieh admits his exact approach might not translate to every company and every worker. "Zappos is not for everyone. Our culture is not necessarily transferable to other companies. I don't think any two company cultures are exactly the same. But what is transferable is the focus on culture and your values, and the idea of leading by values as opposed to anything else. If I meet with founders of a new company, I encourage them to figure out what they want their values to be and commit to running their company based on those values."

David McQuillen had been working at Credit Suisse since 2001. So by 2004, when he took on a newly created job as director of customer experience at the Zurich-based bank, he had talked with enough well-meaning managers and executives about what their customers were thinking and feeling to know it could be a challenge to spur them into action. "They would say, 'Oh, gosh, that's a problem. I'm really concerned about that. Thank you very much.' And then nothing would happen." So when McQuillen was asked to give a presentation in 2004 about what customers go through when interacting with the bank to a gathering of two hundred top managers in the bank's retail banking group, he and his team saw it as an opportunity to make a game-changing move.

They started with a standard chart to show that customer satisfaction numbers were indicating some problems, particularly with the service that customers were receiving on the phone. "They were all sitting there," said McQuillen. "Some were on their BlackBerrys, talking or typing away and not really paying attention." Then McQuillen, a self-possessed, easygoing American in his mid-thirties at the time, said to the room: "Okay everybody, you see the satisfaction numbers. Let's find out if they're true. We've got a phone up here connected to a speaker system. We're going to call the call center right now, tell them that I've just moved to Switzerland and I'd like to open up an account. Let's see what happens." At that, everybody in the room looked up, and McQuillen thought, *Okay, I'm either going to get fired after this or be a hero.* He wasn't sure which. "Everyone put down their BlackBerrys, and you could just see the fear."

He dialed the call center and spoke to an agent, for all to hear. The call didn't go well. "It wasn't very good. But it could have been great; it didn't matter. I hung up the phone, and the room just erupted in discussion. 'Wow, it should have been like this, or that.' The quality of the call didn't matter. What mattered was that these people all of a sudden were brought face to face with the experience. I realized in hindsight the fear on their faces was because they had no idea what the customer experience would be, and that was scary to them."

But it got their attention. Suddenly everyone clearly saw problems that all the customer satisfaction numbers and focus group reports in the world wouldn't have brought home to them as quickly or directly. McQuillen knew he had come upon a powerful tool. Giving the executives in the company a real-life taste of what their customers experienced every day garnered their buy-in. "By having the stakeholders there, going through what a customer goes through, it just generates this empathy that they can't deny."

After that, McQuillen and his team came up with a more formal program for giving executives at the bank a real feel for their customers' point of view. With support from the CEO, McQuillen's team came up with a guided tour. "We took each person individually. We had it very structured. Like when you go to Italy and you have a tour book, we had a guidebook to the Credit Suisse experience." Executives would visit three branches and wait in line for a teller or use the ATMs. They got on the website. They called the call center. And each executive filled out a credit card application. Then they talked about how good each experience was. "It was superficial in a way," says McQuillen, "because it was only very small types of exposures. But we were making them be a customer of the bank rather than a manager of the bank. And it worked. People cared. It was exactly what we wanted."

McQuillen is quick to point out what is relatively unique about their approach: "There's a big difference between what we tried to do and what a lot of companies do. Because when I talk to other companies, they say, 'Oh, well, we do that. Our manager, he spends a day a year sitting at the grocery counter serving customers or answering the customer service line.' And I say, 'Great—a perfect way to find out what it's like to be a frontline employee of your business, not a good way to find out what it's like to be a customer. I recommend both.' You need that empathy for what the employees go through. But if you're a restaurant manager, for example, you need to eat dinner in your restaurant.

"We came to recognize that nothing ever changes without the empathy that's generated from immersions in the customer's point of view. That's the magic thing. When we bring people in and they go through the experiences, we do not need to spend a week preparing a big Power-Point presentation with all our recommendations. Because afterward, they go back to their desks and start fixing things. They just start. They don't need us to deliver the PowerPoint. These are not bad people. They have just built a bad experience. They followed the wrong process. And once they see that, they fix it."

After reaching most of the bank's top executives and showing the value of the experience immersion approach, they were able to use the same technique in other projects within the company.

Bojan Blecic is vice president of customer experience at Credit Suisse and began working in McQuillen's group early on. Before Credit Suisse, Blecic had worked as an architect in Berlin and Switzerland and then started his own company designing and building interactive, multimedia websites during the dot-com boom in the late 1990s and early 2000s. Then he came to the bank to help build the first renditions of some of the company's websites.

As soon as he entered the banking world, he noticed that "everybody was just doing things from a bank point of view. There were plenty of project managers who had clear tasks. They had to deliver something by a certain time and in a specific budget. If they did that, they were a good project manager and they could get a promotion. But nobody was taking care of the user—the clients. After the project manager is already on to the next project, someone else has to deal with any problems that come up for customers."

It reminded Blecic of something he said every architecture student hears in the first weeks of university classes. "You learn that there are two kinds of architects: the ones who build for themselves and the ones who build for people. And you can walk through any city of this world and recognize their buildings." Blecic had opted to become the kind who built for people, always focusing on the needs of the people who would be using the building when making design and building decisions. As he got into tech work, he applied that same philosophy. But he found that such thinking sometimes clashed with the way things were commonly done in the banking world. "Products and processes were just designed with a different logic behind it—the logic was about time, money, and practical bank needs. They had not involved the user. They were speaking their own language, and they expected users to look for things according to their structure and their logic."

It wasn't until Blecic became part of McQuillen's customer experience team, soon after it was created, that he found his home at Credit Suisse. Blecic's mix of tech and architecture skills fit perfectly with McQuillen's team's mission. McQuillen likes to tell a story of how Blecic was able to help people right from the start. A group that designs and processes applications for new accounts within Switzerland came to McQuillen asking for help in redesigning their new client contracts because customers were making so many mistakes.

"Now Bojan had never in his life redesigned a client contract," says McQuillen. "But he is a clever guy. So when the project team came in and wanted to do a survey of customers to ask what they don't like about the contracts, Bojan said, 'No. We're going to do observation-based work here.'" Blecic then instructed the project managers to bring everyone who had anything to do with the contract into a room the next day—the people who wrote the contract, the people who processed it, their supervisors, everyone. When they had all assembled, Blecic brought in some clients and some of the relationship managers who work with the clients. He took out a stack of blank contracts, passed them around, and asked the clients and relationship managers to fill them out.

McQuillen remembers, "We've got a great picture of people filling out the contracts, and you see these guys with their heads in their hands, staring at it, like this." He mimics them looking down with frustration, and sighing. "All the people responsible for the contract had never seen that before." When the customers and relationship managers were finished, the people who designed and processed the forms had finally witnessed customers making the same mistakes that other potential customers had made. So without any focus groups, they were able to identify the problems and fix them. "Through that exercise, Bojan helped them reduce errors by 50 percent—just by experience immersion." Now, McQuillen says, "anyone who wants to work with our team—if they want to redesign a branch, or redesign a website, or a form—we ask if they have gone and used that branch and observed customers, or used that website, or filled out the form, as a customer. If they say no, we say, 'We're going to help you do that.'"

For most website redesign projects, Blecic sets up a usability lab in which customers are asked to perform a task on the site and to explain or think aloud as they go through the process. All of it is recorded on screen shots and video and audio. There is a room attached to the labs where interested parties can observe. McQuillen says they require the project managers to be present in that room for all the labs. "We say, 'You as the project manager are going to sit and watch all sixteen labs. If you don't feel that you have time, then clearly it's not important enough to you. So it's not important enough to us to do this project.'" They also require all the other people involved with the Web project to sit in on at least some of the labs too. McQuillen says that might include "the head of the department, the IT person who built the system, the customer service person who has to handle the requests from that page, and any other stakeholders."

McQuillen describes what can happen. "We've had labs where the IT guy sits there and says, 'I don't know what the problem is. This website is awesome.' Then customer one comes in, and he can't use the site. The IT guy's typical response is, 'Stupid customer. Obviously not a good one.'

"Then the second customer comes in. Same thing. So then he says, 'Stupid lab. You obviously are picking the wrong kinds of customers. The real customers who use this, they don't have a problem.'

"Number three comes in, and we say, 'By the way, this is a heavy user of this kind of site. It's exactly the kind of person who we're targeting with this.' Then they can't use it. Finally, the IT guy says, 'Maybe there is a problem.'

"And number four, number five, number six, all have the same problem. By the end, the IT guy has come around and starts to say, 'I think what we could do is to change this, and that'll fix it.' We even had a project where the IT guy was changing the prototype after every test. So he was improving it on the fly, after everything he saw.

"It's the only way to get people on board with the customer focus. We could do all the labs, come up with a report, give it to the IT guy, and he'd go, 'No, I don't believe it.' But if he sits there and he watches it and he sees all these people have a problem, he can't deny it."

The labs often unify usually disconnected groups within the company too. "All these different people deliver a certain part of the customer experience. Normally they point fingers at each other when there is a problem. Then they see the customer there, who doesn't care about any of these people. He's just trying to use the website or use a building—whatever. And they all say, 'Oh, well that's kind of your problem, and that's kind of yours, and that's kind of mine. Maybe we better all work together if we're going to fix that.' Then we just stand back and let them solve the problem. We've done our work."

Blecic says contact with the customer is key. "The more we bring internal people together with customers—the more that we put them into the position of actually listening to clients—the more something changes, and changes fast. Because it's not us just being the experts who know everything about clients. It's them, sitting in the same room with us and perceiving, one-to-one, what is going on with clients. We just enable them. Quickly, they start to talk about the real important things and forget all the political—or non-customer-centric—issues. So we have the chance to improve things that it would take, under normal conditions, a lot more time to improve. It becomes about understanding the customers' values, the customers' motivations, the customers' concerns, and then somehow finding a way to balance that with what the company wants, the value for the company."

In other ways as well, McQuillen's team employs observation to get closer to the customer's experience of their bank. Stephan Kuebler has spent hundreds of hours simply observing customers in Credit Suisse branches in Switzerland. "We want to find out more about the unspoken needs of customers," says Kuebler, another member of McQuillen's customer experience team. "So it's really important to observe customers using ATMs. We can find out so much more—if things work right, or not—when we watch them instead of interviewing or asking them about how they use things." Kuebler goes into the branches and just watches, trying to be unobtrusive and not make customers uneasy. "You really have to be patient. Sometimes you stand there for a few hours. And of course, you need to be invisible so the customers don't notice you."

He might see customers with confused expressions on their faces, who go out and come back a minute later. At that point, he would ask them what was wrong. "It's a combination of observation and interviewing. I approach them and say, 'I just saw you using our ATM. I am from the bank. We are interested in knowing what is working well for customers and what is not.' Customers are excited that someone from the bank really is interested in their opinion and asks them about their experience. Sometimes the customers see us, and they ask, 'What do you do here?' When we explain, they say, 'Wow, this is amazing.' They really like that people care about what's going on in the branch."

During some of his observation time, Kuebler takes photos. Back in the experience team's stylish office—a large, open, airy room where nine Zurich-based team members, including McQuillen, sit at individual workstations—Kuebler has posted a wall of photos documenting the kinds of things he sees in the branches that need fixing. For example, he has a few photos of an area in the middle of a branch where people stop to write their checks and fill out forms before standing in line to speak to the teller. Since Zurich is a city in which many people walk or travel by the extremely efficient public tram system, most people carry a briefcase or backpack. In a few photos, customers who have to put down what they are carrying to fill out checks and forms are standing at the counter with their bags on the floor, wedged between themselves and the counter, or awkwardly placed between their feet so they don't lose track of them. Kuebler saw that they needed a ledge about halfway between the counter and the floor where they could set their bags while they fill out their paperwork. Now all the branches have that feature. "There are so many details. But it is the sum of the details that has an impact."

McQuillen says the main goal in all they do is to use those details from their findings to help make their customers' lives better. They have figured out, for instance, where customers look in different parts of a branch, so they can "start to put things in places where they are going to communicate to our customers, keep them occupied, make them feel they are not waiting so long, be more pleasant. We showed the people who were designing these branches and in marketing. We said: 'Hey, guys, think about the customers. Understand their behavior. Then you will be more successful.'"

McQuillen doesn't consider their work very mysterious. "It's intuitive and obvious to us. Sometimes we do think, *Gosh, we should really make this sound more complicated*. Because when we say, 'We're going to go stand in the branch all day and watch customers,' it just sounds so simple. But empathy is the foundation of it all. Without empathy, forget it, nothing else will work. So when we hire people for this team, we hire more on personality type than on skills. Like Stephan, he's got it. He's got the personality, the observation, the curious mind."

The customer experience division is part of the marketing department at Credit Suisse. But McQuillen describes his team as an internal consultancy within Credit Suisse. They work across all divisions, helping with projects to design or redesign any part of the customer experience, be it physical spaces, web pages, forms, or any other touch point that customers have with the bank. The fact that his group functions within the corporate structure, not as outside consultants, says McQuillen, helps them establish the necessary trust and credibility to effect change. But he stresses how imperative it is that they always act, and are perceived, as independent customer advocates, first and foremost.

"We help people be more successful by being customer-focused," says McQuillen. "And some of it is painful. People come to us and we have to say to them, 'You know what? Sorry, but no customer understands this.' And that can be hard because you have very smart people who worked on this thing, and they say, 'Well, I understand it.' And we say, 'Yeah, I know you understand it, but you've got your master's in this.' You've got to have people who can just be honest like that and are independent, not political, and can tell the truth and help people. Without that function it would always break down into people caring about their own thing, turf wars."

McQuillen says that his colleagues in customer experience have gotten frustrated at times with how slowly changes come. "They've said, 'We know what that experience needs to be. Why can't we just go make it happen? If we owned that, we could just design it.' I've said, 'Yeah, okay. But if we owned it, we would start caring about it too much. We would start becoming biased. We would go native. We couldn't be objective anymore. We don't need to own it. We just need to get the owners to think the way we do about the customer. And if they start doing that, great, then they will only come to us on big projects where they really need us and deal with the little stuff themselves.'"

Since the early days of McQuillen's now infamous call to customer service at the meeting with two hundred managers and executives listening in, the idea of paying attention to the customer experience has become more prominent in the company. No small feat in a multinational institution that is more than 150 years old.

In achieving this, McQuillen has identified three essential elements that have to be present for a business to be truly client focused.

"One is client insight. You have to know who your customers are, what they're doing with you, how they feel about it. That means your company needs to gather feedback, it needs to manage that feedback, and it needs to do something about it. It's not enough just to do the satisfaction survey. You need to manage that data you get back: analyze it, draw conclusions. And you need to get it to people who can act on it. It's the act part that most businesses fall down on."

The second element McQuillen sees as essential is "a client culture where employees intuitively think about the customer. So the first thing that comes to their minds is, 'How is this good for the customer?' or 'How can I make the customer happy?' or 'What is the experience that the customer is going to have?' I've been in entire conversations, entire management board meetings, where the customer is never mentioned. Two-hour agenda, all internal stuff. The wrong focus. There needs to be an intuitive sense of, 'Great idea. But how does that help the customer?'"

McQuillen is convinced that their processes will further a client-focused culture that works for the benefit of all involved. "You show me a bad experience, and I can tell you how it was built. Someone didn't pay attention. Someone didn't think it was important. The root cause probably isn't customer service; it's a poorly designed product that's generating an overload of complaints to customer service. And if you really get back to what's causing the problem and you talk to those engineers, and they fix it, then customer service doesn't have to deal with a hundred broken things every day on this one product, because it's built right the first time. People might blame customer service. But it's probably not their fault, because they want to do a good job. There's something else going on. Maybe it's an overall problem, a sickness in the corporate culture."

McQuillen adds that a client-focused culture also must include empowered employees. "You have to give them the tools: the thinking tools, the processes, the support, the equipment, and the training to be customer focused. You can't just say, 'Let's be customer focused.' You have to show them and tell them how to do it. And then reward them for it. When I sit down at a table in a customer-focused culture, the first thing we talk about is, 'Okay, who are we doing this for, which customer group, and what do they need, and how does this meet those needs?' That's a customer-focused culture. In a non-customer-focused culture, they say, 'Hey, look at this thing I created. Isn't that cool?' And then they say, 'Yeah, cool. Great. Let's launch it.' No discussion about who it's for, what the benefit is, whether it's good, the impact it's going to have. So with the client culture, you need to engage the employees, enable them, and I say you should reward them. If there's no personal benefit for being customer-focused, then why should I do it? If it doesn't get me promoted, if it doesn't make me more money, if it doesn't give me more pride, if it doesn't give me more recognition, why do it? So you should be rewarded for being customer focused."

The third thing McQuillen believes must be in place for a client-focused company to emerge, in addition to client insight and a client culture, is an ongoing awareness of exactly what the customer experience is at the company. That element is at the heart of his team's work. "You know who your customers are. You've got a business that's thinking about customers. Now what kind of experience are you delivering for them? This means you define the kind of experience your business should be providing customers. Most businesses have never done this. They've done maybe something for their brand. They have a brand that represents what a company stands for. But what kind of experience are they providing customers? What does that mean for their website? What does it mean for their buildings? What does it mean for their processes? What does it mean for their people? All these touch points, how should they behave in order to give a certain kind of experience?"

When McQuillen talks, he is very careful always to cite everyone who works with him and their part in the process. He doesn't seem comfortable taking credit for too much of the work, although he is clearly the leader of this pioneering group, and he practices what he preaches. He enables those who work with him to do what they do best. He brings it out in them. And they bring it out in each other.

McQuillen is not sure where his zeal for this kind of work originated. But he says he first started noticing a need for it just after business school in London, when he took a job at Accenture working on Internet strategy. "Everyone else was talking about business models: 'A good business model for the company online needs to be this.' And I was writing about how it doesn't matter how good your business model is if no one can use this website. It doesn't matter how good your offer is if I can't figure out how to buy it. If I look back on my work experience, that's when I realized that I was focused on this interface between the business and the customer. And I couldn't give a crap about how it actually got delivered, in terms of operations."

McQuillen grew up in Erie, Pennsylvania, the oldest of three kids. He doesn't think anything in his upbringing particularly instilled a sense of fairness in him. But he definitely has one, and it seems to drive him in his work. "I can't reflect on any moment in my life where I became aware that I cared about it, but I just can't stand it when people are treated unfairly. I hate it—it drives me crazy—when people are rude. And maybe that's what it is with customer experience. Customers are spending a lot of money to have their account here at Credit Suisse. It's unfair to treat them poorly. They deserve a good experience. It's not fair to charge customers all this money, and we're not giving them a good experience because we can't be bothered. That doesn't work."

Outside the office McQuillen is an avid long-distance cyclist. He has biked for days across Europe, and he and a friend pedaled across Tibet in 2004, raising money for a literacy program. "Cycling, to me, has always represented exploring. Being out there. Seeing how far I can go. It's not the challenge of conquering the mountains. It's 'I wonder what's over there on the other side of that hill.' And I think that's what we're doing in customer experience. We're exploring. That's probably why I like this work, because it's a journey, it's an exploration. I've got fellow explorers who are sympathetic and excited and we have an interesting place to explore, which is Credit Suisse. The customer experience is an adventure, I guess."

Apparently it can also become an obsession. Kuebler says once he started noticing things that were badly designed in the banks, he found himself using the same powers of observation in other parts of his life. "When you start doing this, you never stop. When you go on holiday, you still have your eyes open, you look at the details." McQuillen reports the same syndrome. "You don't ever turn off when you leave the bank. And to me, I'm not working, I'm just examining customer experiences. When I walk into a restaurant, or a hotel, or a movie theater, or a bookstore, whatever—I usually start with, 'How do I feel here? Are they treating me well? Is this good?'"

While they have found acceptance within Credit Suisse, McQuillen makes it clear that his team still has lots more work to do. "Our next stage is to become institutionalized as part of the way Credit Suisse works. There are only nine of us, but we need all forty thousand employees at Credit Suisse to work the way we do. So that's why we always teach the people we work with how to do our work. We don't think it's so complicated that you couldn't do it. We just have to show you the process, teach you how to watch, then you can go and work with your own customers."

McQuillen says he and his team also look to other companies for inspiration with working on that kind of culture change. In the summer of 2008, he sent Blecic to two American companies doing innovative work in customer experience management, Staples and Cisco, on a kind of executive exchange program. And McQuillen and his team also learn from others they admire, such as Zappos. "They have become legends in a very short period of time. They are good to their employees. They've got a great work environment. They're covering all the bases, in terms of creating a customer-focused business. A company like ours can look up to a smaller company like Zappos.

"But in some ways, effecting change in a company like that is different from effecting change in a business this big. In a small company, you just have fewer humans to deal with. And you can go to one guy who is performing many roles and talk to that person. And the guy is like, 'Yeah, that sounds great.' And then it's done. Here you have to talk to the head of security. You need to talk to the head of real estate. You need to talk to the head of supply management. You've got to talk to the head of banking. The bigger the company, the more specific the jobs get, and the more humans you have to deal with and persuade."

And in a multinational company like Credit Suisse, people from many different nationalities have to work together. "I've got nine cultures on my team," says McQuillen. Blecic is Croatian, Kuebler is Swiss, McQuillen is American, and the team also includes people from Finland, Germany, Scotland, Italy, Korea, and the Czech Republic. "And God knows how many cultures we're dealing with out in the field. How do you get a Chinese project leader to deal with an Italian head of security, while talking with a Swiss branch manager? So I think that's the biggest difference. In a bigger company, there's so much more momentum behind anything, good or bad." As a result, change can be a more entailed process.

McQuillen is hopeful that more and more companies will come to see that in doing well by their customers, they also do well for themselves. "If you deliver positive experiences, then people are going to want to come back, right? Not only that, but positive experiences keep your costs low, because when you deliver bad experiences and you have people calling you, it costs you money. Do delivering positive experiences is good for business."

Every day, billions of people who are customers engage in transactions with millions of people who work at companies in customer service. At any one moment, each of those transactions can either go well or go badly for one or all involved. And every one of those moments is a verdict on how well a company has mastered the art and the science of customer service. Those moments are also a reflection of the way we, as customers, handle the times in our lives when all systems aren't go and we have to maneuver through other people to get what we need or want.

Our billions of everyday transactions are both simpler and more complicated than they appear. But while the infrastructures that support them are continually in flux, the intangibles at the heart of each positive encounter remain constant on all sides: trust, respect, empathy, caring, and even some fun—within companies, and between companies and their customers.

9.　Your Tweet Is Important to Us

New Chapter for the Paperback Edition

By now, most people know that companies and customers are interacting on social networking sites such as Facebook and Twitter. Believe it or not though, one of the most successful pioneers of providing customer service on social networks is Comcast. That's right, the same company that was forced by bad press, increased competition, Mona "the Hammer" Shaw, and Bob Garfield's site ComcastMustDie.com to take a hard look at what they put their customers through, is now a leader in helping customers via Twitter and the rest. When I spoke to Comcast's customer service head, Rick Germano, in early 2008, he was charged with transforming the company's battered reputation by ramping up its customer service. That meant, among other alterations, Comcast hired and trained more customer service workers to answer phones, and became more accommodating to its 24.1 million customers in scheduling repairs.

But perhaps the most groundbreaking hire Comcast made was when they brought in Frank Eliason in 2007, who assembled a group of five employees to monitor mentions of Comcast anywhere people were interacting online—and offer help quickly. It's lucky Comcast did that too. Because in 2008, two-thirds of Internet users visited some sort of social networking site, from blogs, Facebook, and Twitter to LinkedIn and You-Tube, Nielsen reported. And 2008 was the first year that people were spending more of their Internet time on social networks than on email.

When Twitter was founded in 2006, it became the next big thing in tech circles. In 2008 and into 2009, it made its mark in the general public. Visitors to Twitter increased 579 percent, from 2.7 million visitors in December 2008 to 18.1 million visitors in December 2009, according to Nielsen.

While Eliason and his team had staked out a presence on most areas of the Internet where Comcast's customers were talking, Eliason's Twitter page @comcastcares was the anchor of their social networking effort. Customers who had a problem with Comcast learned that if they tweeted about it, they often got a faster and more satisfying response than they would from calling customer service.

By 2010, Eliason had more than doubled his team to eleven and they had become a leading example of customer-service social networking done right. As of early 2010, they had helped more than 150,000 customers through all their social media channels. While that is far less than the 308 million customer phone calls that Comcast's 24,000 customer service representatives took in 2009, the social networking group set a tone for the rest of the company and set a standard for other companies to follow.

Eliason, who has a background in call centers, says the forthright culture of social networking has helped open up the atmosphere within Comcast, beyond customer service. "The real-time nature of social media, and the need for speed, has changed the corporate culture. Many companies have a culture of squashing things. But encouraging employees to be out there as individuals in social media and to be open creates a whole different internal feeling at the company."

For instance, if there is a service outage in a particular area, Eliason tells his team to inform customers of the outage, even when the company isn't sure what's causing it. That might not seem like much. But in the past, admitting there was an outage to customers before they knew how to fix it would have made some people in product development mad, because they didn't want anyone to mention anything bad about their product. Eliason says the traditional company line in product development used to be: "Our product is the best, these things don't happen." But Eliason has been able to use Twitter, in particular, to show product development people that "Yes, they do happen, it's obvious. An outage is happening right now." When it does, the Comcast Cares team shares as much as they know with their customers when they know it. And even if those in the company who rarely talk to customers don't like that approach, he says, "customers appreciate that candor."

Also, Eliason's team is showing Comcast that it can learn useful things by merely listening to its customers on the Web. So when a football game went off the air in mid-play, customers began tweeting about it. Eliason and his colleagues saw right away that DirecTV viewers were also tweeting about missing the game. So they knew that it was not their system's fault, but a larger problem with the station doing the live feed. They were able to tell their phone agents, who could immediately tell those who called in what was happening. They also got the message out to their Twitter followers, who then relayed it to others. "We can tweet," says Eliason, "and hit a million people right away."

In addition, the instantaneous quality of these interactions helps save needless work. In the past, Eliason says, if a football game feed went dead like that, phone agents would have gotten the first alert calls. Each agent would have to fill out a ticket on each call. Eventually, the routing people might notice lots of tickets on a particular problem and they would call in engineers, who, in the case of the lost game feed, would not have been able to help. "It would take lots of time to figure out. And if the problem wasn't because of us, we wouldn't know that. Meanwhile the agents wouldn't know what to tell customers. Now we know immediately."

Comcast's story shows that engaging with customers online in real-time conversations about their company is becoming essential for survival in the new corporate landscape. It boils down to upper management choosing to be a part of it. "Customers are talking," says Eliason, "whether you are out there or not." By engaging in those conversations, he says, a relationship can be built with customers, even unhappy ones. If a company isn't paying attention to what is being said to them, or about them, online, bad feelings "just boil, and boil, and boil, and foster a hatred for the company. If you continue to build up that mistrust, you have trouble. But responding on Twitter or other online forums is a way you can build trust and earn respect with customers." For Comcast, it has paved the way to repairing their reputation.

Social networking can also assist in building the reputation of a newer company. Most employees at Zappos have a Twitter account. It's not required. But CEO Tony Hsieh tweets all the time, as he has almost from the beginning of Twitter in 2006. By early 2010, Hsieh's account, @zappos, had more than 1.5 million followers. In 2009, he wrote a post on his Zappos blog with the headline "How Twitter Can Make You A Better (and Happier) Person," in which he sung the praises of tweeting and talked about how he learned to do it, even within its 140 character limit: "Think of each tweet as a dot on a piece of paper. Any single tweet, just like any single dot, by itself can be insignificant and meaningless. But, if over time, you end up with a lot of tweets, it's like having a lot of dots drawn on a piece of paper." That turns into a "total picture," he said, of the person who is tweeting. Then when you view those pictures together, of all the people in a company, you can see the character of the place.

"I have to admit," Hsieh wrote, "like probably most other people, when I first joined Twitter I felt a bit uncomfortable publicly announcing what I was doing and what I was thinking. But because radical transparence was part of the culture of tweeting, I decided to give it a try and be as transparent as possible, both for myself personally and for Zappos. What I found was that people really appreciated the openness and honesty, and that led people to feel more of a personal connection with Zappos and me compared to other corporations and businesspeople that were on Twitter."

Since I spoke to Hsieh in 2008, he has written a book that distills his story and the company story, called *Delivering Happiness: A Path to Profits, Passion, and Purpose,* which was published in 2010. Zappos continued to thrive, and in 2009 it was bought by Amazon. Its reputation for particularly adept customer service has become legendary, and from all reports, keeping that intact was a precondition of the Amazon sale on both sides.

The amazing growth of Zappos was in sync with, and assisted by, the rise of social networking. Maura Sullivan, a manager at the Zappos call center, has been at the company since 2003, and she has seen how social networking has enhanced their customer service culture. "Tony was the big one who started Twitter here. It wasn't for our customers at first. It was for us to build tighter bonds internally with co-workers and employees. We have such a family environment already, and it has helped us strengthen that bond as we have grown." She says she finds that it helps her get to know her employees and it helps them get to know her. Twitter became the Zappos water cooler, where employees gathered and talked about things not related to work. "I would tweet," says Sullivan, "that I went for a run in the morning and wasn't the sunrise beautiful? And I'd come into work and four or five people would say to me, 'Yeah, it was a great sunrise' or 'I didn't know you were a runner.' It broke down walls between us."

Now Zappos has a group of employees, similar to the Comcast Cares team, that engages in online conversations about Zappos with customers. And the customer service department has its own page, @Zappos_Service. "I guess some companies use Twitter as a marketing thing," says Sullivan, "to sell or gain customers. For us, just like email and live chat, it is just another touch point for our customers," meaning it is one more place where the people who buy from them can interact with their employees.

For all the gushing about Twitter and "social media" (a term Sullivan says Hsieh doesn't like), the people at Zappos know that telephone customer service is still their most powerful tool. A tweet from Hsieh confirms that. "Even though it's low-tech, one of the best forms of social media is the telephone. (That's why our 1-800 number is on every page.)"

In 2009, Zappos averaged about 5,000 to 6,000 calls per day (that works out to around 2 million calls per year). And in December 2009, their peak month, they averaged about 12,000 calls per day. In early 2010, there were more than 350 phone agents at Zappos, and Sullivan says they will have hired about 100 more by the end of the year.

"The phone is our best branding device," says Sullivan. With more than 10 million customers, "we don't get to talk to all of them. So once we get a customer on the phone, that's our time to shine. We want to make sure they get that Zappos experience, and have a lot of fun."

It's a refreshing attitude for a customer service department to foster. But Zappos's success also reflects how common courtesy and manners are in such short supply in our public interactions today. "Working at Zappos," says Sullivan, "has opened my eyes to how we treat each other in the world. People have their defenses up when they call us because they're expecting to get the same type of service they've gotten everywhere else. So even if we just say, 'Yes, I'm happy to help you,' it puts them in a comfortable spot. And they say, 'Oh gosh, this is different.' So we get rave reviews. Maybe that's because people's expectations are so low." Sullivan sums up their formula for interacting with their customers and their employees—online, on the phone, or in person—this way: "It's about doing the right thing, and giving people the benefit of the doubt."

Social networking has not been a cure-all for what ails many companies when it comes to customer service. Companies that didn't treat their customers well before they got on Twitter, won't magically learn to relate to them well through social media. But there is no question that the people in charge of making decisions about how customers will be treated are paying attention to the shift in power that social media is spurring.

Brent Leary is an Atlanta-based business blogger and consultant to companies that want to improve their relationships with customers. He is particularly versed in how companies use social media. He says from 2005 to 2010, the landscape changed significantly. "Social media has given customers a voice like never before, and companies are listening now. These new tools are changing everything, and everybody has to adapt, both the companies and the customers. Customers are getting a taste of what it is like to have a say in things, and be heard, and to organize. Companies that have been kind of slow to respond don't have that luxury anymore. They are going to have to change the way they view the relationship between customers and companies. A lot of them still think they have the upper hand."

The stories that keep appearing in the mainstream media about fed-up customers taking to the Internet have woken up many companies to the angry masses that are sometimes right outside their gates. In 2009, a musician whose guitar was mishandled by United Airlines did not get much response from the company when he complained through regular channels. So he took to YouTube and did a short, clever, well-produced music video called "United Breaks Guitars." It went viral and the company had to work extra hard to repair the damage, not only to the musician's guitar, but also to its reputation. And in 2010, film director Kevin Smith famously tweeted about being thrown off a Southwest Airlines flight because he was too large for just one seat. He had more than 1 million followers, and Southwest—a company that has been ahead of the curve in using social networking for customer service—responded with Twitter apologies, as well as apologies in the mainstream media.

Partly because of social networking's influence, companies are having to turn to customer service, more and more, to take the lead in proactively preventing such mistreatment of customer complaints and concerns. Public relations, marketing, and even legal are starting to recognize that the traditional business model that marginalized the customer service function (and hence the customer) is no longer viable. "These tools actually allow customers to have much more say in who they do business with," says Leary. "Because customers can reach so many more people and companies to make decisions about where to spend, they have many more options. Companies have to understand that they need to change the way they get customers and keep them. Because it is really easy for customers to replace them now."

In some cases, all this has made upper management aware that they have to devote more resources to customer service than they have in the past. "Service is becoming a more important part of a lot of companies," Comcast's Eliason says. Social networking between companies and customers is also starting to give customer service a more prominent role within the company pecking order. That is good news for customers.

Eliason says Twitter and other social media are like real-time focus groups. But the information flows both ways now too, so customers can voice their issues and the company can respond, all in real time, creating "a good convergence between marketing, PR, and service. Historically in any company, it would take forever to get messaging out. Marketing would review it, PR might review it, and legal might review it." But now, says Eliason, "customer service must be prepared to communicate with customers instantly."

The only problem is that no one channel of communication can be the savior of customer service. If a Comcast customer's problem is that his or her Internet connection is down, for instance, then tweeting isn't the way to get help. Or if the Comcast Cares people are good, but the phone system is exasperating and agents aren't empowered to solve problems, customers still will be put off. Eliason realizes these things, so he cautions that "social media is not a fix for customer service. Companies have to get their other channels in line with their social media," and make sure they project the same values, innovation, and attitude on the phone, the website, and in other lines of communication. "You have to find ways to bring it all together," he says.

So even though social networking has become a bright, shiny, new object in the world of customer service—and even though Twitter, Facebook, YouTube, and others are starting to help customers get more attention from the top brass, and customer service gets more support in the bottom line—the basics of good customer service still apply. "Everything we have done in social media," says Eliason, "is centered around what you would do in service. To me, it's customer service 101."

In fact, a company's relationship with its customers is only as good as its weakest link. And that weak link, often, is the customer service call center. So even if a company becomes a star in social networking, it must redouble its efforts to address its most pressing customer service issues wherever they occur in the company. Because if a call center is still marginalized in the corporate hierarchy, and its workers are still treating customers poorly on the phone, all the tweeting in the world won't fix that.

Appendix: Updates Since the Hardcover

The world of customer service is ever-changing and often evolving. Since the hardcover edition of this book, some of the people I wrote about have moved into other jobs. Companies have changed and grown, and new issues and leaders have emerged.

Here is a brief update of one notable story.

• David McQuillen—CEO Buy-In

David McQuillen left Credit Suisse in Zurich for a similar position, as head of customer experience, at OCBC Bank in Singapore. One of Asia's biggest banks, OCBC has operations in fifteen Asian countries, including Japan and China.

McQuillen was recruited and hired by OCBC's CEO, David Conner, formerly with Citibank, and the chairman of the board of directors, Cheong Choong Kong, former head of Singapore Airlines. "The CEO is convinced the only way his bank is going to succeed is if they differentiate themselves from competitors by delivering the best customer experience in their markets." McQuillen said he was convinced to leave Switzerland and move his family to Singapore because he saw that the bank was "taking the mission of transforming their customer experience very seriously. The customer service mind-set comes directly from the top."

I spoke to McQuillen as he was just getting started in 2010. While McQuillen was not sure how it would play out, he was encouraged to have the chairman and the CEO "fully behind this." At Credit Suisse, he said, "we were buried in the Chief Operations Officer's department and maybe would meet with the CEO once a year."

One of the things I concluded after all my travels and visits to call centers and talks with people all over the industry is that the commitment to customers has to come from the top of a company. At companies like FedEx and Zappos, the CEOs had told me that. And I saw it in companies that hadn't taken that mission seriously until they were finally forced to, like Sprint and Comcast.

Credit Suisse had made an attempt at it. McQuillen was proud of what he and his team were able to accomplish there and of the support they got from many in the bank. But their efforts mostly evolved from their own work and that of their team. I remember that when I visited them in Zurich they seemed to spend a lot of time working to educate and convince many people in many parts of the bank that changing their mind-set was worth the effort.

McQuillen called their work at Credit Suisse "a grassroots movement. We were gradually working our way up to the executive level, transforming the culture from the bottom up. We saw at Credit Suisse that this grassroots movement was going to take a lot of time and a lot more energy. What's exciting about OCBC is that the movement for change is also from the top down. I'm not saying that one is better than the other. It's just different. When I got here, I found a lot more is already being done at the grassroots level than I expected. So here we already have more support from the top and in the grassroots." By *grassroots*, McQuillen means the people who implement the corporate strategies, the mid-level managers who run the call centers, the branches, the website, product development, operations, and IT.

He says he will employ some of the tactics he used successfully at Credit Suisse to help employees learn more empathy for their customers, such as asking employees to go through what their customers go through, so they can better understand the customers' needs and make their experience better.

McQuillen reports directly to Conner and is heartened to see that customer experience is on the agenda of executive management meetings. He is also especially interested to see how CEO buy-in will affect the process of change that needs to take place at the bank.

—⁓—

Here is an update of a trend that has expanded since I wrote about it in the hardcover edition.

• Alpine Access—Growth in Home Sourcing

JetBlue was a pioneer. Now many companies, including FedEx, have begun to integrate at-home agents into their call center operations. Other companies are also thriving as outsourcers of at-home agents and the creators of virtual call centers. I originally visited one of those home-sourcing companies, Cloud 10, based in Denver. In 2009 it was bought by its Danish investor, Transcom. Its CEO, Sean Erickson, helped with the transition and by 2010 had moved on to other opportunities.

Another leading home-sourcing company also based in Denver is Alpine Access. It started in 1997 and by 2010 had 2,800 employees working full-time and part-time from home in thirty-seven states. Revenue has increased every year since they began.

Alpine CEO Chris Carrington says that growth in home sourcing, combined with the downturn in the economy, has meant that now when his company advertises 200 positions, they are likely to get anywhere from 10,000 to 20,000 applicants from all over the country.

"Five years ago," Carrington says, "we would have been lucky to receive 25,000 to 40,000 applications a year. In 2009 we received in excess of 120,000 applications. People's perceptions have changed. They see this as a viable career. The supply of workers has increased because the credibility of this job has grown among workers and companies."

Now Alpine and other home-sourcing companies have started consulting with clients who might not want to outsource, but do want to set up their own virtual call centers with agents working from home. Carrington is optimistic that the model will only grow in popularity.

—∿—

McQuillen's quest—to help companies become proactive and design their customer experience, instead of just reactively relegating problems to plain old customer service—is one of the most exciting ways that innovation is changing customer service.

Taking agents out of factory-like call centers and setting them up to work from their own homes, is infusing some humanity and dignity back into the work.

What started as the telephone customer service industry in the early 1980s will enter its fourth decade in the 2010s. Increasingly, the industry has had to adjust to the new ways customers can connect to them—from 800 numbers, faxes, and websites to email, texting, and social media. But as the channels for connection increase, so too do the opportunities for companies to get their interactions with customers wrong, or right. Which way they go ends up being the result of choices made at the highest levels of corporate governance.

With Americans alone making more than 43 billion calls to customer service a year, the attention that companies give to how they interact with the people who buy what they are selling is a huge part of how we, as human beings, treat each other in public. Good customer service can be something that makes the world a better place. Or bad customer service can add obstacles to doing what we need to do in our lives each day, and make the world a more discordant place. Only companies can choose the path to good, by giving their customer experience the resources and attention it deserves.

How would our lives change if the head of customer service at a company were paid second only to the CEO? What if being a customer service agent were a well-paid, coveted career position, and one that led to upper management? What if everyone in a company were focused first on how their actions affected their company's customers? From all I have seen in my exploration, it is clear that the few companies that have been able to foster such elements in their culture have thrived, even during downturns. It is the kind of thinking that can change the way we feel about the companies in our lives. It can make the world a better place.

It is also good business. Companies that innovate and expand their attention to and care for their customers will have the edge in this decade, and this century. Those that don't might do okay in the short-term. But ultimately, as has been demonstrated time and again, they will fall on their own customer neglect.

Acknowledgments

When I started this book, it was not a sure thing that companies would be open to a journalist who wanted to explore how they operate. But I was fortunate to meet people who not only allowed me into their companies, but were committed to helping me find and understand the real stories behind their work. Without their assistance this book would not have been possible. I am extremely grateful.

At TeleTech I thank K. C. Higgins, who is the kind of fair, effective, and professional PR executive that all journalists hope to find and that all companies should seek to cultivate. She protects her company's interest without sacrificing the truth. I also thank CEO Kenneth Tuchman for giving me such unprecedented access to his company. I thank Brian Delaney and Cormac Twomey for helping me see the big picture. I thank John Yanez for traveling to Buenos Aires for my visit and for his invaluable insights once I got there. I thank Martin Sucari for his warm Argentinean hospitality and for letting me see clearly how the Buenos Aires office works. And I thank all the call center workers in Buenos Aires who let me ask them lots of questions. I also thank the other TeleTech executives in Buenos Aires who spoke with me and shared their thoughts, feelings, and experiences, including Matthew Trebb, Miguel Lecuona, Diego Mainetti, Pablo Riccheri, Leonardo Misrahi, and of course, the venerated call center supervisor Pablo Martelli.

At FedEx my thanks go to Sheila Harrell, who took so much time with me and shared such important perspectives. I also thank her colleague Sherri Tipton for going above and beyond the call of duty whenever I asked. I thank Jess Bunn, Bill Margaritis, and Diane Terrell for allowing my work to happen and for help at crucial points along the way. Thanks to FedEx CEO and founder Fred Smith, who graciously took time with me and gave such helpful insights. I also thank June Fitzgerald, Le Anne Symonds, and Matt Ceniceros for help in coordinating my interviews. Special thanks to Kathy Anderson, and to Dante Williams, and to all whom I interviewed at the call center. And thanks to Maisha Allen.

At JetBlue, Cris Palauni made my visit flow without a hitch and was supremely helpful and kind at every point along the way. I also thank Frankie Littleford for sharing her vast experience in customer service and for opening her call center to me. Thanks to Bryan Baldwin in the New York office. I thank Michelle Olsen for taking me to the homes of Bonnie Jacobson and Suzy Dall, and I thank them both for welcoming me and letting me see them at work. I also appreciate Marlene and Tom Goudie for welcoming me into their home and their lives. And I am grateful to Kristal Anderson.

At Credit Suisse in Zurich my greatest thanks go to David McQuillen. He was unfailingly accommodating, fun, and full of mind-opening insights. Much gratitude also to Bojan Blecic for his patience, kindness, and intelligent perspective. David and Bojan are both masters of the art of the customer experience. Stephan Kuebler and Tiia Tuisku taught me much about empathy for customers and about the depth that is possible when focusing on the customer's point of view. I also interviewed and learned from so many other people at Credit Suisse. I am grateful to Peter Angehrn for his time and for allowing me such access to the marketing area of the company, and to Helena Jordao for her time and the time of most of her staff. Thanks too to Bill Staikos for his American viewpoint and for help in navigating Zurich. And great thanks for sitting down to interviews also goes to Martin Petr, Alex Nippe, Marcel Sieber, Alexandre Robert, Susanna Neyen, Sissi Vandenbrouck, Alexander Gier, Christian Gut, Michael Ruetti, and Roland Helfenstein. Thanks also to Anna Brugnoli for coordinating my visit.

At Xceed in Egypt I am especially grateful for the help and perspective of Ossama Nasmi. I thank all the Xceed call center workers and their manager, Ahmed Amin, and Ghada Essam Shawki at Xceed as well. I also am indebted to Khaled Shash at Raya Contact Center for his illuminating observations and for his graciousness. Many in the Egyptian government were also open and knowledgeable and generous with their time, their assistance, and their frank insights. I thank Mohamed Omran, Mohamed Magdi, Amin Khairaldin, Hani El Kolaly, and Noha A. El Sheikh. I also thank Ahmed Reda for his help in coordinating my visit. And special thanks to Mai Medhat for going out of her way to help me navigate around Cairo and the Smart Village.

At EDF Energy in Great Britain I thank Kevin Gatens for his openness and hospitality on my visit there. I also thank Joy Thompson, Dan Pritchard, and Hanna Spence.

At Nuance Communications great thanks go to Peter Mahoney for his insights and to Kristen Wylie for her help in making my visit go so smoothly. And special thanks to Stephen Springer, Robby Kilgore, and Julie Stinneford for taking so much time with me in Boston and New York, and for being so open and thoughtful about the art and science of their work.

At GetHuman.com and Kayak.com in Boston I thank Paul English for all his help. I also thank Lorna Rankin at GetHuman.com for her good help. At Cloud 10 in Denver I thank Sean Erickson for sharing his experiences in the customer service industry and for giving me such a useful overview of the work-at-home trend in call centers. At Zappos.com CEO Tony Hsieh is as open, accessible, and full of enthusiasm and commitment to customer service as everyone says he is. I also thank Renna Coulson for her help with all things Zappos. At SOCAP I thank Beth Thomas-Kim for taking so much time with me and for offering a valuable overview of the industry. At GetSatisfaction.com I thank Thor Muller for a few long conversations that helped me see what seems to be part of the future of customer service. At Amtrak thanks to Matt Hardison and to Karina Romero. And at Comcast I thank Rick Germano and Jenni Moyer. At Sprint thanks to Eronia Singleton and Scott Sloat.

Many other people in the industry guided me as I found my way. Most are quoted in the book. I am grateful for their input.

Scott Broetzmann at Customer Care Measurement and Consulting was particularly helpful and encouraging at so many points in the research and writing of this book. His ability to interpret and convey in laymen's terms the inside technicalities and peculiarities of the business made him a touchstone for me throughout this project. I also thank Mary Jo Bitner at Arizona State University for putting the challenges of customer service in perspective. And Mark Grainer of Customer Care Measurement and Consulting helped me understand the background of the industry.

Keith Dawson at Frost & Sullivan spent many hours discussing the world of call centers with me from his unique vantage point of covering the industry for so many years as the editor of *Call Center* magazine and now as a consultant. I was a fan of his writing before we spoke and was not disappointed as he answered every question I threw at him thoughtfully and with precision.

Peter Ryan at Datamonitor also provided important perspectives and analysis, particularly on foreign outsourcing. In addition to talking to him, I was able to get so much good background from his extensive writing on the subject. Claes Fornell at the University of Michigan helped me understand customer satisfaction measurement. He also maintained good humor throughout our talks, even when I turned to him to help me comprehend the ways of his native Sweden.

Ben Popken at Consumerist.com was a great interview and runs a fantastic website that has helped change customer service for the better. I thank Vincent Ferrari for being so open with me and so welcoming. I also can't complain for a second about the Rev. Will Bowen and his graciousness in taking time to talk to me. And I thank Ralph Nader for talking to me and being so encouraging.

Pete Blackshaw could not have been nicer even though he was busy gearing up for the release of his own important book when we spoke. And I had more fun interviewing Bob Garfield than just about anyone, ever. For other assistance, I also thank Jeff Jarvis and Greg Brummer.

At SpeechTEK and destinationCRM I am grateful for help from the staff of Information Today. And I thank all the journalists and consultants whom I didn't get to interview personally, but whom I was lucky to quote in pivotal places. And I thank Andy and Allison Cates for their ongoing support and friendship, and for connecting me with Ken Van Vranken at Fujitsu, who gave me useful background on the outsourcing business.

In Argentina I thank Patrick McDonnell with the *Los Angeles Times* for good meals and good advice. And I thank Rodrigo and Guiti Benadon for their hospitality in Buenos Aires. I also thank Gustavo Weidemann, CEO of Next, and Rodrigo Rollan, a supervisor in the technical support call center at Next, for showing me their homegrown Argentinean company.

In Egypt I thank Hebba Bakri at the Hotel Longchamps for making me feel at home and sharing her thoughts about Egypt, women, outsourcing, and the world.

In my writing, I had wonderful support in so many ways. Three people stand out in particular.

First is Linda Raiteri, who read every word I wrote before anyone else. Without her patient, wise, and intelligent feedback and her enduring support on a daily basis I am not sure I would have been able to do this. She is a writer's writer and a dear friend.

I am also extremely grateful to Martha Jane Diana, the best transcriber I know. She converted the hundreds of hours of taped interviews for this book into written form more efficiently and effectively than I could have ever done. She was also a pleasure to work with and offered support and feedback way above and beyond the call of duty.

And Chris Tague was a tough second reader, who always kept me on my toes with her thoughtful and perceptive comments and suggestions. I am grateful that she was willing to help me.

I also got further important feedback on the writing from two very good friends: Martha Huie and Lisa Sisson. They came in at just the right time with just the right observations and suggestions.

And I thank other colleagues who are also friends for their continued support and inspiration: Michael Flamini, Kayce Freed Jennings, Lisa Freed, Judy Freed, Kevin Sack, Marty Gottlieb, Lenlee Heep,

Leesa Travis, Jim Hoppin, Eli Brown, Bobby Smith, Jack Doppelt, and Zack McMillin.

Many friends were also there for me through the whole process. In ways personal and professional they helped me with this book. And of course, their calls are always very important to me.

I especially thank Ellen Cooper Klyce, who is like a sister to me and is the only other surviving fellow member of the Tuffy McAdams Society. She has been there for me in many ways that I never expected (and she probably didn't either) but for which I am so grateful. I also thank Amanda Cowan, who helps me keep my visions of success alive even against all the evidence; and to her husband, Jim Cowan, for helping her do that for me and for being so good to her too. For many good dinners and much-needed family time I thank Merry Mariano, Andy Mariano, and Carolyn, Allie, and Jake Mariano, and Robert and Alice Davis.

For political discussions, and fun, and friendship at just the right times I thank Paula Casey. And for support in writing and life I thank Janann Sherman. I also thank Happy Jones, Jocelyn Wurzberg, and Bobby Bostick for their faith in me and my work.

My friends around the United States and the world are treasured even at a distance. I am grateful to have in my life and always keep in my heart Vivienne Jenkins; Anne Cumberland and Shona and Lorna Gascoine; Anthony, Michelle, and Elliott Hobson-Curran; Lisa, Daryl, Anna, Margot, Tillie, and Ruby Sisson; Karen Jozefowicz; Junius Harris and David Lebow; Nina and Marshall Zaslove; Sandy, Tim, Andrew, and Emily Ainger; Karina Spero and Stephen Simms; Maria and Jerome Berg; Aleece Hiller and Janet Boyer; Jean and Dan Rothermel; and Nina and Grace Weinstein.

In Memphis there are many who offer support and friendship whenever I call. I feel very lucky to have in my corner Sharon Bicks; Marcia Bicks; Ben Wilson; Anabel Conrad and Iddo, Theo, Jesse, and Dinah Patt; Lurene, Chris, and Maddox Kelley; Suzanne Bonefas; Judy and Fred Wimmer; Donna Sue and Wayne Shannon; Frank and Carol Fourmy; Craig, Linda, and McKenzie Leake; Anna, Shawn, Maya, and

Riley Kelly; Connie Kelly; Jenny, Keith, Sydney, Sadie, and Summer Tomes; Cookie Ewing and John Sanford; Elisa Blatteis, Matt and Lilly Roberts; Michael and Libby Dacaetani; Melissa Thornton; Elaine Robertson and the entire Robertson family; and Luella Cook.

I am also thankful for the support of my professional and personal efforts in Memphis from Bob Fockler; Vicki Grimes; Pitt and Barbara Hyde; Teresa Sloyan; Kim Tobin; Gretchen McLennon; Lauren Taylor; Paul and Phyllis Berz; Harriet Stern; Dan Murrell; Aurelia and Billy Kyles; Dwayna Kyles; Ben and Frances Hooks; Rachel Shankman; Susan Snodgrass; Penny Aviotti; Deannie Parker; Beverly Robertson; Jim and Jeanne Johnson; and Hans and Marcia Faulhaber.

And I thank Judy Haas and Gordon Bigelow; Margaret Metz and Bill Stegall; David Tankerley; Kim Brisco; Susan Murrmann; Henry Nelson; Leanne Kleinmann; Bob and Christina Klyce; Nancy and John Knight; Susan, David, and Julia Weber; Bill and Susan and Erin and Joey Remijan; Roy and Pam and Carly Haithcock; Tom and Gini Mitchell; Robert Gordon and Tara McAdams; Leah Bray Nichols; Steve Cantor; Karen Lebovitz; Leah Fyfe Stokes; Joe and Lynne Pizzirusso; Dana Sachs; David, Angela, and Emma Less; Rosalyn Willis; Babs and Jef Fiebelman; Brooke Prudhomme; Kimberly Meeks; Ema Mosby; Tony Horne; Joe Birch; Jeremy Jones; Kathy Kasten, Nathan and Andrea Bicks; Patrice Eastham, and Sam, and Buck; Scott Graves; Craig Brewer; Cheryl and Corey Messler; Gary Stella; Marge and Dick Routon; Sundance Raiteri and Sophie Yellin; and everyone at the Memphis Farmer's Market and the Memphis Literacy Council.

One person provided some very necessary ongoing diversion from the everyday grind of writing this book—my godson Graham Kelly. He was patient with me when the work got in the way of our time together and always a delight when we did hang out. He is a light in my life. I am also grateful to his sister Arabella Kelly for her loving spirit, and to his father Shawn Kelly for friendship that endures. Graham's grandparents Paulette and Carl Kelly are a constant and loving support to me too. And I thank the rest of the Kelly family for our enduring bonds.

Christie Watts Kelly is always with me in all my writing, and in the rest of my life every day too. I miss her so much and thank the Watts family for their continuing connection. Jennifer Watts Hoff is my honorary little sister, and her friendship and support bolster me in my work and my life. I am also grateful for the friendship of Tripp Watts, who is like a brother to me. And I thank Christie's parents, Gail and Dean Watts, and her sister Heather Watts. And thanks for support from Christie's aunts Janie Spartaro, Emily Card, and Judy Watts.

Then there is my own family. I send out ongoing gratitude to my aunts and uncles and cousins. I'm so glad we all keep in touch and still are in each other's lives. Tom and Carol Gilmer; Charlotte and Jack Samuels; Jack and Michelle Yellin; Joye and Stuart Sabel; Steve Kleiner; Richard, Hera, Nick, Mark, and Hannah Evans; Brad, Mariam, and Sam John Gilmer; Dwight, Laurie, Carrie, Jake, and Jon Evans; Joan and Dick Brown; Louan and Kathy Jo Torres; Richard and Roger Brown; Arnold, Devra, and Peri Lupowitz; Freddie Lupowitz; Carol and Michael Berman; Tamra Feldman; Gail Feldman; and Arthur Yellin.

My brothers Doug and Tom are, as always, a joy in the good times and a buffer in the not-so-good times. Their love and support through the years are an anchor for me. I am also supremely fortunate to have the love and support of their dear wives, my sisters-in-law Shari Finkelstein and Jean McDonald. And I am ever grateful for the bedrock friendship of my original sister-in-law, Linda Yellin Kleiner, who was the wife of my oldest brother, Chuck. I miss him all the time, but feel lucky that he left me with such a supportive friend/sister.

My nephew Peyto Yellin is another light in my life, as are my nieces Chloe, Isabel, Cole, and Lara Yellin, and my great-nephew Ezra Yellin. It is my delight to watch them all grow and blossom into such amazing people. Loving them unconditionally and cheering them each on through life is a role I relish.

Yet again I thank the people at Free Press. First and foremost, I thank my editor, Wylie O'Sullivan. She is a pleasure to work with, and knew just what to say and do at all turns to make sure I got this book written and to shepherd it through to publication. Her professionalism, good judgment, and smart input got me through the process and inspired me along the way. I thank Nicole Kalian for her excellent work as a publicist. I also thank Liz Stein for acquiring the book and for helping it come to be. I thank J. D. Porter, Donna Loffredo, Sydney Tanigawa, and Sharbari Kamat for their assistance in putting this book together. And I thank Beverly Miller, Celia Knight, Suzanne Donahue, Shannon Gallagher, Giselle Roig, Carisa Hays, and Elisa Rivlin. And I am grateful for the care and nurturing that Dominick Anfuso and Martha Levin have given me and my work throughout the course of this book and my first book.

I am also grateful to everyone at the Zachary Shuster Harmsworth agency. I feel very lucky to have them all on my side. Most especially I thank Jennifer Gates, who is the reason I have any kind of career in publishing. She is an ideal ally and agent, and her commitment to me and my writing defies explanation, given all the ups and downs she has seen me through in the last decade. But I am thankful that she has been there always to look after my interests and to listen, advise, laugh, and cajole me into getting the work done.

And finally, I thank my parents, David Gilmer Yellin and Carol Lynn Yellin, who are with me every day in my writing and in my life. Not even their deaths can diminish the power of the love and guidance they have given me.

Notes

Chapter 1:
Random Acts of Rudeness

Page

2 **To be fair:** Steve Farkas et al., *Aggravating Circumstances: A Status Report on Rudeness in America* (New York: Public Agenda, 2002).

4 **Govan, who also happens to:** Scott Goldstein, "And the Customer Service Award Does NOT Go to . . . ," *Chicago Tribune*, August 17, 2005; Don Oldenburg, "Demonizing the Customer," *Washington Post*, November 13, 2005.

6 **"It had never occurred to me to":** Neely Tucker, "Taking a Whack Against Comcast," *Washington Post*, October 18, 2007.

8 **In a speech in early January:** Stephanie Mehta, "Cable's Consumer Electronics Makeover," Fortune.com, January 7, 2008; Bob Fernandez, "At CES, Comcast Promises New Services," *Philadelphia Inquirer*, January 8, 2008.

9 **In a blog for *BusinessWeek*:** Jena McGregor, "Comcast's Customer Service Woes: Do Investors Care?" BusinessWeek.com, January 22, 2008.

9 **But a Fortune.com news brief:** Dailybriefing.blogs.fortune.com, February 14, 2008.

11 **Well after his Swedish soldier days:** American Customer Satisfaction Index, www.theacsi.org.

12 **And measuring it from the consumer's:** Claes Fornell, "The Science of Satisfaction," *Harvard Business Review*, March 2001; Karen Christensen, "Interview with a Customer Satisfaction Guru: Claes Fornell," *Rotman Magazine*, Winter 2003.

15 **But the study went on:** Customer Care Measurement and
Consulting, "Customer Care—The Multimillion Dollar Sinkhole: A
Case of Customer Rage Unassuaged," October 2003.

15 **The Customer Rage Study:** Customer Care Measurement and
Consulting, "2004 National Customer Rage Study: A Case of
Customer Rage Unassuaged," November 2004; Customer Care
Measurement and Consulting, "2005 Customer Rage Study,"
November 2005; "Results of the 2007 National Customer Rage
Study," November 2007.

18 **"My name is Stavros":** Stavros Papadopoulos is not the landlord's
real name.

Chapter 2:
What Would Alexander Graham Bell Say Now?

Page

20 **She sent the youngest of:** James C. Rippey, *Goodbye, Central; Hello,
World—A Centennial History of Northwestern Bell* (Telephone Pioneers
of America, 1975), p. 321; Telecommunications Virtual Museum,
Heroes: Mildred Lothrop, www.telecomhistory.org.

22 **Vail's ideas about humane treatment:** Kenneth P. Todd, Jr., *A
Capsule History of the Bell System* (New York: AT&T, 1997).
http://www.porticus.org/bell/capsule_bell_system.html.

24 **In November 1882:** "Through the Telephone," *New York Times*,
November 12, 1882, p. 5; "Swearing by Telephone," *New York Times*,
December 28, 1882, p. 5.

24 **By 1902, swearing at operators:** "Telephone Swearing Illegal," *New
York Times*, September 16, 1902; "Mustn't Swear by Telephone," *New
York Times*, July 24, 1902.

26 **Casson also foreshadowed:** Herbert N. Casson, *The History of the
Telephone* (Chicago: A. C. McClurg & Co., 1910).

27 **Corporate executives also commissioned:** Richard Mathais,
"History of Winnetka's Telephone Service,"
www.winnetkahistory.org/gazette/thingsplace/telephone_history.htm;

www.atlantatelephonehistory.info/part1.html; pbskids.org/wayback/tech1900/phone.html; "Telephone Operators," www.ieee-virtual-museum.org.

27 **The women came to be called "hello girls":** Richard John, *Telephonmania: The Contested Origins of the Urban Telephone Operating Company in the United States, 1879–1894* (Chicago: Great Cities Institute, University of Illinois at Chicago, June 2005).

28 **Despite the civilizing influence:** Jim Blount, "Female Operators Key to Phone Service for Decades," [Cincinnati] *Journal-News*, December 6, 2006.

28 **An anonymous poem:** www.telephonetribute.com/images/de_ivy/topfeb3.jpg.

30 **The 1906 article:** "The Passing of the Telephone Girl: A Retrospect," *New York Times Magazine*, March 4, 1906; "Does Away with the 'Hello' Girl," *New York Times*, November 3, 1892.

31 **The consultants found:** "Do You Say 'Hello'? Is Jaw Stiff? Then Your Phone Manners Are Bad," *New York Times*, August 1, 1950.

32 **Then he waxed poetic:** Isadore Barmash, "Retailers Termed Complacent About Customers' Complaints," *New York Times*, November 14, 1965.

33 **It didn't gain as much strength:** John Morris, "Businessmen Call for Self-Reform," *New York Times*, November 13, 1969.

34 **By the early 1970s:** A. Edward Miller, "Consumerism's Other Half," *New York Times*, January 17, 1972.

35 **Companies such as:** Leonard Sloane, "Watchdogs from Within—Corporate Ombudsmen Respond to Consumers," *New York Times*, March 21, 1971.

35 **Suspicion lingered about:** Leonard Sloane, "Consumers Spur Industry Response," *New York Times*, January 7, 1973.

35 **In the mid-1970s:** Better Business Bureau, "What the Better Business Bureau Is—and Does, How It Serves Customers and Business,"

advertising supplement, *New York Times*, November 21, 1976. The study was conducted by the market research firm of Yankelovich, Skelly and White.

35 **An academic survey:** Elizabeth Fowler, "Management—Two Studies on Consumer Attitudes," *New York Times*, November 18, 1977.

36 **In 1976, Gerald Ford's:** Technical Assistance Research Programs, *Consumer Complaint Handling in America: Final Report* (Washington, DC: U.S. Office of Consumer Affairs, Department of Health, Education and Welfare, 1976). One of the other creators of the Customer Rage Survey, Mark Grainer, also wrote the White House Study. He is Scott Broetzmann's partner in his consulting company.

38 **That was in 1987, but much:** Stephen Koepp, "Pul-eeze! Will Somebody Help Me? Frustrated American Consumers Wonder Where Service Went," *Time*, February 2, 1987.

Chapter 3:
"You're Going to Listen to Me"

Page

43 **Reporting in the aftermath:** Randall Stross, "Digital Domain; AOL Said, 'If You Leave Me I'll Do Something Crazy,'" *New York Times*, July 2, 2006.

44 **AOL did seem to learn:** Stross, "Digital Domain."

45 **But Dawson went on to stress:** Keith Dawson, "Super-Empowered Angry Customers," Parts 1–5, CallCenterMagazine.com/blog, November 14, 2006–December 11, 2006.

45 **Consumerist was created by:** http://www.consumerist.com/ consumer/faq/faq-167445.php.

47 **One of the first consumer rebellions:** Jeff Jarvis, "Dell Learns to Listen," *BusinessWeek*, October 17, 2007; Jeff Jarvis, "Dear Mr. Dell," buzzmachine.com, August 17, 2005.

48 **A few months later, much to:** Jeff Jarvis, "Love the Customers Who

Hate You," *BusinessWeek*, February 21, 2008; Dell, press release, April 6, 2008.

49 **John Westphal, who started:** Charles Wolrich, "Top Corporate Hate Web Sites," Forbes.com, March 8, 2005; Amexsux.com.

50 **The practical influence:** Ed Keller and Jon Berry, *The Influentials* (New York: Free Press, 2003).

51 **Blackshaw also writes:** Pete Blackshaw, "Attention? I Don't Want Your Freakin' Attention!" clickz.com, November 27, 2007.

58 **Claus Møller:** The book, *A Complaint Is a Gift* (San Francisco: Berrettz-Koehler, 2008), by Janelle Barlow and and Møller, was revised and updated in 2008 to include two new chapters about the Internet.

63 **That was the claim of:** Toni Whitt, "Where High-Tech Meets Low Opinion," *Sarasota Herald-Tribune*, April 18, 2008.

63 **A Verizon employee told:** Richard Mullins, "Verizon Workers Caught Between Sales, Service," *Tampa Tribune*, April 8, 2008; Nina Kim, "Verizon Employees Protest in Tampa," *St. Petersburg Times*, July 21, 2007.

63 **Almost a year later, in:** Richard Mullins, "Verizon Customers Broadcast Problems with Service," *Tampa Tribune*, March 26, 2008.

64 **A Verizon spokesman said:** Whitt, "Where High-Tech Meets Low Opinion."

64 **Only two customers:** *Tampa Tribune*, www2.tbo.com, from comments on Richard Mullins, "2 People Air Verizon Woes at Tampa Council Meeting," May 1, 2008.

65 **St. Petersburg Times columnist:** Sue Carlton, "Even Your Complaint Is Now Bundled," *St. Petersburg Times*, April 29, 2008.

66 **In late 2005, English:** Bruce Mohl, "Sick of Automation? Dial O for Human," *Boston Globe*, November 6, 2005.

69 **Right around that time, in May:** Jane Spenser, "In Search of the Operator—Firms Spent Billions This Year to Make It Hard to Find One;

How to Reach a Real Person," *Wall Street Journal*, May 8, 2002; Ralph Nader, "Call Waiting," The Nader Page/In the Public Interest, www.nader.org/interest/050902.html.

Chapter 4:
To Send Us Your Firstborn,
Please Press or Say "One"

Page

73 **Then there were the *Saturday Night Live* skits:** *Saturday Night Live* transcripts, season 31: Heder (episode 2, October 8, 2005) and Banderas (episode 15, April 8, 2006); http://snltranscripts.jt.org.

76 **By the beginning of this century:** Daniel Hong, "An Introductory Guide to Speech Recognition Solutions," Datamonitor, August 2006.

82 **At one time, Yahoo!'s:** Steve Coomes, "Calls to Order," *Pizza Marketplace*, February 14, 2003, www.pizzamarketplace.com.

90 **Still, the Internet has:** "The Institutional Yes—An Interview with Jeff Bezos," *Harvard Business Review*, October 2007.

90 **Arkadi Kuhlmann, the founder:** Jena McGregor, "When the Boss Goes to Work in the Call Center," *BusinessWeek*, October 22, 2007; Craig Newmark, "How to Succeed in 2007," *Business 2.0*, February 28, 2007.

91 **"Our customers don't contact":** "The Institutional Yes."

92 **But not everything they:** http://clicheideas.com/amazon.htm.

95 **One of the first questions:** Dale Hrabi, "Blind Date," *Radar*, September 5, 2006, http://www.radaronline.com/features/2006/09/blind_date.php.

96 **Rosalind Picard is:** Liz Karagianis, "Emotional Intelligence—Teaching Machines to Care," *Spectrum*, Spring 2006.

98 **Speech analytics applications employ:** Donna Fluss, *2007 Speech Analytics Market Report* (West Orange, NJ: DMG Consulting, 2007).

98 **Some of the analytics tools:** Tom Keating, "CIA Using CallMiner

Word Spotting?" February 10, 2005, http://blog.tcmnet.com/blog/
tomkeating.

99 **When Bell Canada:** Ryan Joe, "At Bell, Your Voice Is Your Password,"
Speech Technology Magazine, October 1, 2007.

100 **A study by the British:** ContactBabel, "The US Contact Center
Operation Review—Executive Summary," 2007; Lauren Shopp, "Call
Center Report Advocates for Use of Biometrics in Identity Verification,"
Speech Technology Magazine, July 24, 2007.

Chapter 5:
The Other End of the Line

Page

103 **Anderson goes to the next slide:** Albert Mehrabian, professor
emeritus at UCLA, developed this communications theory during
his doctoral work on nonverbal communications in the 1960s, and he
continued working on it throughout his academic career.

119 **The 2006 report also:** U.S. Department of Labor, Bureau of Labor
Statistics, *Occupational Outlook, Customer Service Representatives*
(Washington, DC: U.S. Government Printing Office, May 2006, May
2007).

120 **The study concluded that most people:** Allan Hall, "Secret to a
Long Life—Get Even More Often," *Sydney Morning Herald,* March 21,
2006, www.smh.com.au; Katy Duke, "Faking Happiness at Work Can
Make You Ill," *British Medical Journal*, March 31, 2006, www.bmj.com.

120 **A British academic study:** Christine A. Sprigg, Phoebe R. Smith,
and Paul R. Jackson, "Psychosocial Risk Factors in Call Centres: An
Evaluation of Work Design and Well-Being" (Sheffield: University of
Sheffield, Health and Safety Laboratory, and UMIST, 2003).

121 **Another academic study:** Catriona M. Wallace, "The Sacrificial
HR Strategy in Call Centers," *International Journal of Service Industry
Management* 11 (2000): 174–185.

121 **Professor Zapf, the head:** Katy Duke, "Faking Happiness at Work Can
Make You Ill," *British Medical Journal*, March 31, 2006, www.bmj.com.

121 **The introduction to one customer service:** http://phonerant
.blogspot.com.

122 **Another customer service rep writes:**
http://xanik266.wordpress.com/2007/10/03/what-customer-service-
reps-have-to-deal-with.

124 **In an entry called:** http://CallCenterPurgatory.blogspot.com, 2004–2007.

125 **He has come to believe:** http://xanik266.wordpress.com/category/
personal/work/customer-service.

126 **In an entry entitled "Apathy":**
http://thesupervisorofhell.blogspot.com/2005/07/apathy.html.

127 **But for all the Internet:** Phyllis Korkki, "Still That Need for a Human
on the Line," *New York Times*, October 7, 2007.

128 **A report on customer:** ICMI, "ICMI's Contact Center Outsourcing
Report—Key Findings," September 10, 2007,
http://icmiglobalreport.com.

128 **India has gotten:** www.convergys.com/company/company-overview.php.

129 **The concept of work-at-home agents:** Sue Shellenbarger,
"Outsourcing Jobs to the Den: Call Centers Tap People Who Want to
Work at Home," *Wall Street Journal*, January 12, 2006.

132 **Another unexpected niche:** Dave Kolpack, "Fast Food Technology
Company Honored," *Bismarck Tribune*, October 10, 2007.

132 **At-home agents:** Jon Swartz, "Inmates vs. Outsourcing," *USA Today*,
July 6, 2004.

133 ***BusinessWeek* ran an article:** Jena McGregor, "The Other Indian
Outsourcer," *BusinessWeek*, November 6, 2006.

Chapter 6:
The Next Available Agent: John, Juan, Sean, or Sanjay

Page

144 **Since then, outsourcing:** *CIA Factbook* (Washington, DC: U.S.
Government Printing Office, 2007).

144 **The fact that Argentina:** World Bank edustats, 2006.

151 **The November 2004 *New York Times*:** Saritha Rai, "An Industry in India Cheers Bush's Victory," *New York Times*, November 4, 2004.

152 **The newspaper went on:** Rukmini Shrinivasan, " 'I Made an Indian Girl Cry, You Can Do It Too!'" *Times of India*, January 11, 2005.

152 **A month later, in February 2005:** Rama Lakshmi, "India Call Centers Suffer Storm of 4-Letter Words," *Washington Post*, February 27, 2005.

153 **"Das, who quit":** Mike McPhate, "Insults from America," *New York Newsday*, January 11, 2006; Mike McPhate, "Outsourcing Outrage," *San Francisco Chronicle*, November 17, 2005.

153 **Call center workers and their abusive:** Amrit Dhillon and David Harrison, "India Has Last Laugh in Call Centre Sitcom," *Sunday Telegraph*, January 29, 2006.

154 **At that, the agent:** Chetan Bhagat, *One Night at the Call Center* (New York: Ballantine Books, 2007).

154 **Around the same time all this backlash:** Sudhin Thanawala, "India's Call-Center Jobs Go Begging," *Time*, October 16, 2007.

156 **A May 2006 ribbon-cutting:** Larry Luxner, "A Nearshore Niche in Nicaragua," *CRM Magazine,* July 2006.

158 **ProNicaragua even negotiated:** Anand Giridharadas, "Outsourcing Works, So India Is Exporting Jobs," *New York Times*, September 25, 2007; Lawrence Casiraya, "eTelecare Opens Call Center in Nicaragua," Inquirer.net, August 16, 2007.

159 **The Smart Village also houses:** www.Xceedcc.com.

163 **Still, women not wearing:** Michael Slackman, "Voices Rise in Egypt to Shield Girls from an Old Tradition," *New York Times*, September 20, 2007.

173 **Not everyone sees it:** Paul Sims, "Teenagers Get Lessons in Working in Call Centres," *Daily Mail*, July 23, 2007.

174 **Stirring up negative:** Matthew Taylor, "School with Call
Centre Training Site in Classroom Criticised for Lowering Pupils'
Expectations," *Guardian*, July 23, 2007.

174 **Hylton Red House students:** Taylor, "School with Call Centre
Training Site," *Guardian*, July 23, 2007.

177 **The 2004 article went on:** Chidanand Rajghatta, "A Small Frown in
America," *Times of India*, February 14, 2004.

177 **A *BusinessWeek* article:** Mark Scott, "Luring Customers with Local
Call Centers," *BusinessWeek*, July 24, 2007.

Chapter 7:
The Solution Is the Problem

Page

183 **"CRM emphasized the importance of":** Donna Fluss, "Executive
Interview: Donna Fluss, Principal DMG Consulting, LLC,"
contactcenterworld.com, March 29, 2004.

183 **In 2004, telecom industry:** Brad Smith, "CRM Rides Out the
Storm," *Wireless Week*, February 15, 2004.

184 **Lee's study found:** Dick Lee, "Implement CRM or Become
Customer-Centric," destinationcrm.com, July 1, 2006.

185 **In recent years, the uses of:** Erika Morphy, "Barack Obama: First
CRM President?" *CRM Buyer*, April 8, 2008.

186 **Since the 2003 AT&T Wireless:** Gartner, press release, April 22,
2008.

190 **Those expectations have:** Aspect Contact Center Satisfaction Index,
2005.

191 **Accenture started to prescribe:** Accenture, "Superior Customer
Service Capabilities: Key Factors in the Journey to High Performance,"
May 2007.

193 **Immediately, the story was all over:** www.sprintusers.com/forum, July
2, 2007; Planetfeedback.com, July 7, 2007; gizmodo.com, July 5, 2007.

194 **A few months after MSN:** Jenna Goudreau, "Sprint Nextel: Last in Customer Service," *BusinessWeek*, July 27, 2007.

194 **In December 2007:** Spencer E. Ante, "Sprint's Wake-Up Call," *BusinessWeek*, February 21, 2008.

196 **One of Hesse's early:** Ante, "Sprint's Wake-Up Call"; Sprint Nextel Corporation Q4 2007 Earnings Call Transcript, February 28, 2008; Michal Lev-Ram, "Sprint's Dreadful Customer Service Is CEO Hesse's No. 1 Priority," February 28, 2008, techland.blogs.fortune.cnn.com.

197 **And another reader said:** Diane Stafford, "$40 Million to the Sprint CEO, Pink Slips to Thousands," March 28, 2008, workspacekc. typepad.com.

197 **In April 2008, an ABC News:** Dan Harris, "CEOs Rake It In When Their Companies Tank," ABC News, *Nightline*, April 30, 2008.

198 **Hesse had his work:** Sprint Nextel Q1 2008 Earnings Call Transcript, May 12, 2008.

198 **In that conference call:** Sprint Nextel Q4 2007 Earnings Call Transcript, February 28, 2008.

202 **In the 1985 book:** Karl Albrecht and Ron Zemke, *Service America: Doing Business in the New Economy* (New York: Dow-Jones Irwin, 1985), p. 18.

204 **More than twenty years later:** Karl Albrecht, "The Second Coming of Service?" karlalbrecht.com.

212 **A paragraph from:** Accenture, "Superior Customer Service Capabilities: Key Factors in the Journey to High Performance."

Chapter 8:
Absolutely, Positively

Page

236 **In 2005, *BusinessWeek* said the company:** Kimberly Weasel, "A Shine on Their Shoes," *BusinessWeek*, December 5, 2005; Bill Taylor, "Why Zappos Pays New Employees to Quit—and You

Should Too," Harvard Business Online, May 19, 2008, http://
discussionleader.hbsp.com/taylor/2008/05/wy_zappos_pays_new_
employees_t.html.

238 **A bulwark of the Zappos culture:** Zappos.com/core-values.zhtml.

239 **Every year the company:** Zappos, *07 Culture* (Las Vegas, NV:
Zappos, 2007).

Index

About the Author

Emily Yellin is the author of *Our Mothers' War*, and was a long-time contributor to the *New York Times*. She has also written for *Time*, the *Washington Post*, the *International Herald Tribune*, *Newsweek*, *Smithsonian Magazine*, and other publications. She graduated from the University of Wisconsin–Madison with a degree in English literature and received a master's degree in journalism from Northwestern University.

Yellin decided to write this book while waiting on hold one day in her freezing cold house only to argue for hours with customer service at a home warranty company before convincing someone to come fix her broken furnace. She currently lives in Memphis, Tennessee.